10+

ALSO BY SYLVIA CARY:

JOLTED SOBER:
GETTING TO THE MOMENT OF CLARITY
IN THE RECOVERY FROM ADDICTION

*IT MUST BE FIVE
O'CLOCK SOMEWHERE*

THE ALCOHOLIC MAN

10+

WOMEN WITH LONG-TERM SOBRIETY TALK ABOUT LIFE, LOVE, FAMILY, WORK, AND MONEY

Sylvia Cary, M.F.C.C.

LOWELL HOUSE
LOS ANGELES

CONTEMPORARY BOOKS
CHICAGO

Library of Congress Cataloging-in-Publication Data
Cary, Sylvia.
    10+ women with long-term sobriety talk about life, love,
family, work, and money/Sylvia Cary.
        p. cm.
    Includes bibliographical references and index.
    ISBN 1-56565-004-2
    1. Women alcoholics—United States.2.Women alcoholics—
Rehabilitation—United States. I. Title. II. Title:10 plus.
III. Title:Ten plus.
HV5137.C37   1993
362.29'2'082—dc20   92-26570
                                                              CIP

Requests for such permissions should be addressed to:

    Lowell House
    2029 Century Park East, Suite 3290
    Los Angeles, CA 90067
    Publisher: Jack Artenstein
    Executive Vice-President: Nick Clemente
    Vice-President/Editor-in-Chief: Janice Gallagher
    Director of Publishing Services: Mary D. Aarons
    Design: Tanya Maiboroda

Manufactured in the United States of America

10 9 8 7 6 5 4 3 2 1

CONTENTS

FOREWORD

Sylvia Cary's first book, *It Must Be Five O'Clock Somewhere* was, in my opinion, one of the seminal studies that clearly defined the trauma of the woman alcoholic. Told in the first person, it chronicled the confusion of a seemingly successful and intelligent woman who finds herself drawn into helplessness/loss of confidence, destroyed personal relationships, and, ultimately, loss of self-worth.

Having found nothing in the current literature that examined the phenomenon of continuing recovery versus recidivisim, she set about to determine those factors that ensured success versus the characteristics and/or behavior patterns that led to relapse.

The result is *10+*, a thoughtful and provocative study of recovering women alcoholics who have successfully maintained their sobriety for ten or more years. Her interviewees were willing and cooperative and were eager to share with other women—those who were still chained by chemical addiction—their own experiences, their strengths, and ultimately their hopes in five areas: life, love, family, work, and money.

Although their backgrounds and their histories covered a wide range of ethnic, religious, economic, and educational factors, the basic theme of their recovery was very similar.

This eminently readable book—although targeted for the recovering woman at whatever stage—has such wisdom and insight that I recommend it for general reading for male and female alike. The pain and sorrow, and ultimate recovery, recounted by the subjects in *10+* applies to anyone who is experiencing severe life stresses and problems.

The stories of these 21 women, and their insights and solutions, might just be the catalyst for readers to examine their own lives. *10+* offers the collective wisdom of "ordinary"— hence remarkable—women.

—Muriel M. Zink,
author of *Step by Step*
November, 1992

WHAT'S IT
LIKE BEING
IN THERE?

At a Los Angeles press conference to welcome a visiting Indian yogi master—a man reputed to have been enlightened for 25 years—a group of mostly young reporters fired off questions, each one more esoteric than the last: Can you define Buddhist nature? What's the significance of visualizing wild animals during meditation? How do you know when you're in your last reincarnation? Can anybody learn to levitate? Is it okay to take drugs for spiritual purposes?

The questions went on and on, with the master answering them as best he could. Finally a young woman stood up. After scrutinizing the orange-robed man sitting before her in the glare of the television lights, she said: "What *I* want to know is, what's it like *being* in there?"

People laughed. The simplicity of the question was refreshing. Besides, she had asked what they all secretly wanted to know anyway but were afraid to ask: What's it like being inside the head of an officially "enlightened" human being? What kinds of thoughts does such a person have? Does an enlightened person see more than the rest of us?

It's the same kind of curiosity a lot of us have about other types of special people—the celebrity, the genius, the great artist, Mother Teresa: What's it like *being* in there? In the world of addiction, the still-practicing alcoholic or addict wonders what it would feel like to live without the obsession to drink or use drugs. What would it be like to be inside the head of somebody who's been sober for 15 or 30 years? Despite all the addiction literature that has flooded the marketplace over the last decade, surprisingly little has been written describing the experience of long-term sobriety.

In my last book, *The Alcoholic Man,* I set about to remedy this situation at least in part by interviewing 18 recovering alcoholic men, half of whom had had 10 years of sobriety or more. In *10+* I've gone even further. All 21 of the women interviewed have been sober for at least 10 years, and in one case, 50 years!

What both books make clear is that sobriety is not a stand-still deal. Changes keep happening. As the years of sobriety go by, the recovering person realizes that they think differently, feel differently, work differently, love differently, parent differently, spend differently, handle troubles differently, and relate to the world differently. "I look back on my life before sobriety, and it's like looking at another person. I don't even recognize myself," said one of the interviewees. Another commented, "My drinking life was a horror. If I'd known at the time how miserable I was, I'd have jumped off a bridge. I'm glad I was too drunk to know."

WHO GETS THEIR ACT TOGETHER?

During a recent Alcoholics Anonymous (AA) meeting attended by about 35 recovering men and women, a young newcomer listened politely as others shared their week. Finally she could stand it no more and raised her hand to speak. "If anyone here has any ideas about how to organize your life," she pleaded, "I'd really appreciate it if you'd speak to me after the meeting!"

Again, it was one of those refreshing comments that made everyone in the room laugh. Who *doesn't* wish that all it took was a few "pointers" to learn the art of living! The trouble is, it takes a tad more than that—which may be why psychologist Abraham Maslow once pointed out that barely 10 percent of us ever manage to get our act together in life, or become what he termed *self-actualized.*

Some people don't seek self-actualization because their lives are too rooted in the struggle for daily survival, and others don't seek it because it's hard work. These others are not willing to be that uncomfortable. When life offers them an opportunity to make a change, they pass. They figure that if personal growth isn't a required course, why bother?

We see the same statistics in addiction recovery. Barely 10 percent of those who try for lifelong sobriety actually achieve it. The rest return to drinking or to other mind-altering substances.

An obvious question here is, If change is so hard, why do even 10 percent of us bother with it? The answer is, because of the perks. There are a lot of perks to becoming self-actualized and to getting sober. If you don't do the work, you don't get the perks.

As you'll see after reading the interviews with the recovering women, across the board they seem happier, healthier, wiser, more honest, more energetic, more responsible, more positive, more creative, more sensitive, more loving, more efficient, more socially aware, and so on, than do their still-practicing alcoholic sisters. In fact, it sometimes seems as if they're better off than women who've never been alcoholic at all. Like the proverbial broken leg that heals stronger than it was before it was broken, these women came from behind and then shot way ahead. By virtue of being in AA, they were offered some structured opportunities that helped them begin to learn the art of living—opportunities that most people aren't lucky enough to get. The AA twelve steps are really a kind of blueprint for meeting life's challenges. Plus, each AA member is privileged to be able to work with a personal sponsor who facilitates their progress by sharing wisdom and offering direction and guidance. Alcoholics Anonymous, in fact, offers the kind of practical help in life that has led many people to say, "It's too bad *everybody* can't be an alcoholic and get to go to AA!"

WHY ALCOHOLICS ANONYMOUS?

All 21 interviewees in this book obtained and now maintain their sobriety in Alcoholics Anonymous, which is the oldest (nearing 60 years) and largest (2 million members in 115 countries) self-help group for alcoholism and chemical dependency in the world.

I picked AA women to interview for a number of reasons. First of all, convenience. Since AA is worldwide, finding women to talk with was easy. Where else could I have tracked down a woman who's been sober for more than 50 years? Another reason is AA's consistency. Every interviewee uses approximately the same terminology, has basically the same philosophical approach to recovery, and defines key words the same way. These universal factors are what makes AA a natural laboratory in which to study the recovering alcoholic woman.

Even though the women interviewed are all *in* Alcoholics Anonymous, this is not a book *about* Alcoholics

Anonymous. AA is simply the stage on which each woman's drama of personal transformation is being played out. In keeping with the AA tradition of not being compensated for sharing their "experience, strength and hope," as the program puts it, the women want readers to know that, aside from each of them receiving a complimentary copy of this book, they were not paid.

ABOUT THE INTERVIEWEES

The recovering women interviewed for this book, all of whom have a minimum of 10 years of continuous sobriety, represent a cross-section of backgrounds, religions, economic circumstances, and personality types. Their ages range from 32 to 83. Eighteen of the interviewees were born in the United States, three in Europe. Some had backgrounds of privilege, some of poverty. Currently, one-third of the women are married, two are widowed, and the others are either divorced or single. Two are gay. Two are twins—one identical, one fraternal.

SPECIAL CONCERNS OF SOBER WOMEN

Because of the influence of the women's movement, much has been made of the "special concerns" of the woman alcoholic— maybe too much. My own experience from working with hundreds of alcoholics of both sexes is that the longer a person stays sober, the less difference one's sex makes. In Alcoholics Anonymous, which is remarkably democratic, men and women are treated about the same, and their recovery processes are virtually identical.

However, in early sobriety women do share some special issues: stigma, for one. The double standard, though less stinging than it used to be, still exists. The female alcoholic or addict is more harshly judged than the male.

All sorts of negative moral implications continue to plague the alcoholic woman—everything from being sexually promiscuous to being a bad mother. And whereas drinking has always implied virility for men, it has absolutely no positive connotations as far as a woman's femininity goes. This stigma forces the alcoholic woman underground. She hides her addiction longer, and better, than her male counterpart. By the time she finally admits her problem and asks for help, she has usually gotten more sick. Sometimes it's too late, and she even dies. "Stigma about being an alcoholic will be around until scientists find out just what's missing in us alcoholics, or what we've got extra that we shouldn't have that makes us react funny to alcohol," says one of our interviewees. "Until then, we're just going to have to put up with the stigma and go on about our business."

Even after a woman rises above stigma and asks for help, treatment itself can be a tricky issue. She may need hospitalization but be unable to get it because she doesn't have the money or the insurance; it's no secret that most women in the U.S. are much less financially secure than men. If she goes to Alcoholics Anonymous (or Cocaine Anonymous, Narcotics Anonymous, or Pills Anonymous), which is free, she may have a hard time showing up regularly because of what she sees as pressing personal or family obligations. Being a woman is part of her problem—she puts everyone else's needs before her own, including her health needs.

Newly sober men have their problems, too. In some circles, for example, it's considered unmanly not to drink. Men who are trying to stay sober may be teased and pressured by their buddies. A woman can turn down a drink and not feel socially awkward, but a man who turns down a drink may feel humiliated. If his friends give him enough heat about it, he'll succumb.

However, after 10 years of sobriety, most men and women have learned how to handle all these special concerns. For the woman, stigma has become practically irrelevant. According to one interviewee, "At this point in my life, I absolutely refuse to be ashamed of being an alcoholic. It may not be the first thing I tell people, but it's usually not the last. There are times, in fact, when if I *didn't* tell somebody I was a recovering alcoholic, I'd feel as though I was betraying myself—by sharing it, I might be helping somebody. To hold back out of embarrassment or a desire to look good would be criminal."

DEFINING ALCOHOLISM

There are probably as many definitions of the word *alcoholism* as there are alcoholics, yet there's no one *official* definition. We don't even know for sure what causes alcoholism yet, so until we do we'll have to muddle along with a variety of conflicting descriptions.

For years, AA literature has described alcoholism as "an obsession of the mind combined with an allergy of the body." That definition still applies. In fact, today it seems more on-target than ever because over the last decade or so, a lot of scientific research has pointed to a genetic involvement in addiction. In other words, maybe alcoholism is in the genes, but as yet this hasn't been proven.

Starting back in the mid-fifties with the American Medical Association, alcoholism has been called a "disease." Some people like this definition because it releases alcoholics from any kind of moral stigma, which makes it easier for them to face their problem and get help. Other people don't like this definition because they feel it lets the drunks off the hook.

A definition of alcoholism that the average citizen often uses is "drinking too much." Someone will say, "I quit because I was drinking too much." AA members who hear this tend to smile. To them, it's a term that just tries to "pretty up" what it really is.

If you walk into an AA meeting and listen to the members talking, you'll find that the term *alcoholism* is used generically. It's an umbrella term that covers both alcoholism *and* drug addiction, or a combination of the two. That's because ever since the fifties and sixties, when drugs entered the picture, most people who show up in AA are addicted to a mishmash of mind-altering chemicals. Alcohol may be their drug of choice, but a "pure" alcoholic, someone who uses *only* alcohol, is basically a relic of the past.

However, if an individual's primary drug is something other than alcohol, he or she is likely to end up in some other anonymous group such as Cocaine Anonymous, Narcotics Anonymous, Pills Anonymous, or Marijuana Anonymous. Some people go to these meetings in addition to AA.

One definition of *alcoholism* that I like is a little formula: Alcohol + Problems = Alcoholism. It means that if a person has a problem in *any* major area of life, and that problem can in any way be traced back to drinking (or drugging), then the person has alcoholism. What major areas are we talking about? The ones that are usually mentioned are emotions, work, love, family, finances, health, and community. If a person has a problem at work, in her marriage, with the law, or even with the IRS, addiction may be at its root.

As alcoholism affects these areas of a woman's life, so does sobriety. That's why I've structured this book the way I have. I've taken the major life areas and created a chapter on each. Through these interviews, you'll see that the longer a woman has been sober, the more likely it is that she's doing better and better in each area of her life. The road may be bumpy in spots, but she's left the roller coaster of early sobriety behind.

Who's an Alcoholic?

Let's keep it simple: in Alcoholics Anonymous, you're an alcoholic if you *say* you are. Period. It's called "identifying" as an alcoholic. No one is ever formally diagnosed by anybody else, nor is a person's self-diagnosis ever questioned. As AA members put it, "We don't judge each other or take each others' inventories." There are men's meetings, women's meetings and mixed meetings.

Within AA, there are speaker meetings, discussion meetings, and participation meetings. There are also open meetings and closed meetings. Open meetings are open to the general public. Closed meetings are for those who identify as alcoholics, who are each willing to say, "I'm an alcoholic." The purpose of closed meetings is to give the alcoholic a chance to talk freely without the fear of being judged by outsiders who may not understand the disease of addiction.

If you do choose to speak out at an Alcoholics Anonymous meeting, then AA expects you to be willing to identify as an alcoholic by saying, "I'm an alcoholic." If you choose to speak out at a Cocaine Anonymous meeting, then CA expects you to identify as an addict by saying so. There is currently some controversy over cocaine addicts who attend AA meetings yet still identify as addicts rather than alcoholics. AA worries, and perhaps rightly so, that if the organization loses its strict *alcohol* focus and gets too watered down, it will lose its impact. Others disagree and believe that AA should be the giant umbrella under which *all* chemical dependencies are welcome.

THIS IS SOBRIETY

In a book based on women with long-term sobriety, it is obviously very important that we have a consistent definition of what the term *sobriety* means. It's got to be a definition that all 21 interviewees agree on, otherwise the interviews would be meaningless.

The *official* definition of *sobriety* in Alcoholics Anonymous is "freedom from alcohol." But again, because of the influx into AA of people who abuse other substances as well, the definition of sobriety has been *un*officially expanded to take that into account. Therefore, the word *sobriety* now means freedom from alcohol *as well as* freedom from cocaine, marijuana, mind-altering pills (prescription or otherwise), heroin, designer drugs—anything that affects you from the neck up. This is the definition used by all the women in this book. The only exceptions to this rule are medications used for operations, specific illnesses, psychiatric conditions, and physical pain.

What Is a "Slip"?

A slip is a relapse. It happens when the alcoholic (remember, that means alcoholic or addict) drinks or uses again, and occurs when the recovering person ingests or uses *any* mind-altering chemical on purpose, no matter what the amount. One beer, one sip of gin, one pill, one hit off a marijuana cigarette, constitutes a slip.

When an AA member slips, he or she is expected to be honest about it and start his or her "time" all over again. How much time a person has is very important. In some parts of the country, AA people celebrate their progress by "taking a chip" as they reach each stage: Printed chips that look like poker chips are handed out to members who've achieved 30 days, 60 days, 90 days, 6 months, and 9 months of sobriety. When the AA member reaches a year of sobriety, he or she gets a cake, complete with candles. Every birthday or anniversary after that is celebrated by "taking a cake."

Monitoring one's sobriety is left up to each AA member. Nobody stands at the door and smells people's breath or looks in their eyes to see if they're "really" sober and clean. That kind of thing would empty out AA in no time flat! However, asking someone "How long have you been sober?" is definitely not considered a rude question in AA, not like asking someone their income or age. If the person being asked hems and haws or doesn't give a straight answer, then the questioner is likely to suspect that the person isn't really sober—because 99.9 percent of AA members can give you their length of sobriety instantly! Length of sobriety is a badge of honor. In fact, in some parts of the country, whenever AA members speak up at a meeting they give their sobriety dates as well as their first names.

But even if a member clearly lies about his or her length of sobriety, they'll rarely, if ever, be challenged about it directly (except, perhaps, by a sponsor or close friend). AA believes that sooner or later the member who lies will feel enough pain over it to "fess up" and fly right.

The Moment of Clarity

As you read the sometimes harrowing accounts of the women in this book, an important question is bound to come up: Exactly *how* did these women stop drinking and using? Was going to AA all it took? Or was something else involved?

My view is that in practically every case of addiction recovery, something else is involved, and that something else is a psychological phenomenon known as the "moment of clarity" experience. Outside of addiction recovery circles, this phenomenon remains one of the world's best-kept healing secrets and has yet to find its way into mainstream thinking. But inside AA, the concept is well accepted. You hear people refer to their own moment-of-clarity experiences all the time.

The experience is similar to what is called a "spontaneous remission" in medicine. It's a sudden *aha!* that heals. When the alcoholic has a moment of clarity, his or her obsession to drink or use drugs (which *is* addiction) disappears or loses its wallop. Once that occurs, abstinence becomes relatively easy.

The moment of clarity can go by other names— moment of truth, spiritual experience, surrender, awakening, turning point, transformation, grace, or even left-right brain shift. For each person, the moment-of-clarity event is different. For some people, such as AA's co-founder, Bill Wilson, it's a dramatic, *kaboom*-like event complete with blinding white light. For others, it feels like nothing more than making a decision, or having a good idea or perhaps a quiet realization that their addictive behavior has to end. For example, after years of drinking, a woman might look at herself in the mirror one morning and announce, "Today's the day I quit," and then she'll do it.

That's a moment of clarity.

Some alcoholics are lucky: their moment of clarity comes out of the blue and zaps them sober forever. Others have to work for it. But, in much the same way as scientific insights are more likely to occur in an individual with a prepared mind, a moment of clarity is *more* likely to occur to a person after some effort and deliberate preparation. This preparation can include going to AA meetings, reading about addiction, talking to other recovering alcoholics, working AA's Twelve Steps (the therapy part of the program), meditating, and so on. Eventually, one of these actions may *trigger* a moment of clarity and can result in a healing from one's obsession to drink or use, which may last forever.

The Day I Was Jolted Sober

As you read the interviews in this book, you'll notice that in almost every instance the woman's moment-of-clarity experience was triggered by an internal or external event—a trauma, a life-threatening situation, a dream, a memory, a feeling, a new bit of information, a confrontation, even a throwaway line uttered by someone else. At no time was faith in a quick recovery a requirement. Skeptics experience moments of clarity just as often as anyone else.

I was one of those skeptics.

As a graduate student in clinical psychology at Boston University, I was taught that there's no such thing as an overnight cure, especially from something as complex as addiction. Recovery, I was told, happens in a linear way, slowly, step-by-step, over time. People get better in bits.

When I went to work at Boston State Hospital, a huge mental hospital with more than 3,000 patients, I'd occasionally hear stories about some of the patients (they were alcoholic as well as mentally ill) who claimed to have had overnight cures after going to the hospital AA meeting in the auditorium on the third floor. I always dismissed such tales as unscientific and quackish snake-oil stuff. My training had taught me that alcoholism was only a symptom of an underlying emotional disorder, and until *that* was fixed, the symptom of drinking would remain intact. It was the mid-sixties, and neither I nor my colleagues had any idea that alcoholism was an illness in itself, or that it could be healed in an instant.

Meanwhile, in my personal life, I was drinking like a fish. Alcoholically. It started off simply enough after I got married to a psychiatrist. Each night we'd have a nice, relaxing martini before dinner. In no time, it progressed to two martinis before dinner, then three, then martinis instead of dinner. It took only eight years for gin to wreck my marriage, derail my career, interfere with my ability to parent my two daughters, and begin to erode my health. Convinced that our growing marital problems as well as my drinking were his fault, I left my husband. To my surprise, I didn't drink less, I drank more. Over the next two years it

got to be ridiculous. I couldn't go one night without getting drunk. Ultimately, I decided to attend a local self-help
group for alcoholics. I went in not expecting much.

I arrived a few minutes late and took a seat in the
back. I felt silly being there, felt I was wasting my time.
How could something as superficial as a meeting help
me? Even if it worked, I guessed it would still take me two
to five years to get enough insight into why I drank to
stop. Sitting there, I could feel that familiar old gin urge
lurking inside me, like an organ in my body. (I later came
to see that urge as the obsession.) All I knew was that as
long as that urge was there—and I couldn't imagine it *not*
being there—I was doomed to keep drinking.

Then, suddenly, "it" happened, right after the coffee
break. I was listening to the speaker, a TV actor. He was
funny and I was laughing, something I hadn't done in a
long time. The next thing I was aware of was a little
thought that seemed to arise spontaneously from somewhere in the right side of my brain and waft its way gently
across my mind. The thought was, *They're sober; I'm not. I
think I'll listen and do what they say.* By the time the thought
arrived at the left side of my brain my whole world had
changed. Suddenly I had a worldview shift, and I saw my
situation from a new perspective. The denial had dropped
away. I saw clearly that I was an alcoholic and that the
solution was simple beyond words: Stop drinking alcohol.
No more alcohol, no more alcoholism. This moment of
clarity empowered me with the ability to choose between
drinking and not drinking, so I consciously chose *not* to.
Finally, when I checked inside myself again for that familiar old gin urge—the obsession—it was gone. It had simply disappeared.

That happened 20 years ago, and I haven't had a
drink since. It came out of nowhere and changed everything. It was a powerful moment in my life, *the* most powerful. Although it was not dramatic like Bill Wilson's

moment of clarity, it nonetheless made a believer of me. Today I know beyond the shadow of a doubt, because I've experienced it, that the cure for addiction, no matter how far down the alcoholic or addict has gone, can occur in a no-cost split second. It's getting to that split second that's tricky!

After two years of sobriety, I started working as a psychotherapist in the chemical dependency field, and I've been there ever since. After 12 years of sobriety, I married again. Soon after that, I published my first book, then my second, *Jolted Sober*, which is all about the moment-of-clarity experience—15 years of research findings on a psychological phenomenon that takes place in a flash!

Maintenance Work

The loss of the moment of clarity, and the return of the obsession to drink, is every recovering alcoholic's worst nightmare. The idea of being out there again, out of control, unable *not* to take a drink is terrifying. But the truth is that no matter how long a woman has been sober, she's never home free. Some of the women in the book have had slips, so they know. If a woman stops the sobriety maintenance work, stops "working the program" as AA calls it, then she becomes more vulnerable to a slip. One day the universe just barges in and repossesses her moment-of-clarity healing, replacing it with her old obsession to drink. If she wants sobriety after that, she has to start all over again from Day One.

Therefore, for most recovering alcoholics, routine maintenance work is a must at any stage of sobriety. As you'll see in Chapter 8, the woman with 50 years of sobriety probably goes to nearly as many AA meetings today as she did when she was new. *That's* how she racked up 50 years!

SOBRIETY FIRST

The sole purpose of the existence of Alcoholics Anonymous is sobriety—how to help the alcoholic stop drinking and stay stopped.

As you'll see in the pages ahead, whenever life threw one of our recovering alcoholic interviewees a curve, she had to find a way to handle it *other* than by drinking or using. Said one jokingly, "Whenever I've had a problem in sobriety, I've had to consider a number of different ways of dealing with it. I've considered murder. I've considered suicide. I've considered running away. But I've never considered drinking over it!"

If you add up all the years of sobriety represented by the 21 women interviewed in this book, it comes to a total of 406! That's 406 years of accumulated wisdom about how to handle every imaginable life problem without resorting to alcohol or drugs. This passing on of wisdom from one person to another is exactly how AA works, a never-ending chain of one recovering alcoholic helping another by sharing experience, strength, and hope. To take the utmost advantage of these 406 years of wisdom, I've combed through the chapters and pulled out some of the most helpful pointers in each. These goodies appear at the end of each chapter in a Sober Tips List, which I hope you'll find useful.

Look upon the wisdom distilled from these 406 years of sober experience as a kind of portable support group. If you know somebody in recovery, share *10+* with them. It will give them hope, and reassure them that there's life after sobriety—in fact, a very good life. If you're in recovery yourself and can't get to an AA meeting, pick up *10+* and take it with you. It was created to inspire and motivate you at every stage of your recovery. What helped the 21 women in this book can help you, too.

2

S O B E R

F E E L I N G S

Feelings? I didn't want to know
anything about them! I wanted to
be exempt from feelings.

—Dolores, sober 14 years

Drinking can be cured in seconds—by not drinking. As Alcoholics Anonymous points out, when you take away the "alcohol," what you're left with is the "ism," which is the *feelings* part of the disease. Getting a handle on feelings, something that's considered serious business in AA, can take years. In fact, the recovering woman is warned that if she *doesn't* learn to identify and deal appropriately with her feelings on a daily basis, the frustration, resentment, and confusion that results from repressing and ignoring these emotions may lead her back to drinking.

A feeling is a reaction—happy, sad, mad, glad. Newcomers to sobriety, most of whom have spent a lifetime avoiding looking inward, are notoriously bad at pinpointing how they feel. In fact, their usual response to the question "How do you feel?" is "I don't know." Typically, they confuse feelings with thoughts, opinions, and beliefs.

17

They begin sentences with "I think" instead of "I feel." They intellectualize and deny feelings they don't approve of or think they shouldn't have, such as anger. Some decide that being angry is bad, so whenever anger comes up they push the feeling away. After a while this habit of not acknowledging the truth becomes so ingrained that they can no longer answer life's most pressing questions: "Am I happy?" "Is this job (or man) for me?" "Do I trust this person?" "Should I get involved in this experience?"

People who aren't clear about their own emotions also tend to be bad judges of others. They pay attention to words instead of deeds, which makes them vulnerable to abusive partners, associates, and employers.

In recovery, the feelings that tend to surface first are depression, anger, fear, and guilt, with a little joy thrown in. Getting in touch with your feelings sounds like a great idea in the abstract, but in reality it's very uncomfortable. The actual experience of depression, anger, fear, or guilt *hurts.* These are the very feelings that the alcoholic drank to escape in the first place! And, while unpleasant feelings don't *cause* alcoholism, the alcoholic discovers that alcohol and other mind-altering chemicals do a good job of anesthetizing these emotions and preventing them from entering consciousness.

I used to have a photograph on my office wall of a beautiful flower pushing its way up through a crack in an asphalt driveway. The picture reminds me of what happens when people stop drinking and using and their feelings begin to push up through the layers of mental "asphalt" into consciousness, where they are finally *felt.*

Babies don't have problems with feelings. When they're happy, sad, mad, or glad, they know it and show it. But in households where it's not okay to express certain emotions, infants learn that, for survival's sake, it's smart to hide the truth. As they grow older, they get so good at hiding the truth that they end up fooling themselves. Once upon a time they might have known that a tight knot in the stomach probably meant "No, I don't want this," but after years of ignoring this kind of clue, they forget what it means.

Recovery programs such as Alcoholics Anonymous have ways of helping people get reconnected with their long-lost feelings. Members are encouraged to attend lots of meetings, and by listening to others talk about *their* feelings, they'll be better able to identify their own. They'll also start learning the art of interpreting those crucial physiological clues, like the woman who discovered that whenever she gets a certain kind of headache, it's a warning sign from her intuition. She says, "As soon as I start feeling that tingling in my head, I know that I'm probably doing something I shouldn't be doing, and that if I don't stop, I'll get a terrible headache. If I stop, the tingling usually goes away."

Another handy recovery tool to help people identify what they're feeling is the Feelings List at the end of this chapter. This isn't an official AA document, just a list of feelings in alphabetical order. A recovering person who has trouble pinpointing how he or she feels can run down the list and see what words ring a bell. I know one recovering woman who's been carrying her tattered Feelings List around with her for five years.

Undoing the damage a woman has done to her emotional life can take time. Even after two or three years of sobriety, she may still avoid her feelings or rush to rationalize them away. I heard one of these women describe an upsetting experience she'd had with her new therapist. She said, "I was at my therapist's office, and I went to use the bathroom. No sooner was I in there than the therapist started pounding on the bathroom door, insisting that I let her in. I didn't want to, but I did. Then she proceeded to hike up her skirt, pull down her pants, sit on the toilet, and pee right in front of me. I was shocked. I mean, I hardly knew this woman! It seemed like a very inappropriate thing to do."

Then the young woman launched into her rationalizations, which allowed her to discount her true feelings: "I didn't dare say anything to the therapist about how I felt because I figured it must have been *my* problem if I was so uncomfortable. *I* was the one who needed to change, right? I was just too uptight and puritanical. It probably shouldn't have bothered me. After all, *she* was the therapist!"

Obviously, this woman hadn't progressed to the point where she could trust her own feelings. It's not that her intuitive machinery wasn't working—it was working just fine. In fact, she was able to pick up some really good clues: her feeling of shock, her feeling of physical discomfort, and her feeling that something wasn't appropriate. But because the situation involved a credentialed psychotherapist, she disregarded these clues and concluded that she must be wrong and her therapist must be right!

Had she trusted herself, she'd have seen that she had choices of how to react. She could have (1) locked the therapist out of the bathroom, (2) let the therapist in and then exited, (3) told the therapist that her behavior seemed inappropriate and was making her uncomfortable, or (4) changed therapists. But for women in their early years of recovery, these options seem all but impossible. In fact, most don't even *think* of them.

Now, there's nothing wrong with using our intellect. We need it for many things, including balancing our checkbooks and reading maps. The point is, when it comes to making decisions, we need to draw on the wisdom of both our intellect *and* our intuition.

IDENTIFYING CHARACTER DEFECTS AND TACKLING LOW SELF-ESTEEM

In early sobriety, the recovering alcoholic woman doesn't present a very pretty picture. Not only is she dishonest about her feelings, but she's also a walking list of what AA calls character defects. Character defects are emotions, personality traits, and behaviors that get in the way of one's personal growth and happiness. They can also get in the way of the growth and happiness of others! In other words, the recovering alcoholic isn't always a joy to be around.

Some of the more common character defects that AA members are encouraged to deal with include:

fearfulness	secretiveness
anger	self-centeredness
blaming	irresponsibility
denial	negativity
resentfulness	manipulativeness
emotional dishonesty	perfectionism
defensiveness	impulsiveness

These traits are so limiting that AA feels they are downright dangerous. Unless the recovering alcoholic woman acknowledges them and gets rid of them, they may drive her back to drinking.

All too often, *low self-esteem* is used as a catch-all phrase to explain bad behavior that results from the kinds of character defects mentioned above. It's certainly true that feelings of worthlessness and a lack of self-respect plague many recovering alcoholics who engage in this behavior. But does low self-esteem cause bad behavior, or does bad behavior exacerbate low self-esteem? AA's view is that no matter what the source, the only cure for low self-esteem is *good* behavior. Sooner or later, nearly all alcoholics discover that the way they feel about themselves is directly related to their actions. Do bad, feel bad; do good, feel good. It's that simple.

While most recovering alcoholics have many of the character defects mentioned above, certain defects are especially troublesome, as we'll see in the three interviews in this chapter. Our first interviewee, Dolores, has had to deal with excessive fearfulness and secretiveness, traits she admits have severely limited her life and have kept her isolated and wary of risks despite 14 years of sobriety . However, because of her intense desire to maintain her sobriety, she has become increasingly willing to work on these character defects even though it makes her uncomfortable to do so.

For years, Frances was plagued by her near-crippling perfectionism both before and after sobriety. That, plus her explosive anger, muddied her relationship with her daughter, nearly cost her her marriage, and came close to driving her back to drinking.

Julie had to overcome her co-dependency, which no doubt sprang from the fact that she came from a highly dysfunctional family in which her alcoholic father died a tragic death in a fire just before Julie turned 11. She's been out to "save" men ever since.

When we act out our character defects in our lives, we become acutely uncomfortable. It's nature's way of saying "Don't do that!" For alcoholics, there's always the danger that this discomfort may lead to drinking, so it's in the alcoholic's best interest to pinpoint her character defects as soon as possible and deal with them.

IS OUTSIDE PSYCHOTHERAPY NECESSARY?

In Alcoholics Anonymous, there are two schools of thought about seeking help outside of AA. Some members feel that AA is a full-service therapy program and that getting outside help is unnecessary. Others feel that AA works even better when it's combined with outside psychotherapy. There are no rules about this one way or the other. It's left up to individuals to decide what *they* think they need in order to stay clean and sober.

Some of our interviewees chose to get outside psychological help and some didn't. One commented, "I get more out of AA than I ever got from any of the psychiatrists I went to before I got sober." Another said, "Psychotherapy gave me permission to really go for my dreams."

What most of the interviewees agreed on, however, is that therapists who don't understand addiction and don't understand Alcoholics Anonymous can, with all good intentions, do more harm than good. They can influence their AA member/patient to rely more on the therapy than on AA, which is often a prescription for disaster. AA relapse statistics suggest that the alcoholics who are most likely to drink again are those who stop going to meetings, where they get to rub shoulders with other recovering alcoholics. In fact, it's this "rubbing shoulders" phenomenon that seems to be crucial to long-term recovery, as AA's co-founders, Bill Wilson and Dr. Bob Smith, discovered. Whenever two or more alcoholics get together and share their "experience, strength and hope," as AA phrases it, magic happens. This is the thing that non-AA-oriented psychiatrists and psychotherapists don't seem to understand.

One of our interviewees, who is a mental health professional as well as a recovering alcoholic, has a few critical things to say about some of her colleagues. "The therapists who don't know about addiction, but *think* they do, drive me crazy. For a while there I thought the mental health field was finally beginning to accept that alcoholism is a disease and not a symptom of some neurosis. But lately I've noticed a sort of backsliding into the old ways of thinking. Once again, therapists are rooting around in the alcoholic's psyche, looking for psychological explanations for addiction. Most of them would deny this, of course, but that's what going on! I think anyone who's in AA and is contemplating getting outside therapy needs to be aware of this bias on the part of so many mental health specialists."

The purpose of all therapy, whether it's AA therapy, psychotherapy, spiritual therapy, or any other kind of therapy, is to heal. When the alcoholic woman stops drinking and using and signs up for healing, she finally gets a chance to start becoming the person she was on her way to becoming when her journey was so rudely interrupted by her addiction.

DOLORES, SOBER 14 YEARS

*Basically, I'm still a person who doesn't
want anybody to get to know me.*
                                    —Dolores

Dolores, 36, is a sweet-faced, slightly overweight phone company technician. She was born in Idaho, the daughter of a minister father and a schoolteacher mother, neither of whom drank. She says, "I was the only alcoholic I ever knew." She has two younger brothers. She got sober at 21. Later that year she married a man she met in AA who's considerably older. He's black and she's white. They're still married and have no children.

"I think I was born an alcoholic and born with low self-esteem because there's no other way I could have gotten that way growing up in my family!" Dolores says. "My parents were kind and accepting, and yet I felt unworthy and alone. My parents not only loved me, they told me that they loved me, but I heard them through alcoholic ears, and I just couldn't accept it. I still felt unworthy and alone. Automatically, I stuffed my feelings down and kept them down with food. I ended up a shy, overweight loner with braces. When I hit 12 and it started being important to be cute, I withdrew even more into books and good grades."

Dolores remembers being timid and fearful "of everything" from an early age. "I saw a TV show recently about infants and temperament. They waved a mobile in front of two babies, and one of them took it all in and was delighted and smiled about it, and the other baby was terrified. He couldn't handle it, and he cried. Of course, I identified with the kid who couldn't handle it and cried. Fear was just a part of me. Even when I was happy, underneath there was always that fear, and it never took much of anything to bring it out. In school I was a rule-obeyer. I never could stand the thought of getting into trouble or getting negative attention. I was also pretty straight-laced and I had a whole list of things that I would 'absolutely never do.' Of course, once I started drinking, I ended up doing most of them."

Alcoholism Waiting to Happen

Dolores appears to have been an alcoholic right from the start. "The very first time I drank, I had a blackout, was in a minor car accident, hid from the cops, and threw up. I found it all real exciting."

However, she held back from drugs. "I wasn't street smart, and I was terrified of the whole subject of drugs, so I just drank in my room by myself. I don't think my parents were even aware of it. I shut my door."

Dolores went on to college, where she was still a good student and still a loner. "But I didn't have a clear purpose. I'd sign up for a course, and then I'd drop it. I didn't know who I was or what I wanted."

Eventually she dropped out of college and went to work. Her drinking increased. She'd drink on her lunch hour and after work. Sometimes she'd pass out in her car in the parking lot. "Nobody ever bothered me. I was definitely watched over." But one night she woke up in her car and it was already dark. "That really scared me— enough to call AA." She went to one meeting but didn't stay. "I thought I was too young and too intelligent to be an alcoholic. It didn't occur to me that if I was so smart, how come I was so drunk?"

Dolores kept drinking. It was a moment-of-clarity experience that got her back to AA. "I was drunk in my car, when suddenly I felt this presence there with me, a kind, safe, loving presence, and it gently put its arm around me, and I felt moved to get out of the car, walk down the street and into a church, where I talked to a minister about my drinking. He told me to get my fanny to an AA meeting." Dolores did, and she's been sober ever since.

"It's Just in My Head"

No sooner did Dolores get sober than the job of learning to recognize her feelings began. "I was starting from ground zero," she says. "I'd buried my feelings for so long that I was convinced I didn't have any. All my life, my heroes had been people who were stoic and never talked about their feelings, who were *above* feelings, so when I had a feeling I'd discount it by saying, 'Oh, it's just in my head.' But my AA sponsor [someone who's been sober longer and acts as a kind of mentor] wouldn't let me get away with that. She'd tell me to simply note how I was feeling, without judgment, without trying to decide if it was a good feeling or a bad feeling, and just to *feel* what it felt like.

One day I said to her, 'You know, I went to the beauty parlor and they cut my hair wrong—but that's just in my head.' She said, 'Maybe they *did* cut your hair wrong. You know, sometimes your feelings are *valid.*' Wow! Until she said that, I don't think I'd ever considered that possibility.

I remember thinking, *Maybe my feelings are real. Maybe there's really something happening here after all!"*

Trusting Your Gut

Next, Dolores began to learn how to read the messages her body gave her. "Today, if something doesn't seem right, whatever the reasons, I'll get a real strong poke or jab in the pit of my stomach, the kind of feeling I used to ignore."

One incident took place at work. "I do technical work, computers and wiring, and my employer presented me with a situation where I'd have to go places at night to work, and it felt unsafe to me. I got that jab in the pit of my stomach telling me 'No,' not to do it. It threw me into a tailspin because I was afraid if I said no, I'd lose my job."

She asked for time to think it over. With encouragement from her AA sponsor, she talked to her boss about her misgivings. "His response was, 'What's the problem? You get to go out to all kinds of new places. It'll be fun.' But I knew I couldn't do it, not feeling the way I did. And it wasn't just because I was afraid. I'd walked through other fearful stuff in sobriety. It was a stronger feeling than that. It felt *valid.* It didn't have to feel valid for anybody else."

Next, Dolores tried to get her employer to guarantee her that she'd have escorts on the job, but he refused. Dolores finally realized that she'd have to be willing to risk losing the job in order to honor her intuition. Fortunately, it didn't come to that. "Seeing that I meant what I said, my boss finally let me transfer to another department, where that type of work wasn't required. The whole experience was a valuable lesson to me about having enough faith in my inner self to do what *it* says, not what other people say!"

The longer she's sober, Dolores says, the more open she is to the little as well as the bigger intuitive messages from within. She sees them as gifts. "I'll be walking down the street, and suddenly a thought will just pop into my head, like, 'Why don't we just go by such-and-such a bookstore?' So I'll go to the bookstore and find a book I've been looking for. These thoughts are more like suggestions than commands. I kind of play with them and have fun."

Another area where Dolores trusted her intuition was in marrying Albert, a man she met in AA. Albert has now been sober 20 years. "I didn't go looking for a relationship," Dolores recalls. "When you're an introvert and stay in your room all the time, you don't meet too many people, but Albert and I hit it off immediately. I felt safe and comfortable with him; we understood each other. When he asked me to marry him, I didn't think twice about it."

How did her parents react when Dolores decided to marry a black man? "Albert wasn't exactly what they had in mind for me," Dolores says. "They'd always taken great pains to teach us kids that we're all human beings, but of course that was in the abstract. In reality, they had a hard time with it. They tried to act like it was okay, but it wasn't easy for them. Eventually, they came around and now they see what a great guy he is. Albert and my dad are buddies now."

Taking on new experiences in sobriety can stir up old feelings. Dolores was surprised to find that being married to a black man stirred up her old feelings of fear, especially fear of rejection. "I was afraid that somebody would see Albert and me together and be upset by it and try to hurt us. When people would stare at us in public, I'd get anxious that they'd attack us. What helped me most was when my sponsor told me, 'When you get stared at, just think, hey, I'm giving them something interesting to talk about.' That put a positive spin on it instead of a negative one, and made it seem like less of a big deal. Since then, most of the fear has gone away."

Dolores and Albert have, so far, decided not to have children. "It doesn't really have anything to do with the biracial factor. We never sat down and talked about how a kid might have a hard time with it, so let's not do it. It's just that neither of us feels the need to have kids. We enjoy our own company too much. When friends visit us with their kids, it's great, and I'm glad when they leave, and they take the kids with them!"

Keeping Secrets

By her own admission, Dolores's first impulse when a feeling starts to well up within her is to keep it a secret. "But I know I can't do that because one thing I've learned in AA is that *talking* about our secrets is what leads to solutions, and I want solutions! I remember back when I was new, I heard an AA woman say, 'You're only as sick as your secrets,' and the instant I heard that I got one of those jabs in my stomach that tells me there's a message there for me. She was reading my mail! So, hard as it is, I make myself talk."

However, when it comes to sharing secrets, Dolores feels that some AAs go overboard. "I know recovering alcoholics who'll tell you things about themselves you don't even want to know! They'll blab on endlessly about their co-dependency issues and their incest issues and their molestation issues and their eating disorder issues, until sometimes I finally have to say, 'Hey, what's all this *issues* garbage! This is Alcoholics Anonymous, so let's not get off track! Let's talk about getting sober and about staying sober, because *that's* what we're all here for!'"

Dolores has never been interested in seeking outside therapy. "Working AA's 12 steps is enough therapy for me," she says. "I'm not down on therapy. What I'm down on is when people get caught between their therapist and their AA sponsor, and they end up in conflict:

'My sponsor says this, but my therapist says that.' I also think it's harmful when AA sponsors tell people, 'If you want me as your sponsor, you can't be in therapy!' I don't think they can know whether or not therapy is going to be helpful to somebody else. I wouldn't think of telling someone not to go to therapy."

Whatever Dolores is doing, it's obviously working for her. She's still sober, still married, still content, and still employed. And she helps others. "The greatest gift of my recovery," she says, "is getting a sense of being human, of being comfortable in my own skin, and even comfortable with my own feelings. Being a secret-keeper, it's a big deal for me to sit here and be interviewed for a book. But when you asked me, I told myself, 'Look upon it as just another little sobriety experiment to see how willing you are to share yourself. Besides, maybe something you say will help somebody else. So go ahead, Dolores, *do* it—and see what happens.'"

FRANCES, SOBER 22 YEARS

> *Everything was going my way and*
> *I didn't want to hear about feelings,*
> *buried or otherwise. I didn't want*
> *anything to upset the applecart.*
> — Frances

Frances, 53, a married businesswoman and mother of two, was born in Plattsburgh, New York, "just south of the Canadian border." She is brisk, tweedy, funny, with a no-nonsense manner. The youngest of four children, she has two older sisters and a brother. The family was rife with alcoholism. Her father, whom she adored, was a judge and a practicing alcoholic. He was subject to terrifying rages, although he never hit Frances. Two of her three siblings are now also members of Alcoholics Anonymous, and the third is *married* to an alcoholic. "The family crest should have been two crossed bottles on a field of green," she jokes.

The Tyranny of Perfectionism, the Tragedy of Denial

In grade school, Frances's sense of self-worth revolved around scholastics. "I'd never went to school to learn, I went to be a star. I was always the smartest kid in the class, and if I wasn't, I acted like it." She was at her happiest in boarding school. "There I felt safe, more at home than at home because I was away from my father's alcoholic rages. I was surrounded by my peers, who respected me and loved me for being smart, and being smart was social currency there. I was elected to everything, and I was a clown." The good feelings stopped at about age 17 when the drinking began. "I became a perfectionist of the worst type," she says. "If I thought I couldn't excel at something, I wouldn't even try. In college I'd planned to be a French major, but when I realized that some of my classmates had been educated in Switzerland and spoke French fluently, I said forget it! I majored in English instead."

Frances is a strong believer in the genetic aspect of alcoholism. "I was an alcoholic from the start. There was never a time when I drank normally, no moment when I crossed over the so-called invisible line. I was *born* on the other side of the line. I was a blackout drinker from my first drink, and I remember it well. I was with a bunch of kids in a lodge on Lake Champlain, and I got totally drunk. Waking up the next morning, not having the slightest idea what had happened, was the most terrifying morning of my life. Luckily, my friends had protected me and I hadn't gotten into a lot of trouble."

When Frances moved to New York, she left the safety
of her network of friends. "With no one to protect me
when I drank, I was taken advantage of a lot." Her answer
to this was to get married. "It was a way of insuring my
own safety," she says. She married Wynn, a man who
didn't drink but was judgmental and punitive when it
came to her drinking. "It was a case of marrying my jailer,"
she says. They later had a son. "For a while it all worked
because I was careful of my drinking around my husband.
On those few occasions when I did get drunk, he was
always there to take care of me. Of course, then he'd punish the hell out of me for weeks afterward—not physically,
but verbally."

When her parents died a year apart, both of heart
attacks at the age of 56, it totally upended Frances.
Instead of experiencing her grief, however, she avoided it
by staying drunk. Then, from time to time, she'd break
out in rages, just like her father used to do when he got
drunk. To further distract herself from her grief, she
started an affair with a neighbor's husband. "It didn't help
my marriage much," she admits.

The neighbor's husband was "brilliant, gorgeous, and
black. When my husband found out that I was having an
affair, he sued me for divorce and for custody of our
three-year-old son on the grounds of moral turpitude,
which I think means not having any morals." She went to
court. "My whole life lay in rags and tatters on that court-
room floor. I don't know how I got through it. I was seeing a psychoanalyst at the time, and he was wonderful.
Every day he'd give me half a Valium, and he'd say, 'Keep
this in your pocket, and if you think you're going to need
it, take it. Otherwise, don't.' There were days when I took
one pill, and days when I didn't. In the end, I got custody
of my son, but I had to promise that I would never see my
lover again, and I never did, not until many years later
when I visited him at a veterans' hospital. He'd been sent
there after being paralyzed in an auto accident. His mind

and his brain were still fine, and he just sobbed the whole time I was there. It was horrible. That was the last time I ever saw him."

Frances's Moment of Clarity

For two years following her divorce and custody battle, Frances continued going to her psychoanalyst—and continued drinking and wrecking her life. "One time I got arrested for drunk driving and had to spend a night in jail; another time I spent five days in a psychiatric hospital for observation after a suicide attempt. Awful things like these kept happening, and I just couldn't figure out what was wrong with me."

One night while watching TV, Frances saw a special on alcoholism. "The actress Mercedes McCambridge was narrating it, and she said that the one thing alcoholics all have in common is that they are powerless over alcohol. *Ping!* That word *powerless* really rang a bell because that's exactly how I felt! That was my moment of clarity. In a flash I saw that alcoholism was indeed my problem because I was completely powerless over my drinking. I called AA, went to a meeting, and I've been sober ever since."

Once she was sober, Frances says, "My life turned around on a dime. I met Peter, the man I'm still married to, we had a daughter, we moved into a new house, and with a partner I started a new business that took off and did well. My life got so perfect that I thought I'd solved all my problems forevermore."

Quelling the Fires Within

Unfortunately, the recovery process isn't that simple. No matter how good life gets, in order to maintain that sobriety the recovering alcoholic will have to deal with her feelings. Frances kept trying to avoid that part of her journey. But feelings, like that picture I mentioned of a flower pushing up through the asphalt, have a life of their own, and as long as there's no alcohol or drugs to keep them down, they *will* be felt sooner or later!

The first feeling that caught up with Frances was rage. It was triggered by a change in her living situation. "When I was seven years sober, my husband accepted a job in Washington, D.C., so we had to move. Suddenly I was in a new place, with a new baby, no job, nothing to do, no friends, and a husband who was working 14 hours a day. Plus, the AA meetings there were different, so I refused to go. Here I was, removed from my perfect little life, and isolating myself from AA, and I was in a rage. I started to hate my husband, and I complained constantly. I'd erupt into rages at the drop of a hat. Poor Peter was stunned. He didn't know how to handle this angry, bitter woman. I don't know why he stayed with me. I started losing weight. My anger was eating me up. One day my husband said to me, 'What *is* the matter with you? This is like a goddamned soap opera. You are constantly nagging me, and bitching at me, and carrying on. I don't even know who you are anymore!'

"I was scared. I thought, *Oh, God, I've become one of those wives that I despise.* Finally, out of pure desperation, I called my old sponsor and she told me that if I didn't get back to AA I'd probably drink. I said, 'But I don't like the AA meetings in Washington,' and she said, 'Nobody's asking you if you like AA! Nobody asks the cancer patient if they like chemotherapy, or the kidney patient if they like dialysis. AA's not entertainment, it's treatment, so for God's sake get back there!'

"Reluctantly, I agreed to go back to AA, but my anger had gotten so out of control that my rages continued. I even turned on our little daughter. One day when she was only about four, I started raging at her in a drugstore. She wasn't even doing anything. She was *never* doing anything.

But I started yelling at her, and out of the corner of my eye I saw the druggist going for the phone to call for help. When he did that, it was like another moment of clarity. Suddenly I *saw* what I'd become. I stopped yelling, and I got down on my knees and asked for help. The rage subsided. I got up, paid for my purchases, took my child by the hand, and we walked out. The rage has never come back. I've been angry since then, but never in a rage."

The outside therapy that helped Frances was going to church. "Going to church helped me unstick some of my long-suppressed emotions and started me on what I call my melting period. Every Sunday I'd go to church, sit down, and let all that sadness and grief that I'd never let myself feel before flood over me, and I'd start to sob. At first I was terribly embarrassed, but after a while I gave up on that because, in fact, I had started to feel better. I suspected there was a connection! I began to think of church as spiritual therapy."

Tackling Character Defects

Once Frances was more at home with her feelings, she was ready to work on some of her more troublesome character defects, such as her perfectionism. "I still thought I had to be perfect and be the star of everything, which is pure arrogance," she says. "My perfectionism kept me captive inside myself, because perfectionism is a trait that advances in front of you like a shield. I knew I'd have to break through it in order to discover the real person who was hiding inside of me."

There's nothing like a little humiliation to begin curing perfectionism. It happened to Frances when she decided to go back to graduate school to get her MBA. "Confidently, I announced to everyone I knew, 'Oh, yes, I'm going to get my MBA.' I liked the sound of that. But when the application came in the mail, I couldn't understand how to fill the damn thing out! I sat in the living room and started to cry. My husband looked at me and asked, 'What are you reading?'

"'I'm reading this application for business school, and I can't figure it out!' I replied tearfully.

"He started to laugh. I said, 'Don't laugh! How am I ever going to go to business school if I can't even figure out the application?' Then I started to laugh. There I was, laughing and crying at the same time, and suddenly I 'got' it—that this wasn't about school at all, it was about my ego. It was about how my self-worth had always come from being a star, and here I was being cut down to size by a stupid application. It taught me something. After that, when people would ask me, 'What are you up to?' I'd say, 'Well, if I can ever figure out the application, I'm going to apply to business school.'"

Tackling character defects, just like getting in touch with feelings, is a long process. Frances admits, "My perfectionism, which I have to keep reminding myself is really arrogance, didn't go away in one fell swoop. Even today, when I'm frightened or feel vulnerable, I find myself reaching for it again, and it's usually right at my fingertips. Whatever it was in my childhood that convinced me that I simply couldn't fail in life and be allowed to live is still strong within me."

That perfectionism flared up again a few months after Frances had entered business school (yes, she finally figured out the application!). It was triggered by failing a calculus test. "Failed!" Frances says. "The very word sent me into a tailspin. I'd had no experience with the feeling of failure before, because I'd always avoided any kind of situation where that could happen. Now, here I was, a grown, sober, married woman, a mother, with my very own house, and yet *this* was my reality—that if I failed a calculus test, I would die. I went home and sobbed as if my heart would break. I was so distraught that my little girl asked me, 'Is Daddy dead?' Now *that* got my attention. I thought, *Frances, all that's really happened to you is you've failed a calculus test.* Once again, I saw so clearly that for me, failure is *death.* There's no difference in my mind. Oddly enough, one of the things that taught me that you *can* come back after a failure was watching basketball. I'd see some player standing at the free-throw line; the crowd would be going nuts. And he'd stand there, calmly centering himself, and then he'd throw. Sometimes he'd make it. But sometimes he'd miss. He'd *fail!* And yet, a week later he'd be right back there doing it again. And I'd think to myself, *How does he do that? How can he fail and not die?* Wow, was that instructive! Again, I *got* it, and the fear of failure began to diminish."

Frances also had to face the fact that she'd been imposing the same standards of perfectionism on her daughter that she'd imposed on herself. "When my daughter was about eight years old, she was having reading problems in school, and I remember screaming at her, 'What do you mean you can't read! If you can't read, then you can't be a part of this family!'" Needless to say, Frances had to learn to lighten up on her child just as she'd had to learn to lighten up on herself. When it came to Frances's marriage, one of the character defects she had to work on was her addiction to relationship drama. Getting used to not raging and living in peace and serenity was hard! "At first I thought that the absence of drama in our marriage meant that I didn't have any kind of real feeling for him! Today, I realize that I love him totally, that life without him would be unthinkable, and that it's probably the *absence* of drama in our marriage that's kept it together so long. Without AA, I would never have known these things."

The Joy of Rediscovery

Frances sums up: "To me, the whole purpose of the sobriety journey is to go back to *get* yourself, to reclaim that person you were intended to be when you were born. When I became an alcoholic, the flame went out. I lost my identity. To rediscover it, I had to stop drinking. Today, everything has changed. My work life has changed. The *way* I work has changed. What I want has changed. What I look for has changed. How I react and respond to people has changed. It's all totally different.

"The other day I was driving along and I caught myself singing. It dawned on me that I was joyous. Imagine, me joyous! At first, I thought that joy was the *one* feeling that I'd never had, not even in childhood. But then I began to realize that joy was, indeed, a familiar feeling, but that I'd suppressed it, killed it, along with all my other feelings. Somebody in AA once said that you can't throw away just one side of a coin, and now I understand exactly what that means. If you turn away from pain, you also turn away from joy. When I was drinking, I did both.

"So, driving along that day, feeling joyous, I said to myself, 'My God, *this* is who you are—this happy, joyous, fun-loving, funny, outgoing person, with a ton of friends. You have been returned to yourself!' It's so incredibly exciting to finally feel at home in my own skin."

JULIE, SOBER 22 YEARS

> *I think we're born with the ability to know our feelings, but it gets talked out of us. I was brought up to believe that people who express certain emotions don't have good breeding, so I never dared tell the truth about how I felt.*
>
> —Julie

Julie, 44, an exceptionally pretty, divorced mother of a 21-year-old daughter, was born in Chicago, the second daughter of alcoholic parents. She works for a marketing and public relations firm. Her father, a businessman, was frequently in and out of drying-out centers, and her mother, according to Julie, "did a world-class job of hiding her own drinking and hiding my father's drinking." Her sister is 11 years older. "Perhaps I was the late-in-life baby who was supposed to save the marriage, or get my father to stop drinking, but it didn't work," Julie surmises. At birth, it was discovered that Julie's right leg would never develop normally, and she had to use a walking brace. At 14, her leg was amputated, and she got an artificial leg. For the past few years Julie has been in a committed relationship with an older man who is also a member of Alcoholics Anonymous.

A Child's Pledge

"I adored my father, and he was always extremely gentle with me," says Julie. "I was always the one who could make him smile, and the one who was sent in to subdue him when he was drunk, and therein lies a pattern I've had with men all my life: Go in with the sunshine, rescue them, and they'll love you forever."

Julie didn't have to be told that alcohol was the family problem. "Kids *know*," she says. "As young as three or four, I used to look at my father, and look at his bottle, and say to myself, 'Whenever that bottle appears, everything goes wrong, so why doesn't he just *not* use it anymore?' And I made that pledge that so many thousands of children of alcoholics have made: 'It will *never* happen to me!'"

When Julie was nine, her parents divorced and her father moved away. Then, just two days before her 11th birthday, her father was killed in a fire. "He'd thrown a party to celebrate the launching of a new business in another state, and of course he drank too much. After everybody had left, it's believed that he fell asleep on the couch with a cigarette in his hand, and that's all it took. At first, my family tried to hide from me how he died, but before long I learned the truth and *again* I said, 'It'll never happen to me.'" After her father's death, her mother's alcoholism escalated. "It felt like such a betrayal," Julie says. "I remember thinking, *Well, one down, one to go!*"

Despite her physical handicap, Julie went to schools and camps for normal children and excelled at many things, including horseback riding. "I had my father to thank for that because, from the time I was a tiny little girl, he'd always made me get back up on the horse—both literally and figuratively—and that's what I did and what I've been doing ever since."

The Early Clues

The first signs that Julie had an addictive nature showed up at age 14, when she was in the hospital having her leg amputated. "They'd put me on Demerol, and one day the orthopedist came into my room and said, 'The nurses tell me that you like this stuff too much. You'd better be careful,' and then he turned around and left. Well, I was instantly indignant, which in itself is a symptom of alcoholism! His statement was like an arrow that hit the bull's-eye. It was the same feeling I was to get later on in my life when people would say things to me like, 'There's something wrong with the way you drink.' I'd get furious. Anyway, after I went home from the hospital, the very first time my mother went out, I went to the liquor cabinet and found something to drink. It was totally automatic. I didn't even give it a second thought."

Now that she was outfitted with an artificial leg instead of an ugly brace, Julie found school a less socially awkward and painful place. "Finally I looked more like everybody else. I could even dance. And thanks to alcohol, I could talk to boys without being terrified. Alcohol became my solution." However, in speculating about the causes of her addiction, Julie is emphatic. "I don't believe for one second that my alcohol problem had anything to do with my leg, or with what I saw going on at home. I am totally convinced that alcoholics are born with alcoholism. The seed is within the person, and it's only a matter of time before it springs out. When I took that first drink, I liked it better than any other feeling I'd ever had in my whole life. It was instant nirvana. All the pieces suddenly came together. That drink made me whole."

Although Julie went on to junior college, her heart wasn't in it. "I wanted to be a singer. I'd studied singing for years, so while I was in college, I did some coffeehouse performances. Then I dropped out of school and started singing in nightclubs. To overcome stage fright, I'd have a few drinks in order to go on stage. The trouble is, drinking not only calmed me down, it killed my ambition and made me lazy and fat. Drinking became my career. One night I was with my mother and for the first time I dared to drink in front of her. She was drinking, too. After a few drinks each, she suddenly turned on me and, summoning all her alcoholic vengeance, she shrieked, 'You're just like your father when you drink!' It stung terribly, but it was true."

When the Cat's Away

Julie met a man who introduced her to the martini—and she ended up marrying him. "Once we were married, he'd sit back, take a puff on his marijuana cigarette, and tell me, 'There's something wrong with your drinking.'" When he was shipped off to Vietnam, Julie was as relieved as she was afraid for him. She'd grown tired of having a resident guard in the house. "As soon as he left I started getting drunk two or three times a day. Afterward, I'd have horrendous anxiety attacks, which I self-treated with tranquilizers." She got fired from her job. That's when she ran into an old boyfriend. Before long, she was pregnant. "I was in major denial about being pregnant," she says. "I decided that my symptoms were due to premature menopause. I was 21! By the time I finally faced reality, I was 4 ½ months along.

"I decided I wanted to keep the baby, so I stopped taking pills immediately, but I continued drinking. Back in those days few people knew that alcohol could hurt a fetus, but fortunately nothing bad happened, and my daughter was born normal. My husband arrived back from Vietnam just in time for the birth, and because the timing was close and labor had been induced, he really thought the child was his." Julie could have gotten away with her little transgression, but she chose not to. Three weeks later, she told him the truth. When they couldn't work it out, she left him and moved in temporarily with her sister. There, she returned to drinking and pill-taking with renewed enthusiasm.

Julie's Moment of Truth

"Alcoholism was hitting me like a missile. I'm only 5'1" tall, and I ballooned up to 150 pounds. I had skin problems, bladder problems, I was losing my hair, and I was hallucinating. At that point, my sister said two things to me, one brilliant, the other not so brilliant. The first thing she said was: 'I refuse to be a part of your life when you drink.' That was brilliant, because it shocked me into telling her I'd go to AA. But then she said, 'Oh no, honey. I didn't mean *that*! You're not an alcoholic. You just have to shape up and fly right.' That was unfortunate, because it let me off the hook and let me continue living in my denial. Finally, my drinking got so bad that I didn't care whether my sister thought I was an alcoholic or not, I knew I was. It was a moment of truth. I went to AA, and that's where the real journey started."

In AA Julie began to learn that sobriety wasn't just about not drinking or using, that it was about change. But when she learned that it meant facing her feelings, she resisted. "I didn't want to look at feelings. Like my mother before me, I'd learned the habit of denying truth. I wanted to keep everything pretty and make nice-nice, but inside I was like a squirrel in a cage and my life was a shambles. I was afraid that opening myself up emotionally would be like throwing kerosene on a fire, and I wasn't looking forward to it."

The first feeling Julie became aware of was insecurity, or what today would be lumped under the term *low self-esteem*. Behind all her brightness, beauty, and bravado was a scared child. "I don't think I had *any* self-esteem, low or otherwise."

Taking Positive Action

What began to cure Julie of her low self-esteem was taking positive action by starting to engage in behaviors she could be proud of. "I took the actions my AA sponsor suggested, such as calling people on the phone. 'Call somebody newer than you are,' she'd say, 'and *don't* talk about yourself. Ask them how *they* are, how *they're* feeling.' She'd also tell me to see my everyday household chores as self-esteem or growth exercises. These little actions, such as waxing the kitchen floor or straightening out the shoes in the closet, turned out to be important first steps in getting some order back into my life, which helped me to start liking myself again."

Going back to work also helped repair Julie's sagging self-esteem. AA stresses the importance of a job and encourages the recovering alcoholic to become self-supporting, beholden to no one. (We'll focus on work in the next chapter.) During her first year and a half of sobriety, Julie had been living off the remainder of an inheritance from her father, but when that ran out she had no choice but to find a job. "One thing I knew was that being a saloon singer probably wasn't a good idea." She ended up getting a job at a foundation for retarded children.

After working for a while, Julie was astounded to discover how much better she felt. "It forced me to rejoin the human race. When I was drinking, I can remember looking at the commuter traffic on the Chicago expressway and thinking, *They all know some secret about living that I don't know.* I had always felt like an outsider. But after I went to work in sobriety, I no longer felt like an outsider. For the first time in my life, I felt like a contributing member of society, a 'worker among workers,' as AA says. I was now an official commuter among commuters. I was just like everybody else, and I liked that feeling a whole lot."

After a few years of sobriety and working, Julie got married again, this time to a man she met in AA. She continued to work, switching to a job in a marketing and public relations firm. Of her husband, Julie says, "I think I married him because he was one of the few men I knew in AA who wore suits. I was always attracted to the executive type." Ultimately the marriage broke up, but Julie reflects, "I'm grateful to him for the fact that we were together for 15 years, and he was a good father to my daughter. He was able to provide her with the normal family life she needed growing up."

One thing that helped Julie get better at being able to read her feelings was paying more attention to all the accompanying bodily clues. "I get definite physical signals, a knot in my gut, or a little punch in my stomach, like when I was pregnant. Other times my skin feels affected. Initially, I paid no attention to these clues. I didn't trust them. It took me a couple of years to get to the point where I dared make an actual decision based on them. Today, I count on them, even in my work. I find that when

I use both my intuition and my brain, about 95 percent of my judgments about people are right. Twenty years ago I met a woman, and I remember that the top of my skin suddenly felt crawly, and out of the blue I thought, *I'd never leave my daughter alone with this woman.* Then, *Why am I even thinking this?* For some reason I picked up danger. Two years later I found out that this woman had been in prison for killing her husband."

Julie is the first to admit that she's not always right, however. "Sometimes I'll override what I *think* is an intuitive feeling because of a practical need. I've had bad feelings about getting on planes, but maybe it was important for me to get someplace, so I got on the plane anyway. And, here I am, so maybe it wasn't intuition after all. Maybe it was just my old fear of flying. Obviously, I've got some more fine tuning to do!"

To avoid such errors, recovering people need to learn to move slowly, and to balance feelings and intuition with intellect and facts, the right-brain stuff with the left-brain stuff. It's all there for a reason. Says Julie, "I'd be dead if I'd gone chasing off after every gut reaction. Even today, after 22 years, I'll still say to myself, 'Okay, Julie, this *feels* right, but I think it would be a good idea to give it a while and see how it goes. Then I'll check out my so-called intuition with a few other people and see what they say before I do anything about it.' I've learned to stop reacting impulsively by giving things time."

Making the Grade

"I consider my recovery the single greatest achievement of my whole life," says Julie. Nonetheless, she is acutely aware that she still has some character defects to work on, one of which is her tendency to be co-dependent, to try to "fix" and rescue people. "I'm still your basic ambulance chaser!" she admits. "I appear at people's doorsteps with chicken soup and I suddenly materialize at their hospital bedsides. I've sought help for this. I've gone to all kinds of Adult Children of Alcoholics [ACA or ACOA] workshops and seminars. Intellectually, I now understand perfectly well what I'm doing when I try to rescue people: I'm *still* trying to save Daddy! But emotionally it's a whole different story. When somebody who needs saving shows up in my life, a bell goes off and I'm down the fire pole!"

But in spite of any lingering flaws, just how far Julie has come in her 22 years of sobriety hit her a few years ago at a political fundraiser. "I was doing some PR for one of the candidates, and at dinner they sat me next to an ex-governor, and the two of us carried on an energetic conversation for the entire evening. The fact that I could actually *do* that, that I could sit there and hold my own with an ex-governor and feel so comfortable that I didn't even once *think* about wanting a drink, made a big impression on me. It made me realize just how much recovery has taken place inside of me. That night, I experienced the feeling that AA promises us we'll feel if we just hang in: Of and by myself, I am enough. Today, of and by myself, I feel I am enough."

SOBER FEELINGS TIPS LIST

1. Turn to the *Feelings List* at the end of this chapter. This list will be one of your most valuable tools. Photocopy it. Carry it around with you. Use it to identify your feelings.

2. Go to anonymous group meetings. Listen to people talk about *their* feelings. See which ones you can identify in yourself. Label them so you can spot them faster next time they come up.

3. A thought is not a feeling. Learn the difference. A thought is, "He's got a flat tire" or "The Dodgers won." A feeling is happy, sad, mad, or glad.

4. You are what you *do,* and so is everybody else. Don't just listen to people's words, look at their deeds. Behavior is everything. Decent behavior is the real cure for low self-esteem!

5. Begin to trust your intuition, your gut. If something feels inappropriate, it probably *is* inappropriate. Honor that feeling.

6. Your body knows what's okay and what's not okay. Pay attention to bodily clues such as a knot or jab in the stomach, tingly skin, light-headedness, headache, shallow breathing, a sense of shock, or squeamishness.

7. Don't intellectualize your feelings. Anger is not "in your head." Anger is a feeling. Make it real and deal with it.

8. Save your intellect for things like balancing your checkbook and reading maps. Don't count on it for evaluating a love relationship or dealing with a friend.

9. Self-blame ("I'm probably wrong") is sometimes a way of avoiding real feelings. What are your *real* feelings?

10. Make a list of your character defects. How are they holding you up? Start working on fixing them.

11. If you want outside psychotherapy in addition to AA, make sure the therapist (1) is knowledgeable about addiction, (2) understands AA, and (3) supports your going to AA while you're in therapy.

12. Remember, the magic of AA's success is "sharing experience, strength and hope." If you do nothing else, *go to AA meetings* faithfully.

13. Don't bother trying to find out "why" you drank. Nobody knows as yet what causes alcoholism. You can stay sober forever without finding out what made you an alcoholic in the first place.

14. For fun, follow some of your intuitions, as if they were butterflies, just to see where they lead you.

15. Perfectionism is a character defect most alcoholics seem to share. Let it go! Remember, who are you *not* to make a mistake?

16. Tell the truth about how you feel and what you want. It really will set you free.

17. Put sobriety first. Every day, do whatever you have to do to maintain it.

18. You can't throw away just one side of a coin. To feel joy, you must also feel pain, so don't be afraid of pain. Joy will follow.

19. As best you can, keep current with your feelings on a daily basis. Don't let them stack up.

20. The purpose of your sobriety is to become the person you were on your way to becoming when your journey was so rudely interrupted by your addiction.

FEELINGS LIST

abandoned
accepted
admiring
affectionate
afraid
aggravated
alarmed
alienated
amazed
angry
animosity
annoyed
antagonistic
anticipatory
anxious
appreciative
apprehensive
approving
ashamed
aspiring
assured
attracted
aversion
avoiding
balmy
belittled
belligerent
bitter
bold
bored
bottled up
brave
calm
capable
cautious
cheated
cocky

cold
comfortable
compassionate
competent
competitive
complete
concerned
confident
conflicted
confused
contemptful
contented
courageous
cowardly
creative
crushed
curious
daring
defeated
delighted
depressed
desired
desirous
desolate
despairing
desperate
despondent
disappointed
discouraged
disinterested
dislike
displeased
dissatisfied
distant
distracted
dispassionate
distressed

distrustful
dominated
dread
eager
ecstatic
elated
embarrassed
empathetic
empty
enduring
enthusiastic
envious
euphoric
evasive
excited
exhausted
exhilarated
expectant
fearful
friendly
frustrated
fulfilled
furious
futile
glad
grateful
grieved
guilty
gutless
gutsy
happy
hateful
helpless
hopeful
hopeless
horny
hostile

humble
humiliated
hurt
identification
impatient
impressed
inadequate
incompetent
indignant
indifferent
inflamed
insecure
insignificant
inspired
insulted
irrational
irritated
jazzed
jealous
joyful
lonely
longing
loved
loving
lustful
mad
miserable
misunderstood
needed
needy
negative
neglected
nervous
numb
passionate
patient
peaceful

pitying
pleased
preoccupied
pressured
proud
put down
puzzled
rageful
reborn
regretful
rejected
rejecting
rejuvenated
relaxed
relieved
remorseful
repelled
resentful
revulsion
ripped off
sad
satisfied
scared
sensual
serene
sexy
shame
shocked
sinful
sorrowful
sorry
spunky
startled
strong
stubborn
suffocated
supported

suspicious
surprised
sympathetic
tearful
tender
tense
terrified
threatened
thrilled
tired
transcendent
trapped
trusting
uncertain
uncooperative
understood
uneasy
unhappy
unloved
unworthy
upset
uptight
vague
vengeful
vindictive
wanted
warm
warmhearted
wary
weary
withdrawn
withholding
worried
worthless
worthy
yearning
other

3

SOBER WORK

Throughout all my years of drinking and self-destructive behavior, I still wanted to make something of myself. I wanted to be "discovered," only I didn't know at what. I figured that the person who discovered me would tell me what my talent was. That person never showed up. But what happened instead was I got sober, and I ended up discovering myself.

—Gabrielle, sober 17 years

One truth that got temporarily swept aside by the women's movement is that men and women have different priorities. By and large, men focus on work first and relationships second; women focus on relationships first and work second. Once a man gets his work life settled, he feels he can take the time to seek a relationship as his reward (or pay more attention to the one he is currently in), whereas once a woman gets her relationship secured, she feels freer to devote time to her work. Without a secure relationship, even the most career-oriented woman may still have that haunting feeling that something is missing in her life.

Given that this book is about women, I wasn't sure which chapter to put first—the chapter on love or the chapter on work. In the end I decided to put the work chapter first because AA puts work first. AA makes it very clear that recovering alcoholics, both male and female, need to get their work lives in order before they focus on their relationships. Relationships will only distract them from the most important goal: to stay clean and sober.

AA's Work Philosophy

There are a number of reasons why AA puts such emphasis on work. One of them is strictly practical: survival. In today's economy, it usually takes more than one paycheck to support a family. Even if the recovering alcoholic woman is married, she will probably have to go to work or continue to work, whichever the case may be. AA also supports the idea that there's no free lunch. It's important that recovering alcoholics, women as well as men, become self-supporting rather than beholden to others. Taking money from a spouse, partner, parents, or the government, or borrowing from friends, keeps the recovering person in a childlike, dependent position where they are more likely to be influenced by the wants and needs of others. For example, a husband who controls his recovering alcoholic wife through money may not "let" her take the car to go to her AA meeting. Maybe her sobriety threatens him, or he's afraid she'll meet another man. If she had her own money, her own car, and her own independence, she would have a better chance of survival. In this chapter, our first interviewee, Gabrielle, lived on state disability during her first few years of sobriety. But in order to stay emotionally comfortable enough to stay sober, she knew she had to grow up, get a job, and support herself.

As an organization, AA lives by this same self-supporting philosophy. AA refuses to accept free meeting halls (rent is always paid) and does not accept financial contributions from anyone who is not an AA member. In doing so, AA does not run the risk of being influenced by outside individuals or groups who may have their own agendas. Even AA members are limited as to the amount of money they can contribute within a given year. This way, AA stays free of corruption.

Another reason AA stresses work is because most newly sober alcoholics have a lot to learn about the subject! It's a rare alcoholic who *doesn't* have problems in the work area, whether it's office work, creative work, school work, or volunteer work. Some come into sobriety having lost their jobs; for others, their jobs are in jeopardy because of their drinking. AA knows that if the recovering person is ever going to succeed in life, he or she is simply going to have to learn how to be a good worker. Even those who overwork themselves to the point of workaholism are encouraged to look at that behavior as a possible problem, as something they may be doing in order to avoid dealing with other areas of their lives that may be screaming for attention—spouse, kids, friends, health, spirituality, and of course, feelings.

Dragging Character Defects into Work

Alcoholics in their first few years of sobriety typically bring the character defects from their personal lives into the workplace with them. On the job, these people are often self-centered, irresponsible, unreliable, and unproductive. They don't seem to grasp the concept that work takes work. They want instant success, instant CEO status, instant big bucks. They don't want to pay their dues. Many alcoholic employees have deep-seated feelings of discomfort when dealing with authority figures. They may bristle and become defensive when corrected or criticized. Before they got sober, they may have seen their supervisor or boss as a threat, someone who could interfere with what the alcoholic employee most wanted to do—drink and use. The employee may have spent a lot of time and energy trying to hide the addiction problem, resulting in behavior that may have appeared puzzling, secretive, or even deceitful to the supervisor.

After sobriety, these old employee-supervisor tensions are bound to linger for a while, just as they do in a family when one of its members suddenly sobers up. Everyone needs some time to adjust to the alcoholic's new sober role. In this chapter, our second interviewee, Leah, is a good example of a recovering alcoholic who had trouble dealing with authority both before and after she got sober. Her ultimate solution was to start her own company so that *she* could be the boss!

In addition to having troubles with their supervisors, many recovering alcoholic employees can't handle conflicts with their co-workers. They need to learn how to function as part of a workplace team. Women, especially, tend to personalize interoffice conflicts and fail to see that *not* resolving them appropriately can actually hurt business. They may attempt to handle the problem by passive-aggressive means instead of confronting an issue directly. They'll gossip, backbite, and complain to people who are powerless to do anything about it, or they'll passively resist by being late, slowing down their production, or using company time to do personal business. Not only is this destructive to the job and to the company, but it's also destructive to the recovering alcoholic, whose festering resentments may well lead right back to the bottle.

Another thing recovering alcoholic employees may do is drag their unresolved dysfunctional-family issues into work and start reacting to their employers and co-workers as if they were family members. We see this dynamic at work in our third interview with Deanne, an actress and star of a TV series, ended up treating the network executives as if they were the grown-ups and treating the cast and crew as if they were her siblings. By doing this, she held her career back for years.

That's why AA says it's important for members to get insight into their own family dynamics (through working the 12 steps or even through therapy) so that they don't re-create them on the job.

THE AA SLOGANS

To help recovering alcoholics learn to be good workers, AA offers some handy little slogans to hang onto when the going gets rough:

"Suit up and show up" reminds AA members that responsibility, reliability, and persistence pay off.

"Be a worker among workers" reminds them not to hang onto childlike expectations of being "special" at work, and not to demand unearned privileges.

"Principles before personalities" reminds them to avoid taking interoffice conflicts personally and to handle them appropriately.

"Think service" reminds them that while they're on the job, they're there to do what the boss wants them to do, not what *they* want to do.

WORKING SOBER AND LIKING IT

Responsible work behavior, then, is considered absolutely essential to sobriety. The rewards of work, AA says, will come only *after* one's work agreements have been carried out. By utilizing the steps, tips, and tools offered by Alcoholics Anonymous, the recovering person not only learns *how* to work, but also learns that work can be both satisfying and profitable.

The major purpose of Alcoholics Anonymous is to help the alcoholic stop drinking and stay stopped. Obviously, the happier the recovering alcoholic is at work, the less likely he or she is to drink again. Conversely, when a work situation is so stressful that it becomes an actual threat to sobriety, the AA member is encouraged to deal with the situation so that it's no longer so stressful, or quit the job and find something else. AA doesn't view work as the salt mines—far from it. Once the alcoholic has learned how to be a good worker, AA bends over backward to encourage and support each member to find his or her dream. We definitely see this in the case of Gabrielle. After many years of finally learning how to work successfully at a paying job, Gabrielle quit her job to return to school. She eventually started her own business and became a painter.

Finally, whatever work the recovering alcoholic chooses to do, AA insists that it be honest and legal. It's not acceptable, for example, for a now-sober car salesperson to cheat a customer, or for a recovering addict to earn a living by selling cocaine! This is not only for moral reasons but also for survival reasons. The rationale is that dishonest and illegal behaviors cause guilt, which feels uncomfortable, and if a person is uncomfortable he or she might return to drinking. Once again, sobriety comes first.

By following the work guidelines set forth by Alcoholics Anonymous, the recovering alcoholic can do very well in life and discover that sobriety, integrity, a good work attitude, and a good work ethic can turn out to be secrets of success.

GABRIELLE, SOBER 17 YEARS

> *I knew I had talent at the age of*
> *eight when I sold my first painting*
> *for ten cents. I've spent every*
> *moment of my life since then strug-*
> *gling between my need to acknowl-*
> *edge my art and my tendency to dis-*
> *tract myself from my art. Alcohol,*
> *pills, suicide attempts, stealing,*
> *and relationships have all been dis-*
> *tractions.*
>
> —Gabrielle

Gabrielle, 43, a tall, blond painter/film editor, was born in Paris, France, the oldest of three children. She has a sister and a brother. When she was six, her parents emigrated to the United States by way of Canada. Gabrielle was single until the age of 41, when she married an actor she met in AA. The marriage was short-lived. She has no children but is now "considering adoption," she says, "with or without a husband."

Gabrielle's father, whom she describes as a somewhat distant man, is a frustrated painter who has worked all his life in the restaurant business, starting out in the cafés of Paris at the age of 18 and eventually owning and operating his own French restaurant in America.

"He purposely hung onto his French accent to add atmosphere to the restaurant," Gabrielle says. Her mother, a highly critical, emotional woman, taught sewing at a high school and did alterations out of the house. "She had episodes of deep depression. Occasionally she'd threaten suicide, which terrified me, especially because my father, who felt he couldn't handle her, kept telling me, 'You're the oldest, Gabrielle. It's your responsibility to keep your mother happy.' I grew to feel personally responsible for her moods. I knew that if she died, it would be my fault because I'd made her unhappy. For years into my sobriety, I *still* felt responsible for her moods. In fact, I was one of those people who watched the news and thought that the whole world had to be all right before *I* could have a life! Happily, today I no longer carry the weight of the world on my shoulders.

By the time Gabrielle was 19 she was drinking cheap wine nearly every day. "I'd become a regular wino. In fact, a neighbor once said to me, 'Honey, you like to drink a lot!' People were noticing. I'd go to someone's party and drink, and wake up later on their bathroom floor."

Getting Something for Nothing

At the time, Gabrielle looked for ways to sidestep the pain that her family situation caused her. At 15, she started drinking and stealing.

"I'd drink whatever was there—hard liquor, malt, wine—and that gave me the 'false courage' I needed to steal. "I'd always felt deprived, so I guess I needed something to fill up that empty space," she says. "I loved getting something for nothing, but I also think I stole out of anger to prove how stupid people were and how easy it was to get away with things. When my clothes got dirty, I stole more. Once I walked into a store wearing a coat I'd stolen from there the year before. I hung my old coat on a hanger and put on a new coat. Then I walked up to the counter, paid for some underwear, and walked out!

"I liked to steal small but expensive items so I could go back to the store and exchange them for things I really wanted but were too big to steal. When I went to Paris as my high school graduation present from my aunt, I cased the Louvre for small items to steal, but they were too hard to get to. Once I stole a bunch of plants from a nursery, and when I told my therapist what I'd done, she said she needed some plants for her office and asked me to steal some for her. When I started dating my first boyfriend, we'd steal presents for each other. Once he stole a casserole for me, and when I lifted the lid, inside he'd spelled out the words 'I Love You' in white amphetamines. I was touched by his thoughtfulness."

Art was the one area in which Gabrielle felt grounded and in which she excelled. "In spite of all my other craziness, and in spite of the fact that my parents weren't supportive of my talent, I always knew I wanted to be an artist. In school I was lucky enough to have one of the nuns give me a lot of encouragement. I remember painting a picture for Easter, and she loved it. She asked my parents to have it framed, and then she showed it off to all the other nuns in school. By the time I reached high school, I was regularly referred to as 'the artist.' After high school, I took myself to Italy one summer to paint with a group of eight other artists, and another summer I studied watercolor painting at the Royal College of Arts in London."

On a Downward Spiral

Unfortunately, Gabrielle kept stealing and drinking, which had consequences. At 20, Gabrielle was picked up for shoplifting, spent a brief time in jail, and was sent back home (she'd moved out). She got a job at a fast-food restaurant. Meanwhile, her drinking was resulting in the same kinds of self-destructive behaviors she had seen and hated in her own mother, including suicide attempts. "I tried suicide so often it became just something to do, a sort of temporary escape. It never occurred to me it might work."

As a result, Gabrielle became the family's identified patient and "crazy" child and was sent on an endless round of visits to psychiatrists, psychologists, social workers, mental hospitals, and therapy groups. In between, she tried to go to college, but after taking four years to complete a year of coursework, she dropped out. "I was labeled a paranoid schizophrenic by the state, a manic-depressive by a private psychiatrist, and a chronic depressive by another. They all prescribed different pills to cure the problem and, of course, I took them all. I complained about some side effects to one psychiatrist, and instead of taking me off some of the pills I was on, she prescribed more to counteract the side effects."

After one suicide attempt, Gabrielle decided to try Alcoholics Anonymous. But after attending a few meetings, she learned that AA expected her not only to stop drinking but also to stop taking pills, she was shocked. "Then how do you handle sobriety?" was her immediate response. Convinced that life without painkillers was unthinkable, she left AA and went back to drinking.

One night Gabrielle took an overdose—on purpose—and called the Cremation Society. "I told the man, 'Look, I'm in the process of killing myself here and I want to make arrangements to be cremated and have my ashes cast to sea.' I guess it was unusual for the future corpse to call in and make the funeral arrangements, so at first he panicked, but when he saw that he couldn't talk me out of it, he gave me directions. He told me to write a suicide note and leave a check for $250 made out to the Cremation Society along with their name and phone number. I made out a bum check, took more pills, and passed out. My parents found me and I woke up in a hospital. They told me I probably wouldn't live through the night."

At the hospital, Gabrielle drifted in and out of consciousness, and then she had what she refers to today as "a near-death experience."

"[At the time] I had no idea that they were called near-death experiences. I'd had them before, but until I heard somebody describe one at an AA meeting, I didn't know there was anything unusual about them."

She recalls her own experience vividly: "I felt myself start to float up, away from my body toward an airplane that was waiting for me. I wanted to board the plane, but I couldn't because there was this doctor who kept talking to me, working on me, trying to bring me back, telling me all kinds of things, telling me he'd like to take me out on his boat. He just kept talking and talking and he wouldn't shut up. I couldn't answer him, but I couldn't get away from him either, and because of his talking I missed the plane and I had to come back to earth."

Gabrielle recovered, and 12 days later she crawled back to AA. "I was only 26, which is pretty young for an alcoholic to throw in the towel, but I knew I had no place else to go." She's been sober ever since. As for the doctor she saw during her near-death experience, she never did find out who he was.

Because of her history of mental problems, Gabrielle lived on Aid to the Totally Disabled during her first four years of sobriety. She moved into a halfway house for recovering alcoholics. And, to prepare herself to become self-supporting (as AA was encouraging her to do), she enrolled in college to study film production. Her tuition was paid for by the Department of Alcoholic Rehabilitation. She took courses in film editing. After two years, she got her A.A. degree. Through friends in Alcoholics Anonymous (AA is excellent for networking, even though that's not its purpose), Gabrielle landed what was supposed to be a temporary job as an apprentice editor in the film editing department of a movie studio. That first position blossomed into a ten-year career. In the beginning, just suiting up and showing up on the job every day was hard work for Gabrielle. Her work habits were not exactly exemplary. "Frankly, I had a rotten work attitude. I always wanted people to do things my way. Finally a man in AA told me, 'If you're not the boss,

you're there to do what the boss says to do. Period. That's
all you need to know. Someday when *you're* the boss then
you'll get to do things your way.' That helped me so
much. After that I was able to settle in. I turned out to
have a knack for film editing, and I kept getting promoted. I was upgraded from apprentice to assistant film editor to film editor, and I got into the union. Even though
this was the mid-to-late eighties, there still weren't that
many women film editors. People would have killed for
the job I just fell into!"

From State Aid to $60,000 a Year

Gabrielle couldn't have been a better example of the AA
work philosophy. In 10 years she went from being on state
aid to earning $60,000 a year. "That ought to show you
what AA can do!" she says.

The trouble was, the film editing job left Gabrielle no
time to paint. At first painting wasn't that important to
her; getting well again and getting back on course took
precedence. But as the years went by, the urge to paint
got so strong that Gabrielle finally realized that she'd have
to do something about it, otherwise she'd be unhappy.
"I'd had little formal art education, and I realized that if I
was ever going to be a serious painter, I'd need to study
art formally and get credentialed, starting with getting my
B.A. degree."

With the encouragement and support of her AA
sponsor and her network of friends, Gabrielle took a huge
risk. She quit her high-paying job, "which by then had an
American Express gold card that went with it!" she says,
laughing. She went back to school and majored in fine
arts. To support herself, she took another huge risk. She
went into the film editing business for herself, working
out of her apartment. "I'd learned film editing so well
that I could do it in my sleep." Investing in a computer
and a moviola, she started a business providing editorial

film services. The movie studio that had been her former employer became her first client. Her business made a substantial profit even in that difficult first year and is still going well.

Returning to school in sobriety, just like returning to work in sobriety, wasn't easy for Gabrielle in the beginning. "My mind had been so shattered by drinking that when it didn't just snap back immediately, I panicked. My immediate response was to think suicide! I seriously considered the idea of trying to drown myself by putting a rock on my head!" However, thanks to some solid AA advice, she got a tutor instead. She did well on her first exam: "There were two As in the class, and I was one of them," she says proudly. That one success gave Gabrielle enough confidence to stay in school. She graduated with a Bachelor of Fine Arts degree at the age of 40.

At 41, Gabrielle got married for the first time to an actor, John, then 38, whom she met in AA. Unfortunately, it was not a marriage made in heaven; they were together less than two years. John turned out to be one of those impulsive boy-men who proved incapable of handling money, marriage, or responsibility. He left her shortly before this interview took place. "He told me that he couldn't stay married to me because I was 'too healthy'! All my life I was the one who was too *sick* to have a good relationship. Now I'm too *healthy*?! I guess maybe I've changed more than I've been giving myself credit for!"

Looking back now on the early days of their relationship, Gabrielle can see that there were warning signs, but at the time she ignored them. "Even before we got married, John would go into these sudden emotional withdrawals, but I always made excuses for him. I'd say, 'Well, he's tired' or 'Well, actors are high-strung.' But basically, he was immature and everybody saw it but me. In fact, when we went to Paris on our honeymoon and visited my aunt, she said to me in French, 'Well, you've always wanted a child. Now you've got one.'"

The bottom line is that this relationship cost Gabrielle in every area of her life. It cost her emotionally. It cost her financially. It cost her creatively. It cost her hundreds of hours of time that might have been better spent doing something more fulfilling for her—like painting.

Getting Back on Track

But now, even without a relationship to distract her, Gabrielle still manages to find ways to avoid her creative work. She procrastinates, which is common among nonalcoholic artists as well. "The creative process is so easy to get distracted from. I come up with all kinds of things to keep me from my painting. Sometimes I even let errands take precedence over my painting. On my tombstone, instead of 'This woman was an artist,' it's going to read, 'This woman went to the store'!" she jokes.

Things are changing for Gabrielle, however. "The longer I'm sober, the more forceful the creative urge within me becomes, and the harder it is to distract myself. I used to be able to procrastinate and not paint for years because I could drink or take pills or steal to make the discomfort go away. But in sobriety, I can't do that. If I avoid my art for too long, I end up in both physical and emotional pain. The only thing that makes me feel better is getting down to business. Ultimately, the push to create becomes stronger than the push to avoid the work."

Another distraction from work has been Gabrielle's habit of criticizing herself. "I used to get totally paralyzed with self-criticism, with those voices in my head that would say, 'Who do you think you are to paint? You're not a real painter! You're a fake!'" But by attending AA meetings and talking with her AA sponsor about her mental monsters, Gabrielle learned a few tricks to help her through. "Whenever I find myself worrying about what somebody *else* thinks about my paintings, I remind myself of what my sponsor keeps telling me: 'What *they're* thinking is none of *your* business. If they want it to be your business, they'll tell you. If they say nothing, you have to assume everything's okay.' I repeat this over and over to myself, like a mantra, until it finally sinks in. It helps. I know that my job is to be a painter, not an art critic. Being inside other people's heads instead of my own takes too much energy. When I can just stay out of other people's heads, it's amazing how much more I can get done! That's when I'm able to get up the nerve to call galleries about hanging my work, or show slides of my work to art dealers, or start making arrangements for another one-woman show."

Gabrielle is openly grateful to Alcoholic Anonymous. "When I came to AA I didn't have a life. I *got* a life in AA. My sobriety is the most important thing that ever happened to me, and anything I've accomplished is a direct result of that. Sobriety *is* success."

In recent years the real gravy for Gabrielle has been the fact that painting has brought her real joy. "When I stop procrastinating, stop criticizing myself, and finally get down to painting, I feel great happiness. I get a feeling of 'Oh, *now* I know what it is that I'm supposed to be doing! *Now* I know why I'm alive!'"

LEAH, SOBER 14 YEARS

> *My success in business comes from the fact that I know I'm going to succeed. I don't write big marketing plans, or make out elaborate budgets, or do any of those things people do in business. I just go in there, and I succeed.*
>
> —Leah

Leah, 42, an outspoken beauty-contest winner turned businesswoman with wavy, sandy-colored hair and drop-dead green eyes, was born into a military family in Fort Benning, Georgia. She has an older brother and a younger sister. "We moved all over the country, mostly the South, as well as to Panama and Germany. We never lived anywhere longer than three years." She is currently divorced and has a nine-year-old son.

Leah's mother is an alcoholic and is now sober, too, but she is not in AA. Her father was not an alcoholic.

"He was the kind of social drinker that AA members like to laugh at. He'd drink a few drinks, but he always knew when to stop. Whenever he reached that point, he'd push the drink aside and say, 'No more of this for me, thanks. I'm beginning to *feel* it.'" She laughs. "'I'm beginning to *feel* it?' Now, no self-respecting alcoholic I know would ever talk that way! *Feeling* it is the whole point. That's how I know that my father wasn't a drunk."

Leah's father also possessed a strong Midwestern work ethic, which he passed on to Leah, and it's helped her in her own work life. "He'd tell me, 'You go to work to work. If you have a job, you do the best you can do, and if you earn $50 you don't spend more than that.'"

When it came to child-raising, both parents believed in heavy discipline and swift punishment. Her mother was quick-tempered, and if Leah did something she thought was wrong, her mother would hit her. Sometimes those hits became beatings, and Leah quickly learned that by being covert and manipulative she could create situations to get her brother in trouble so he'd get hit instead. Later, her brother got back at Leah by exposing himself to her and eventually by sexually molesting her.

"It started when I was 12 and he was 15. There was never any penetration, just fondling. He has even made sexual innuendos and advances to me as an adult, but he's such a sick-in-the-head creature that I've never directly confronted him about it." As for Leah, she dealt with the sexual and physical abuse by involving herself in three years of intensive psychotherapy between the time she was 9 and 12 years sober.

Rebel on the Loose

In grade school, Leah describes herself as being "defiant, antagonistic, a big-mouth, a ringleader, an instigator—and very popular." She was also athletic and beautiful. "I entered beauty contests, but my self-esteem was so low that whenever I won, I'd think, *They're playing a joke on me.*"

When Leah was 13, her father was sent to Germany, and the family followed. That's where she started drinking. "I instantly fell in with the German crowd, learned German, and drank. The very first time I drank, I got drunk. I started leading a double life. In school, I was this cheerleader who got good grades, and at night I'd sneak out to bars with my friends, follow music groups around, get drunk, get into bar fights, and get picked up by the American military. Once a group of us got drunk and broke into the general's house. It almost caused my father to lose a promotion. My parents were unable to control my behavior. I was bent on having fun and doing what I wanted."

By the time Leah was 19, she was back in America living on her own and was a full-fledged alcoholic. She started college but later dropped out. "Drinking got in the way," she explains. She moved to Nashville, Tennessee, and got a typing job at an insurance firm. "For excitement I drank, went to nightclubs, and hung around with drug dealers. I was attracted to the seedy side of life. I had a boyfriend who was a heroin addict, but for some reason I never took drugs myself. I just drank."

Struggles in Work and Relationships

When it came to her attitude about men, Leah says, "I was always determined never to pretend that I thought a man was smarter than I was if he wasn't. I loved men, but I refused to take second seat to a man's ego. My choices always ended up being disasters. To give you an idea, once I met a very rich, glamorous man on a plane—an alcoholic, of course!—and we started a relationship that ended three years later with our throwing each other out of moving cars."

Of the three women in this chapter, Leah is the one who has allowed relationships to interfere with her work life the least, both before sobriety and since. She's always had a straight-arrow determination to succeed and has put tremendous energy into her work. "I've always been fiercely competitive," she admits.

After five months at the insurance agency job, Leah went to work for an A & R (Artists and Repertoire) man who also happened to be an alcoholic. "Interestingly enough, that man is sober in AA today and working as a disc jockey. He turned out to be a really great person, but at the time, because his drinking was getting in the way of his job—even more than my drinking was getting in the way of my job—it fell on me to do his work. Eventually, he got fired and I got his job, but not his pay! This was back in the late sixties, and I was the only female in Nashville at that time to hold such a position, not to mention I was only 20. It was a very big job. I was responsible for every aspect of putting out a record, from its inception, to setting up musicians, all the way through to the records being pressed and distributed. I had a lot of prestige in that job. It made me feel very important. And they gave me a $20 weekly increase! Now, I knew immediately that a $20 raise wasn't enough, but I was so grateful to have the job that even though the low pay bothered me, it didn't send me to the moon the way it would today."

As time and other jobs went on, however, Leah grew to resent the fact that she'd always end up running things while other people made the money. "One guy whose job *I* was doing was driving around in a Rolls-Royce!" Realizing she'd never get rich working for somebody else, she made the decision to go into business for herself. "Since I had no money and no college degree, I decided that my only option was to capitalize on the one thing that I knew well besides the record industry, which was office work—something I'd always excelled at." Leah started an employment agency for temporary office workers. "In the beginning I had no other employees, so *I* was the temp."

For the first year she worked 18 hours a day, learning as she went. "I also started a typing service on the side to get money to live on, and I'd type manuscripts all night."

The only hitch was that Leah was still drinking. "No matter how smart you are, and no matter how efficient you are, if you're an alcoholic it catches up with you. My work ethic was fine until I took that first drink. Then I lost control over what I did. I had all my rules down about drinking—I was always big on rules—but the moment I got a drink in me, I'd end up breaking them. I'd say, 'I'll only drink this much at this time,' and then I'd break the rule, and I'd have to redraw the line again somewhere else. I wasn't doing an honest day's work. I ran a phone line from my business to my home, so when I was too drunk to go in to work, it would ring at my home, and I'd pretend I was at work. Behind the wheel of a car, I was a menace. I'd drive down streets the wrong way, and then plow back the other way in reverse. I didn't care. I valued nothing. I stopped going to business events and work-related parties. All I wanted to do was go home and drink. If I ever had a drink at lunch, that's all she wrote! Instead of going back to the office, I'd end up in another state. A couple of times I went to bed with clients, which was another rule I said I'd *never* break. Deep down, I'm very moralistic, and this kind of behavior was totally unaccept-able to me. Toward the end, I was just squeaking by on my good looks and on my ability to be convincing, but my business wasn't growing. As long as I was drinking, I was putting a ceiling on my success."

Leah's Moment of Clarity

Leah was never in denial about her alcoholism. "I knew I was an alcoholic. I just wasn't ready to do anything about it," she says. She started going to AA, but she didn't stay. She returned to drinking. However, the second time she went to AA, two years later, she *was* ready. "What I heard there the second time was basically the same thing I'd heard the first time, only this time I heard it differently. The second time I felt a feeling of love in the room that reverberated off the walls and surrounded me, and it was magical. It made me know that AA was what I wanted."

This, Leah's moment of clarity, may not have been dramatic—no white lights—but it was profound. She's been sober ever since. "There was this little flicker of light that flashed through my mind, and I knew there was hope. It was the idea that there was, after all, another way to go. All it took was that one tiny moment, and that was enough."

Back in Business

Even though Leah functioned fairly well as a drinking alcoholic, the difference between working drunk and working sober was like night and day. "Sober, I started making money hand over fist. Everything I touched made money. The reason was that I was there with mental presence, not just physical presence. Because of that, things started clicking. My business began to grow again. My salary went to six figures." When Leah was less than a year sober, a time when many alcoholics are just starting to venture out into the working world again, Leah was able to take some of her earnings and buy herself a present—a Mercedes.

In AA, Leah began to learn that the same intuitive skills she was learning to develop in the area of personal relationships could also be used at work to help her make business decisions. "I kept meeting people who wanted to help me, and I think it's because I was coming from an honest place. My intent was, and is, to do good work. If people get that feeling from you, then they want to do business with you. However, there were times when I had to say no to offers of help, and AA helped me figure out who to say yes to and who to say no to. One time I met the chairman of the board of a major corporation, and he said he'd give me anything I wanted. He was giving me his company as a client, but I wouldn't take it because I *knew* he wanted to have an affair, and that's not how I wanted to do business. In sobriety, if I'm doing something that's not right for me, I know it instantly because I get physically uncomfortable. Sometimes I get a knot in my gut, sometimes belabored breathing, sometimes just a feeling of wanting to escape or get away from a person or situation. Whatever it is, when *it* says no, *I* say no."

After a few years of sobriety, Leah, like Gabrielle, married a man she'd met in AA. His name was Tony, and they had a son, Terry. Again, as with Gabrielle, the marriage turned out to be a mistake. "He was one of the sexiest, most flamboyant men I'd ever met, and I was absolutely passionate about him, but he was also one of the most irresponsible, explosive persons I've ever known," Leah says. "If he was driving and people cut him off, he'd chase them for miles, jerk them out of their cars, and terrify them. I was constantly cleaning up the messes he'd made, until I realized that, if I kept focusing on him, both my business and my sanity would go right down the tubes. Finally I said, 'That's it! That's the end. There is no more.'"

They divorced. Leah adds, "Not surprisingly, he's been a lousy father, too, more damaging to my son than an earthquake. Every time Terry went to see him he'd come back a mess. My son needs a male role model, not an irresponsible, out-of-control person who doesn't even pay child support. I finally had to get a court order to have Terry's visitations monitored, and since then Terry has calmed down considerably."

If Tony is an AA member, why is he still so wild and irresponsible? To this Leah answers, "Tony *says* he's sober, but in my opinion he certainly wasn't sober when we were together, at least not according to the AA definition of sobriety, which prohibits all mind-altering chemicals. He took pain pills—for his 'bad back,' he said—but I think those pills really affected his head. As long as he was on pills he didn't have to feel his feelings, so he wasn't motivated to grow up."

Seeking Balance in Life and Love

Recovery programs teach the importance of balance in the various areas of people's lives. In the work area, at least, balance is what Leah seems to have finally achieved. "In sobriety, I've *purposely* capped my success. I've had opportunities where I could have expanded my employment agency business, gone national, had offices in different cities, spun off into different business endeavors, even had a television show—it's all been in my lap at one time or another—but I made a conscious decision not to get involved in all-consuming work, so I said no to these opportunities. It took me six or seven years of sobriety just to learn that I *could* say no to more business!"

She goes on: "When my son was two or three, I had a shift in priorities. I realized that there was no amount of money, prestige, or success that was as important as having time with my son. Instead of leaving Terry in day-care, I started leaving work at 3 or 4 in the afternoon so I could be with him. I went from working 10 or 12 hours a day to working a reasonable 7 hours a day. I go into the office, I do a good day's work, I leave, I spend time with my son, I go to AA, and that's it. I don't bring the work home. I take days off. I take vacations. I lead a moderate life."

Leah admits that she'd like to balance out her life even more with a good relationship. "I've been successful at work, and now I'd like to be successful at love, too, even though some days I don't know if I have the energy for it! But I think I'm ready for it. I think maybe today I could do some of the things that women do who have good relationships. Maybe now I could be part of a team and share with a man, even if it means playing second fiddle!"

A few months ago Leah had a big insight: She realized that the main thing that's been keeping her from meeting men is her other addiction—gambling. "I come from a gambling family. I've gambled and played cards all my life. And just as I had all kinds of rules about drinking, I've had them about gambling, too. One of my rules was 'Never drink and gamble at the same time.' I stuck to it. After I got sober, I'd frequently go off on gambling junkets, flying here and there, and at least once a week I'd play cards locally. If I couldn't go, I was a lunatic! I'd justify going, saying, 'It's the only thing that gives me pleasure,' which is just what people say about drinking. I was very controlled. I never lost money, but gambling was still hurting me in all other kinds of ways. It was keeping me from dealing with my loneliness. Gambling gave me a rush; it filled me up. When I gambled, I didn't need a man, I didn't need sex, I didn't even need food. What I came to realize was that gambling was just another way for me to numb myself and detach myself from my life, so a few months ago I decided to give it up."

Since then, Leah has been feeling more open to meeting a man, and more prepared to do the necessary work. "All my life I've relied on my looks to draw men in. Men would approach me at the car wash and in supermarkets, so I never even had to work at it. But what worked for me at 32 probably isn't going to work for me at 42, so I'd better get out there and do a little footwork myself."

However, with the confidence that Leah's years of business experience and success have given her, she says, "I *will* succeed at this, you know. I always succeed at what I do."

DEANNE, SOBER 15 YEARS

> *Early in my sobriety, I became a celebrity*
> *and made a lot of money. It made me*
> *extremely uncomfortable. I didn't think it*
> *was okay for me to be rich and famous. I*
> *was guilty and apologetic about it, and I*
> *kept giving my money away.*
>   —Deanne

Deanne, 52, a blond, soft-spoken actress seen frequently on stage and television, was born in Washington, D.C., to two alcoholic parents "who were very much in denial," she says. Recently remarried, she has three grown children from her first marriage. Of the three women in this chapter, Deanne is the one who, at least currently, seems to be achieving that sought-after balance between work and love.

"I was an unwanted child. My parents tried to abort me. They failed." Her parents went on to have five more daughters. The girls grew up on a "gentleman's farm" in Connecticut, complete with animals, a horse and buggy, a full household staff—and absentee parents who spent most of their time traveling. "We were taught to be formal with our mother and father, to stand up whenever either of them entered the room. Nonetheless, they were witty and had interesting friends, and I thought they were glamorous. I adored them."

When it came to feelings, Deanne's parents were experts at denial, and they taught their children to do the same. "In later years, when my sister had a child who died at birth, no one in the family ever talked about or even mentioned it. It was as though the child had never existed."

Whenever Deanne's mother displayed strange, alcoholic behavior, it never occurred to Deanne to protest or complain. "One minute she'd be wonderful to me and tell me I was remarkable, and the next minute she'd be terrible to me and call me a stupid bitch and a whore, and she'd throw things at me from across the room." Deanne just swallowed all her feelings about the matter, and everybody pretended that nothing was wrong.

An Early Introduction to Alcohol

Deanne's father did undercover work for the government. "It was all very secretive and mysterious, and we never knew quite what he did." When Deanne was 11, the family moved to Austria. "We lived in a small village in an idyllic *Sound of Music* setting, but in the village school I went to, the teacher would hit us under the desk with a stick. I didn't even speak the language, and that made me feel even more alone. I shook all the time, and nobody knew why. My mother took me to a doctor who prescribed alcohol, and that's how it all began. Right then and there I learned that booze is medicine. Feel unhappy? Here's a drink. Bad news? Sit down and pour yourself a drink. I remember trying to pour scotch into a spoon so I could take my medicine—I was shaking so much I couldn't get it to my mouth. I ended up taking a swig right out of the bottle."

At age 12, after a year in the village school, Deanne's parents sent her off to boarding school in England to study acting and dance. Even though acting and dance were her passion, and she trained strenuously in both areas for years, she still saw boarding school as her parents' way of getting rid of her. "I felt abandoned, thrown away, and I cried for years," she says. "I cried so much that my teacher would say, 'Would you please go to the back of the room and cry more quietly?' I lived for vacations when I could go home and be with my parents and sisters."

After returning to the United States at 15, Deanne experienced culture shock. "The girls my own age were so developed, so tall, and they all wore makeup and drank at parties. On my first day at school I thought the students were the teachers." In her desperate desire to fit in, Deanne began experimenting with drinking, and before long she was drinking on a regular basis.

At 16, while attending a Shakespearean festival, Deanne met an actor who also happened to be diabetic. "When my parents got wind of this relationship, they shipped me back to school in London to 'complete my education,' but I knew that the real reason was to get me away from him. I stayed nearly a year, but ultimately I dropped out of school to come back and marry him and, eventually, to take care of him." She was only 17. By 18 she had had her first child.

From Caretaker to Enabler

Over the next few years Deanne focused almost exclusively on her role as caretaker. She had two more children, and in addition to nursing her husband's diabetes, she also cared for her mother, whose alcoholism had gotten much worse. "It was the fifties and sixties, and I got caught in that transition period somewhere between Mrs. Cleaver and women's liberation," Deanne says. "My kids and my husband's acting career were my priority. Even though I'd studied hard and was a serious actress, and even though I did a lot of TV and stage work while I was married, both in the United States and in Canada, I still always put 'housewife' in the blank on my passport. I'll never forget the first time I put down 'actress' instead!"

She goes on: "Ultimately, what *I* wanted out of life got buried somewhere. The one good thing about it, at least, was the fact that all that caretaking forced me to keep my drinking in check for nearly a decade. If I'd been more of my own person, I think my drinking would have progressed a lot faster. Even when it *did* progress, it was never dramatic drinking. I didn't fall down, or hide bottles in the laundry basket, or drive across my neighbor's lawn. I drank, you might say, like a lady. In fact, when I finally turned myself in to AA my friends were shocked. They didn't even think I drank."

As a fairly typical at-home housewife/alcoholic, Deanne admits that she was so out of touch with her feelings that she didn't even know how much her life bothered her. "I didn't know I wasn't happy. I didn't know that I had resentments about having to take care of other people. I didn't know that I'd become an enabler. But looking back on it, I think enabling was my primary disease even before alcoholism. Enabling is what always got me into the most trouble. I'd always been taught to be a 'nice' person and to worry about how other people felt, not about how I felt, so if somebody kicked me in the face, *I* was the one who apologized! I ended up enabling my husband, too. He'd go out and sleep with other women, and I'd make sure his bed was turned down and his pajamas laid out for him when he got home."

Deanne didn't stay a happy enabler for long. "I thought I was just fine until one night, for no apparent reason, I tried to commit suicide by running out into the street in front of an oncoming car. Fortunately, I tripped and fell before I reached the path of the car. I ended up bruised and scratched, but not dead. However, the fact that I'd actually tried to *kill* myself without even knowing why got my attention! How very well I'd learned those family lessons about denial!"

Deanne started psychotherapy, and her life began to go off in a new direction. Even though she was still drinking, in therapy she was able at least to begin the process of getting in touch with her feelings. She realized that she was miserable in her marriage and wanted out. She and her husband got a divorce. "Still, it was hard leaving that marriage. I'd met him at 16, and now I was 30, meaning I'd been with him nearly half my life."

Once divorced, and as much out of necessity as for any other reason, Deanne finally started paying attention to the one person she'd always neglected—herself.

Occupation: Actress

While many women who find themselves suddenly alone with three kids to raise might have given up their creative ambitions and settled for the safety of an office job, Deanne chose not to do that. "When I asked myself what kind of work I wanted to do full-time, I think I was intuitively guided in my answer because, without a moment's hesitation, I said acting. I just figured that since I hadn't finished high school, I probably wouldn't be able to get a 'real' job anyway, so I might as well dive back into acting since it was all I thought I could do!"

The bottom line is that, within a few short years, Deanne became extraordinarily successful.

"When my husband and I separated, we sold the house I'd bought years before with a small inheritance, and we split the profits. When that was gone, I had nothing. I didn't even ask for alimony, and there wasn't much in the way of child support because he just didn't have it. I was wearing bargain-basement nightgowns for dresses. So when I got a chance to audition for a part in a TV series, I drove right to Los Angeles. It was amazing that the role was still open. They'd been testing everybody in town. I think if I *hadn't* been drinking at that time I'd probably have panicked and maybe even blown the audition, but I was in blissful ignorance about how really desperate my situation was, so I just showed up, like they tell you to do in AA, and—maybe because I was a fresh face—I got the part. I guess God looks out for drunks!"

To Deanne's surprise, the TV show was an instant hit (it ended up running for 13 years) and it made her both rich and famous.

"I made it as an actress at the very peak of my drinking," Deanne says. That's not a common story. More often, alcoholics are driven into AA by pain and failure, but what drove Deanne into AA was her stunning success. "I got so much attention and made so much money so fast that it totally overwhelmed me," she admits. "I didn't think I deserved it, and that made it even more of a problem."

Countless interviews, public appearances, photo sessions—all of these put so many demands on Deanne's time and energy that she realized she couldn't handle it all and drink, too. To cope, she was clearly going to have to have her wits about her, which meant she'd have to stop drinking. That realization was her moment of clarity! Quickly and quietly, without any fuss, Deanne sneaked into a meeting of Alcoholics Anonymous and got sober.

The hardest part of her success and her sobriety, she says, was the impact both had on her children. "When I got sober, my youngest son was only 9, and I don't know which was worse for him: me being home all the time and drunk and miserable, or me being sober and successful, but never home. On top of working long hours, I was going to AA meetings at night. My older children were somewhat independent, but when my son would see me run out of the house to go to a meeting, after I'd already been on the set of my TV show all day, he'd feel abandoned, just as I'd always felt abandoned when my parents sent me off to boarding school. I had tremendous feelings of guilt about this, even though I *knew* I had to go to AA meetings in order to stay sober and, naturally, I had to work. For working mothers, that guilt just goes with the territory and I don't think there's any solution. Ultimately, I had to stop beating up on myself about it and remind myself that I really did love my children, that I gave them the best I could, and that I did it without a whole lot of help from anybody else."

Whether the work one does is painting, typing, running a business, or starring in a television series, the task of learning how to become a better worker is important. As an actress, Deanne had to learn it, too. "At the time I landed that role in the TV series, I had so little insight into the family dynamics of my childhood that what I did was transfer all my unresolved past issues from home to work. The cast and crew became my siblings, and the network people—the big bosses—became my parents, and that's how I behaved toward them. The network people were the grown-ups and I was the child. Even though I was *starring* in the show, whenever the bosses came around I wouldn't even bother to go up and talk with them. I had so little self-esteem that I was convinced they didn't even know my name. Now, that's not how a mature employee—who's getting very well paid, I might add!— should behave. But I just kept replaying those tired old family scenes from my past, and I think it really hurt my career. But at the time that was the best that I could do. I was incapable of doing any better. It was only after I had a few years of sobriety under my belt and began getting some insights into those patterns of behavior that were set up in childhood that I could see what I'd been doing."

Learning to Say No Graciously

Deanne's inability to say what she felt, and especially her inability to say no, also hurt her career. "I kept all my career decisions to myself. I didn't seek advice. I ended up saying yes to things I should have said no to, and no to things I should have said yes to. After all, I'd grown up in an atmosphere where people said yes when they meant no, so that's what I learned to do, and it just about ruined me. After I became well known, I remember writing in my journal, 'Everyone wants a piece of the cake, and I'm the cake, but I feel like a crumb.' Since I didn't know how to take care of myself, I said yes to everything and got exhausted. I'd say yes to charities, and yes to appearances, and then I'd go home and say yes to my kids, and yes to my sisters, and yes to my friends, and it wore me down. Here I was, sober, successful, making all this money, and I was miserable."

Slowly, trained by AA and aided now and again by some outside psychotherapy, Deanne began to learn how to say no. "At first I wasn't very gracious about it. Now I can say things like, 'I'd love to help you in the future. Perhaps you can get somebody else to do the charity event this time.'"

Deanne's journey into sobriety had one interruption. After three years, she had a slip. The cause, she feels, was that old monster, denial. "For those first few years I think I was still in massive denial that I was a *real* alcoholic," she says, "so I decided—and this is truly insane!—that since I wasn't a real alcoholic, it would be okay for me to practice controlled drinking and have a glass of wine now and then. Now of course, no real alcoholic can do that for long, which is why AA insists on total abstinence. Well, I tried it and at first I congratulated myself because I was able to stick to my plan: Whenever I felt the need, I'd have one glass of wine and no more.

"I did this for six months, and even though I never got drunk, what those few glasses of wine did was put me right back into my old isolation. AA says that we're only as sick as our secrets, and I had a secret again. My secret kept me away from meetings. I avoided AA friends, and I totally isolated myself." Even after she told her sponsor what she'd been up to, Deanne still denied that she'd had a slip. "When my AA sponsor used the word *slip* I was shocked. 'What do you mean, *slip*? I just had some wine!'"

Nonetheless, Deanne's sponsor encouraged her to own up to the slip. At an AA meeting the next day, Deanne raised her hand and started her AA time all over again. "That's why now, instead of having 18 years of sobriety, I have only 15," she says. "And perhaps the most valuable lesson I learned from that slip was the fact that, for me, it's not just alcohol that kills, it's the pain of self-isolation." She's been sticking closer to the program ever since.

Deanne, like so many other women, alcoholic or otherwise, has tried to find that perfect balance between work and relationships, striving not to let relationships distract her from her work. In the beginning she did not succeed. "At times in sobriety I've been involved with a man to the point of obsession. It kept me so focused on what *he* was up to that I didn't stop to look at what *I* was up to. I didn't have to be responsible for my own life."

Since sobriety, she's remarried twice. Her first was to a man who was both physically and verbally abusive. "He'd whack me, then turn around and give me more 'nice' things than anyone else in my life ever had, so I put up with the abuse because the crumbs were so tasty. At times,

that marriage was like a weird re-creation of my relationship with my alcoholic mother, who'd run hot and cold
the same way." Deanne admits that it's probably a lucky
thing that her husband was the one who left the marriage.
"Otherwise, I'd still be in there, trying to make it work,
and it would have killed me."

After that marriage ended, Deanne took time out to
be alone. She didn't date for a year. When she was ready
to step out into the world of men again, she wrote out a
list of qualities she wanted her ideal man to have. She
wanted him to be kind, trustworthy, loyal, faithful, and
loving. "Then I went out and bought myself some pretty
underwear, and I made room for a man's toilet articles in
my bathroom. Two weeks later, I met the man I am now
married to! He's everything I wanted and more!"

But after being in the habit of destructive relationships, making the adjustment, even to a good man, hasn't
been easy. "I used to think that being in a good relationship would be a snap, but my caretaking and co-dependent tendencies have driven me to Al-Anon, where I hope
I've finally learned how to love a man without trying to fix
him!"

Happiness: The Reward for Staying the Course

There's a reason why most of the people who get sober
don't stay sober: it's hard work. Staying sober takes effort.
Having a happy work life takes effort. Having satisfying
relationships takes effort. "I don't always *want* to do what I
have to do to stay sober and keep my life in balance,"
Deanne says. "Sometimes I don't even want to get up in
the morning, or go to AA, or go to business appointments
or auditions, or 'relate' to my family when I get home, but
I *do* it. I tell myself, 'Just do it, and don't drink or use no
matter what, and see what happens.'"

What keeps happening, of course, is that Deanne's
life gets better and better in all areas. She's happy in

marriage and happy in work. "Creativity is sometimes the only thing that can save someone like me with my background," she says emphatically. "It doesn't matter if it's acting or writing or finger painting, it's the thing that can give you back your soul. On the other hand, what I've also learned in AA is that I am *not* my work. Even though my work makes me very happy, it no longer *identifies* me, and I think that's healthy. I'm a sober woman first, and *then* I'm all those other things—actress, wife, mother, sister, friend.

"AA has changed me a lot. And what I want to do next is keep right on growing and changing."

SOBER WORK TIPS LIST

1. Your number one priority is sobriety. Take care of that first. Without it, you won't have any work to worry about.

2. In AA, the goal is to become "self-supporting by your own contributions," so start planning your moves.

3. Write a work autobiography ("inventory"). It will help you get a clear view of your lifelong relationship with work.

4. Write a list of the character defects that are interfering with your work happiness and success. Begin fixing them.

5. Learn some of the helpful AA slogans that apply to work, such as "Suit up and show up," "Be a worker among workers," "Principles before personalities," and "Think service."

6. Your work should be legal and honest; if it isn't, you'll get uncomfortable, and that might lead you back to drinking.

7. Discover, or rediscover, your dream, creative or otherwise. Do something every day toward making it come true. This is how you'll eventually end up getting paid to do what you love to do.

8. Seek balance in all things, including work. This bit of advice is found not just in AA but in ancient Oriental philosophy. Overwork, like any other obsession, can distract you from your feelings, your family, and your creativity, so take note when you see yourself going overboard.

9. If you have stress on the job, don't look for someone to blame or sue. Take constructive action to handle the stress, or quit. Don't keep on being a victim in life.

10. Try to be a cooperative worker. Remember, if you are not the boss, then you are there to do what the boss wants you to do. Someday, when you're boss, you can do things your way.

11. Patience and persistence at work usually pay off.

12. Learning how to interpret your bodily clues may help you in judging certain work situations. Being in touch with your feelings at work is just as important as being in touch with your feelings in your personal life.

13. Secrets of success include having such traits as integrity, responsibility, reliability, punctuality, a good work attitude, and a good work ethic. By the way, people *do* notice these things.

14. Don't drag your unfinished dysfunctional-family business into work with you. Get enough insight into your original domestic dynamics so that you don't re-create them at work and end up getting the same results!

15. Recovering alcoholics with low self-esteem often let themselves get overworked and underpaid. Don't let this be your story. Keep working on your self-esteem by behaving well and doing things you're proud of. Your outside circumstances will miraculously improve.

16. Other people may resent your success. That is their problem, not your problem. It's not a reason for you to run away or drink. It goes with the territory of being successful.

17. Real humility on the job is having a clear sense of who you are and who you are *not*.

18. Learn to say no graciously.

4

SOBER LOVE

Being married to a man who is lov-
ing and reasonable has allowed me
to start thinking of myself as
"deserving." I guess another way of
saying that is that for the first time,
I'm in a relationship where I have
self-worth.

— Lynn, sober 21 years

In the recovery field, there are some unwritten rules about romantic relationships, one of which is "Don't get emotionally involved in your first year of sobriety." The wisdom behind this? Unless a recovering alcoholic has both her feet firmly planted on the ground, she can't expect to pull off a stable relationship with somebody else. For women who are already emotionally involved in a relationship when they get sober, the advice is to stay put for at least a year and give your health a chance.

The only problem with the one-year rule is that it's not long enough. It probably should be a tad longer—say, 10 years! I've seen more women get thrown off-center by bad relationships than by anything else. Women in recovery are just as eager as their nonalcoholic sisters to meet and bond with a supportive, loving companion. Until they've taken the time to come to terms with themselves and their alcoholism, however, it's recommended that they stick to this "waiting period."

Connecting with a person who is healthier, not sicker, is the psychological equivalent of "marrying up" and certainly something the recovering alcoholic woman should hold out for. The trouble is, most newcomers have absolutely no idea what a good relationship *looks* like.

THE LOOK OF LOVE

What *does* a good relationship look like? My own vision of it evokes the image of the pioneer couple pushing West in a covered wagon, eyes on the horizon, thoughts on their goal. For survival's sake, this couple must work together and respect, support, and protect each other, and must feel confident in the integrity and loyalty of the other. They cannot afford fragile egos or petty differences.

Such a relationship is indeed a partnership, one in which both people recognize that there's important work to do, and that together they can do it better. "I know my husband is on my team," says one of the happily married interviewees for this book. "When he's out in the world, and he talks about me, I know he's proud of me and says nice things about me. And I know that if I call him up and say, 'Help, I have a flat tire. Come get me,' he'll be there."

Even though finding a good, stable relationship isn't easy, the good news is that a woman's chances of it are increased tenfold once she gets sober. The clarity she gains from sobriety helps her separate the wheat from the chaff.

THE NEED TO BREAK AWAY FROM LOW-SELF-ESTEEM RELATIONSHIPS

Before she stops repeating the dreary old dysfunctional relationship patterns of the past, the recovering woman who's looking for love will probably go through a series of low-self-esteem relationships. Typically, she'll pick someone who's ambivalent, critical, immature, disloyal, or even abusive. Or she'll pick a person who is out of work, is married, or lives in Tierra del Fuego. They all may come in different wrapping, but the common denominator is that they can't be there for her when it counts. In short, she'll pick a loser—only she won't know he's a loser until she's already emotionally involved. Then, when she starts figuring it out, she'll probably blame herself: "Maybe I have unrealistic expectations," or "Maybe the reason I get so angry at my boyfriend when he stands me up is because my father abandoned me when I was a kid, and it stirs up my abandonment issues." Translation: The boyfriend is a loser, and so was her father. What a coincidence! But getting the woman to face this is like pulling teeth.

My down-to-earth friend Harriet, who is neither a recovering alcoholic nor the product of a dysfunctional family, has no patience with women who get themselves into these low-self-esteem relationships. "I figure if I'm not happy with a man at least 90 percent of the time, to hell with him!" she says.

Obviously, to Harriet, being happy is basic. But to a lot of women it's not—at least not yet. As we saw in Deanne's story in the previous chapter, they gladly settle for crumbs. Those who come from families in which a parent was alcoholic or emotionally absent don't even know what the experience of emotional abundance in a relationship *feels* like, so they don't know what to hold out for. When they start dating, unless they're lucky enough to accidentally stumble upon a good partner right off, they don't know who to hang on to and who to reject. They don't even know what there *is* out there, so they simply settle. "If I don't take this one, I'll be left with nothing," they reason.

In recovery, each woman has to learn what is out there, what she wants, and how to get it.

An extreme example of someone too willing to accept crumbs is a recovering woman I once interviewed (not for this book) who'd been the mistress of a married man for 11 years. On the day I spoke with her she was all smiles because her "honey," who was vacationing in Europe with his wife and kids, had sent her three post-cards. "I expected *one*, maybe, but *three!*" she gushed. "Wasn't that sweet of him to take the time to send three?" Her expectations were just about as high as her self-esteem, but she was oblivious to it.

Someday this smiling mistress may get in touch with her feelings, realize she's been in a typical low-self-esteem relationship, and experience a lot of pain over it. That's exactly why so many recovering women avoid the inner journey: they don't want to know how awful they really feel inside. The whole purpose of the inner journey is to keep current with one's feelings and inner truths *on a daily basis* and to learn how to handle them in an appropriate and constructive way. But when the truth hurts, a lot of people will simply turn away from it, refuse to see it, and avoid taking actions that might remedy it.

A Ship without a Destination

Lucie, a recovering woman in her late 40s, provides a poignant illustration of the unwillingness to look inside one's self for the truth about a relationship. Lucie's boyfriend has been living with her, in *her* house, for two and a half years. When I asked her what she wanted out of the relationship—did she want marriage?—she looked at me as though dumbfounded by the question. She finally replied, "What do I want? Gosh, I don't know. I haven't even thought about it."

This kind of response isn't unusual for women in their first years of sobriety. Their low self-esteem makes them afraid to consider their own worth, wishes, and options. But if a woman doesn't know what she wants or where she wants to go, she'll have no control over where she ends up. She'll be a ship without a destination. If Lucie wants a housemate instead of marriage, then she's doing just fine. But if she wants marriage, and he's not the marrying kind, then she's wasting her time. Plus, she's letting him keep her from taking actions toward getting what she *does* want. But like so many women, she's reluctant to rock the boat. To Lucie, crumbs seem better than nothing at all.

However, if Lucie stays sober, she may come to the same realization that the three women in this chapter—Georgia, Barbara, and Lynn—have come to terms with: Settle only for the whole cake and, until you get it, live on self-respect.

GEORGIA, SOBER 13 YEARS

> *In a relationship, telling the truth is better than stuffing feelings and being in limbo. Scary as truth-telling is, it's better to confront something, because at least that way it moves.*
>
> —Georgia

"I called my mother Mary Martyr, and my father Billy Booze," says Georgia, 49, a petite, brown-eyed beauty with long, curly dark-brown hair. She was born in Oakland, California, the second oldest of four girls. "I think those names are from a book, and they suit my parents perfectly. My father was a sculptor-turned-stockbroker-turned-roaring alcoholic, who ended up brain-damaged, wandering around on Skid Row. To this day, I have trouble every time I see a homeless person. I can't give them money because I'm convinced they'll buy booze with it."

By her own description, Georgia is the product of a dysfunctional family. "My mother was basically help-less. She never learned to drive. She always needed a ride to the grocery store. She was long-suffering and quiet. The deadly silence is what I remember most at home. I was taught not to be verbal, to be seen and not heard, to stuff my feelings, and not to get too happy because I'd be disappointed. One of my sisters was a drug addict and committed suicide, and in later life my mother went catatonic—that's really quiet!—and had to be hospitalized."

Georgia's escape route out of this family was through achievement. "I was artistic, and in school I entered every kind of art contest, and a lot of times I won. I wanted to be a painter, and I even went to college on an art scholar-ship, but I dropped out because of a man. I think I fell in love with him because he hugged me, and since there was no hugging in my family, the first time he touched me it was like Santa Claus. So just to get those feelings, I ended up having sex early, getting pregnant early, and getting married early. I became a person who couldn't be without somebody."

Putting Her "Self" on the Back Burner

Here is where Georgia, like so many women from alco-holic, dysfunctional backgrounds, decided to shelve her own creativity in the hope that a romantic relationship would cure her inner emptiness.

By 19, Georgia had had her first son. By 21, her sec-ond. By 23, her husband had left her for a younger woman—a girl of 14. From there, Georgia went on to a string of equally bad liaisons. "I kept picking unreliable, unavailable, unresponsive types, just like my father." Before long, depression set in. "I killed off my emotional pain with alcohol. I drank at night and had hangovers, but I was a functioning drunk, so every morning I'd get up and go to work as a store manager for a women's retailing chain. It was a responsible position, and I even won All-Chain 'Rep,' but my attitude was awful. Ultimately, I told off the division manager. Even as I was doing it, I knew that I was burning a bridge. I knew that if I lost the job, I'd be sabotaging myself and putting off the chance to become a painter even longer, but I did it anyway, because telling him off was what I wanted to do. Of course, I got fired."

Georgia's personal life wasn't exactly smooth, either. "I was unpleasant and testy with my kids. One time I got so angry at my then-10-year-old son that he shouted back, 'You need a psychiatrist!' Ten years old!"

Out of Body—and into AA

Later on, Georgia sent her sons to live with their father for a brief period so she could regroup as far as her work was concerned. "At the time, I was living in an artist's loft in the middle of a war zone, an industrial, scary place, strictly gang city. I'd have to park my car and run to my front door. One day a friend said, 'Georgia, you drink too much. It gets in your way.' She suggested that I try *not* drinking. I tried, and what I discovered was that I couldn't *not* drink. That, of course, is alcoholism.

"Until I tried that experiment, it had never occurred to me that I might be an alcoholic. I decided to check out an AA meeting, and it was everything calculated to chase a newcomer away. It was in a smoky, God-awful room. The man sitting next to me stank. And I was totally ignored. Still, there was something about the feeling in the room that clung to me. After I got home that night, I parked my car, but instead of running to my front door, I walked, and it was then that I realized that something had happened to me. I was no longer afraid.

"However, I still wasn't quite ready to quit drinking. I'd go to AA, but then I'd come home and drink wine. One night as I started to drink my wine, I had a kind of out-of-body experience. With each sip, I watched all the good feelings from the AA meeting drain out of me, and I felt powerless to stop it. It was a visual image of what alcoholism actually does to a person's soul. The next day I phoned a woman I knew who was in AA and said, 'Guess what, I'm an alcoholic!' She laughed. 'No kidding!' she said. At that moment, I got it."

Georgia eventually discovered that every area of her life was touched by sobriety. But since the healing process is uneven, some areas clean up faster than others. Improving her physical health was easy, but shaping up in the areas of love and work has been hard. "From the start, I began to exercise and eat right. I discovered that if I do anything about 13 times, it becomes a habit. That's been very useful information for me—it's where my alcoholic obsessive-compulsiveness works *for* me. I crave what I do. So the trick is to do only positive things, and to *stop* doing negative things."

When asked to discuss work, Georgia sighs. The subject is painful. Like Gabrielle found in the previous chapter, at 13 years of sobriety Georgia is still not painting as much as she'd like. "Some people don't even know what they want to do with their lives, but I've always known that I wanted to paint." But procrastination gets in the way. "I walk around with paintings in my head that need to be painted. I dream them. But I put off doing them because I find I simply can't be creative when I have bills to pay and the wolves are at the door." She finds that running her business as a commercial artists' rep—managing artists' careers and negotiating contracts and fees—has a way of taking up most of her "painting" time.

Even when she does paint, her perfectionism trips her up; it's a characteristic that many alcoholics share. Behind it, of course, is that old bugaboo, low self-esteem.

Says Georgia, "When I was drinking, my perfectionism demanded of me that every painting be the best I'd ever done. Now that's pressure! I'd have to drink a six-pack of Dos Equis and eat a bag of corn chips just to calm my demons enough to paint. When I first got sober and didn't have anything to numb out my fear, I couldn't paint at all. Finally, I got myself a painting sponsor in AA. He'd tell me, 'Paint junk. Paint something you can stick your foot through. Just paint.' What this did was give me permission *not* to be perfect, and my fear began to lift."

The Love Distraction

Perfectionism aside, Georgia also faces that major distraction from painting: love. "I've always let relationships drain me of creative energy," she explains. "For a while, instead of getting better, my relationships in sobriety got progressively *worse*. My last one ended with my getting a bleeding ulcer. I'd keep letting inappropriate types into my life, and I'd say, 'Oh, I can handle this' or 'I'm just going to practice on this one.' Well, what I've learned is that when I practice, it ends up taking four years! It's like taking a sip of wine—I get hooked again. So I'm finally learning to *listen* to the man! If he tells me up front that he changes relationships every two years because he can't commit, I no longer say, 'I'll be the exception.' Now I believe him!"

Most important of all, Georgia has started to listen to her intuition, that inner voice that votes yes or no on things: "If something inside suddenly says, 'Uh-oh,' I'll pay attention instead of telling myself, 'You don't need to deal with that. It'll pass.' Today when I'm in a relationship with a man, I get very uncomfortable if I sense he's trying to alter my reality on purpose by lying to me. I get a knot in my gut, and a little voice says, 'Wait, something's wrong.' I may not know *what's* wrong, only that something is wrong. In matters of love, intuition is not intelligence. It's a feeling, a sense, an 'Uh-oh!' I realize that I always *had* that voice, I just didn't listen to it. Now I listen to it. Now that voice *is* my reality."

Although Georgia's current relationship is "the best I've ever had," there are some problems emerging. "It's taking a lot of energy and adjustment, and what gets sacrificed is time for painting," she admits. "In order to clear that creative channel for my painting, I need to feel safe in my relationship, and lately I haven't been feeling safe. We've hit a snag because we seem to have different timetables for commitment. I want a committed relationship. I want marriage. I'm tired of serial monogamy. Been there. Done that. I was clear with him about this from the start. I told him, 'Dating doesn't appeal to me. I'm not a go-with or a girlfriend anymore.' At first he said, 'No problem.' We even got engaged. But it's been almost a year since then, and now I'm not hearing anything about marriage. I'm hearing about trips, but there's no mention of a honeymoon. Naturally, it makes me angry. It makes me wonder how honest he's been with me all along. Sometimes I suspect that if men told the truth about how they really feel, they'd never get laid!"

The Courage to Confront

Most women get scared and back off when a boyfriend won't commit. But sobriety eventually gives women courage, and Georgia has kept pushing the issue with her man: "When I confront him, he gets difficult, and I become the target of his anger. The other night he said, 'This marriage thing is a big problem for me. If I marry you, I'll feel like I'm betraying my ex-wife and kids.' Now, I think he really believes this! To me, of course, it's ridiculous! He's been divorced for 15 years, his children are grown, and he's just become a grandfather! But he has all these feelings where his family is concerned, feelings like guilt and anger, but he keeps denying that he's got any unfinished business to take care of. He just doesn't see it. And I find that dealing with someone who's into that much self-deception, maybe even outright lying, is rough. I told him, 'Why don't you go back to her? You're stuck. Go back and get clear on what you want, because this way everybody's trapped and nobody's moving.' That was hard to say, but so far nothing's changed."

Truth Does *Set You Free*

Georgia's relationship is still in limbo. But she's learned, as do most recovering alcoholics, that truth *does* set you free, even if it means not getting what you think you want. "It's been such a relief to speak and hear the truth, even if it means I lose in the end. The fact that he and I have identified the issue and now we're talking openly about it has made me feel less frightened. So, for the moment at least, I'm able to be with him in a very loving space. However, I've noticed that there's a part of me that wants to run, because I know how to run. I know how to leave one relationship and start a new one, but in this case I'm determined not to do that."

While long-term sobriety doesn't guarantee a woman that she'll always get her man, it does give her new ways to handle disappointment. There was a time when Georgia thought she'd die if she didn't have somebody. Today she approaches the whole subject much more calmly. "If this current relationship doesn't work out, I know I'm still going to be okay. Of course, I'd *prefer* to be in a committed, married relationship, but if it doesn't happen, that's fine, too. I've learned to make peace with my loneliness. Besides, I have myself, and I have my sons who are grown now and have turned out to be wonderful people.

"When I got sober, I unfroze and became pleasant again, and my love for my kids came roaring back. It was like a wall was taken down from around my heart. We don't have a silent relationship, like the one I had with my parents. As a child, I was invisible and unheard. So with my sons, I really make an effort to *listen.* I think people need to be heard. We talk to each other, and cry with each other, and tell each other the truth. I have learned to love them without rescuing them. I've learned to let them make their own mistakes. Neither of them has an alcohol problem, but if they did, I think they would know where to get help."

BARBARA, SOBER 22 YEARS

> *I used alcohol, spending, food, and*
> *even addictive relationships to fill*
> *an empty hole in my chest. But*
> *shoveling those things inside of me*
> *didn't make me happy. It's like*
> *shoveling coal into a furnace; it*
> *burns up as fast as it gets in there.*
>
> —Barbara

Barbara, 52, is a sharp-featured, attractive, twice-divorced mother of three who works as a film costumer. She was born in Minneapolis, Minnesota, the only daughter of two nonalcoholic parents. She has two younger brothers. "My mother and dad both came from wealthy families. I don't think anyone from either of their families ever did a household chore until the Depression came along, and both families lost their money. They ended up in the lower middle class. However, my parents handled money, or the lack of it, responsibly, whereas I'm the opposite. I handle money alcoholically. Once I start spending it, I can't stop."

Like Georgia, Barbara let herself get sidetracked from her original dream. "I wanted to be a fashion designer. I was accepted at Parsons Art School in New York, but fear ruled my life in those days and I was too scared to leave home, so I ended up at the University of Minnesota." She later quit college to become a flight attendant, then quit that job to get married, have children, and drink. "I became a housewife drunk. I stayed in the house, drank in the house, and went mad in the house."

The "Stepford" Alcoholic

Not being in touch with her feelings, goals, or wants, Barbara realized that she'd walked into a marital mistake. "I'd married an Arab engineer who was 'Daddy.' He was a very dominant male controller, the best I've ever seen. He wanted to take care of me, and I let him. I turned into a Stepford wife. I had dinner on the table every night. I took speed, and I cleaned the house like crazy. I know I damaged my kids. When you have a damaged person raising little people, they become damaged, too. After all, they had a child for a mother. I think it's scary for a child to be parented by another child, particularly one who's nuts and suicidal. I remember standing over my second daughter's crib in my little green chenille bathrobe, a glass of wine in my hand, crying to this baby that if it wasn't for her, I'd kill myself. She was born a peaceful, placid baby, but by the time she was 13 months old, she was so stressed out that her eyes looked like saucers. Basically, what I did to her was rip her basement out and deny her any sense of safety in this world, which still affects her to this day."

Encouraged by a friend, Barbara started going to AA meetings, but she hated them. "Everybody was so friendly and kissy-face and I thought they were all phony." Out of loneliness, however, she continued to go to meetings and, to her own amazement, ended up getting sober.

After sobriety, it got harder for Barbara to maintain her Stepford-wife front. "I started resenting my husband for controlling me. I began to fight back, first in passive ways, then in aggressive ways. I had violent outbursts. He was always the one in control; I was always the one out of control. At one point I was so afraid that I was going to stab him that I turned myself over to a friend to keep an eye on me for a few days so I wouldn't kill him. Under the circumstances, it seemed like a reasonable idea to get divorced."

Though sober, Barbara, by her own admission, avoided looking at her feelings after the divorce. "Leaving that marriage meant leaving a lot of money, so my immediate concern was my pocketbook, not my psyche," she remembers. "I didn't have time to look at feelings. I had to get a job. Fortunately, coming from Middle America, I had a strong work ethic to start with, and I was willing to work hard. If you wanted me there at 7 in the morning, I was there. I got a job in a costume design studio and was able to hire someone to take care of my kids. Sometimes I worked 15 hours a day."

Two Sides of the Same Coin

When Barbara was ready to turn her attention to love relationships, she realized she had a lot to learn. "Most alcoholics I know have little or no capacity to love anybody as long as they're drinking. I know I didn't. When I married my first husband, I thought I was this warm, wonderful, loving human being. What I discovered was that I was crippled in the relationship area. I wasn't capable of a grown-up marriage, so I picked somebody who wanted a child-woman to care for. After I was sober for a few years I went to the opposite extreme and got into a marriage where I was the mommy instead of the child. Instead of being the controllee this time, I was the controller. I didn't see any of this at first because I had such a strong sexual attraction to this man."

Even though Barbara and her second husband dated for five and a half years before they got married, she still managed to miss the warning signs about possible troubles in the relationship. "Deep down I *knew* I couldn't trust this man. I knew there had been other women when we were supposedly monogamous, but if you don't want to see something, and I didn't, you deny it. I pushed aside the warning signs and ignored my intuition. I told myself, well, once he's with me—the love of a good woman and all that—he'll be just fine. The truth is that throughout the relationship, I kept trying to keep this man in the boat, and he kept trying to jump out. I thought that by being prettier, faster, quicker, better, I'd be able to keep him there. I kept refusing to see the big picture, which was that he didn't want to be kept there. The man could withdraw standing right in front of me, and I wouldn't get it. He never really lied to me. He kept telling me he wasn't happy, wasn't capable of being in an intimate relationship, but I didn't hear. I went right on saying things were fine when they weren't fine. In the end he did the only thing he knew how to do: he had an affair. That was his sickness. My sickness was that I thought I'd die without him. He left me for her, and I spent the next 13 months on my knees, doubled over in pain."

Barbara's Second Surrender

Barbara moved to Sante Fe, New Mexico. In part, this was a "geographic," an attempt to run from her feelings. As she describes it, "The pain of losing my marriage was even worse than the pain of getting sober. I didn't think I was going to be able to survive it. It brought me right up to the edge of drinking again. In fact, I'd all but decided that I *was* going to drink again. But one day, when I was riding on a train to visit a friend, I had what I can only describe as a spiritual experience during which I believe that God touched me and kept me sober."

In Barbara's words, this is what happened: "As I walked toward my seat, I had this thought pop into my head: *I'm going to drink.* There was no question about it; it was a fact. After [what was then] 17 years of sobriety, I absolutely knew I was going to drink. I was in a state of total self-centeredness, with no thought of anybody but myself. Anyone else in my life who might have been affected by my drinking, like my kids, or my friend who'd find me drunk when she came to pick me up at the train station, ceased to exist. I sat down in my seat. I had a book called *For Their Own Good* by Alice Miller in my lap, and I said to myself, 'Before I go into the bar car and order a drink, I'll just spend 10 minutes reading this book.' I have no idea what specific thing it was that I read, only that two hours later I looked up from the book, and I felt hungry. I walked into the dining car and ordered a sandwich. I had no more thoughts of taking a drink."

The experience created a profound and positive shift in Barbara's attitude, often referred to in AA as a second surrender. "I realized that for 17 years I'd been avoiding the inward journey into my feelings, and now it was time. If I wasn't going to drink, and if I wasn't going to die, then I'd damn well better start looking inside."

When Barbara got back to Sante Fe, she started intense psychotherapy. "Of course, the fear of something is always worse than the reality—that old fear of fear itself. For 17 years I'd been afraid of looking at my feelings, and when I finally did, it really wasn't all that bad."

A New Relationship, a New Lesson

In her therapy, as well as in AA, Barbara sought guidance on how to avoid getting into any more relationships with inappropriate men. "I wanted no more men who were daddies, and I wanted no more men who needed mommies. So when I met Charles, who seemed very much an equal, I thought I was on the right track. I was very direct and upfront with him. He knew, for example, that my work as a film costumer sometimes took me away on location for weeks at a time, and I thought that was fine with him.

"Charles was Hispanic, and the only thing that he ever said to me that was like a warning flag was when he told me, 'Hispanic men can't be left.' I remember thinking, What the heck does that mean? but I didn't ask. It simply didn't register with me, and I forgot about it. Other than that, during my year with him I felt centered and strong. He wasn't domineering, like my first husband, nor was he ambivalent, like my second. One day he even stood in front of me and said, 'You've had a hard time with men, haven't you?' and I said, 'Yes,' and he said, 'I'm here to make a difference, to change that.' Pretty romantic stuff.

"Well, four days later as Charles was driving me to the airport to go off on a movie set for about six weeks, he announced, 'My heart has closed down and gone away.' And that was it. The relationship was over. It was the biggest shock I had ever experienced. My second husband's affair wasn't nearly the shock that this was. I'd seen the affair coming, but this I didn't see coming, nor did a lot of other people who knew us. Even a psychiatrist friend of ours didn't see it."

Barbara has reached some conclusions as the result of this last relationship. "Recovering alcoholics are always chanting, 'I want to be loved, I want to be loved!' but I don't think that's really what we want at all, at least not in the beginning. In the beginning what sober people want is emotional *safety*. A 'safe' relationship is one in which you don't have to have real intimacy. However, in a 'loving' relationship you really have to show your ass. You have to get honest, tell the truth, have integrity, share feelings, say what you want, say what you don't want, and that's scary. Coming as so many of us do from unsafe and even frighteningly dysfunctional families, our primary purpose in a relationship is to find safety, not mature love. But I don't think safety and love ride on the same train. You must choose. I used to choose safety. By the time I was ready to choose love, the man I happened to fall in love with, Charles, was still stuck back at safety. *That's* why, when the intimacy level increased, he got scared and ran. And all that nonsense he told me about how Hispanic men can't be left—that was just his escape route! The *real* reason he ran was because we were getting too intimate, too close, too loving, and that made him stop feeling safe."

Barbara adds, "Forewarned is forearmed. Next time, I'm holding out for love."

LYNN, SOBER 21 YEARS

All my life I'd been looking for someone to take care of me. Then I had an awakening, a moment of clarity about love: I realized that I was going to have to first learn how to take care of myself. *If I never dated again, never had sex again, that was going to have to be okay. So that's what I did. And it was after that that I met my present husband.*

—Lynn

"I had a short drinking career, but a long sobriety, so I think that makes my story a little different," says Lynn, 44, a tall, thin, dark-eyed woman with a ready laugh and a head of luxurious dark-brown hair. She drank for 8 years and has been sober for 21 years, nearly half her life. She is in her third marriage and has a daughter, 15, by her second marriage.

Lynn was born in Brooklyn, New York, of a "not atypical middle-class Jewish family," and has one sister 6 years older. Her father was a heavy drinker and may even have been an alcoholic. He died of heart disease when Lynn was 14. "There were no other alcoholics in my family. My mother took pills, and I suspect she'd have become an alcoholic if she'd ever taken that first drink. Fortunately, she did not."

In school, Lynn was considered smart, even a genius. "My whole identity was built around what my mind could do, which turned out to be a trap for me because I couldn't keep up emotionally with the great things that were expected of me. I was one of those kids whose father would say when I got 98 on a test, 'What did you do wrong?' I thought I'd never get anywhere."

Disheartened, Lynn began to feel increasingly insecure. When she couldn't get attention by succeeding, she got attention by being bad, by screwing up. At 15 she started drinking. She graduated high school, but instead of having an exemplary career, "I accepted menial jobs, went to college at night, and went to bars. My social life centered around bars. I drank everybody under the table, and I was promiscuous. A guy would take me out to get me drunk, and I'd get him drunk. My attitude was, 'I'm so smart, I can outdrink anybody!' I rarely ate, only if something was nearby, otherwise I wouldn't. I dropped out of college. I stopped caring about my future or what I wanted to be. I just gave up."

An Abusive Marriage

Even in this frame of mind, Lynn decided to get married. "Mark was alcoholic and a classic batterer, only we didn't call it that then. I had no self-esteem, so I put up with it, but that doesn't mean that I liked it. I never once met an abused woman who liked it. Women stay in these relationships because they're afraid to leave."

After a number of years of continuous abuse, Mark went to AA and stopped drinking. Lynn anticipated that the abuse would stop, too, but it didn't. "He took me along to some of his meetings and I hated them. No wonder! I myself was an alcoholic in heavy denial. It took months of listening before I could finally identify enough with the AA speakers to dare raise my own hand as an alcoholic. Even then my denial lingered, and I half expected them to throw me out because AA is 'for alcoholics only,' and I was taking up valuable space. But guess what? They didn't, so I stayed and I stopped drinking."

Of course, once Lynn stopped drinking, it was inevitable that she'd have to start looking at her marriage. "I'd tell people in AA what was going on at home, but at that time [the early seventies] little was known about the psychology of the batterer, and since the AA philosophy was that we shouldn't point our finger at anyone else and should only look at ourselves, that's what I tried to do in my marriage. I was told to worry only about cleaning up *my* side of the street and not his, and to look at my own behavior and see if there was anything *I* was doing that provoked Mark's lashing out at me. Well, that's a fine philosophy in some cases, but it doesn't work with batterers because anything can provoke a batterer. Mark, even sober, just kept right on punching me out! He'd tear me down, rage, and hit. And I kept trying to prove I was a good AA member and turn the other cheek, but I was miserable. Like the typical battered woman, I kept on hanging in there and taking punishment. When people would tell me to leave, I said that I couldn't because of money, but that was a delusion: I worked steadily, and he was working only sporadically. But my belief system was that I was inadequate and helpless, and for a long time I just couldn't see that it simply wasn't so."

Learning to Trust Her Heart

As Lynn got deeper into her own feelings and deeper into the philosophy of the AA program, she finally began to learn the ultimate AA lesson: *Nobody*, not even your sponsor, can tell you what's in your own heart. It's up to each AA member to decide that for herself or himself. "I knew I'd have to listen to my own feelings and stand up to Mark," Lynn says. "I couldn't keep going along with what I *thought* AA was telling me to do if it didn't feel right for me. Some people are happy to let other people run their lives and tell them what to do, but I wasn't one of them. That was an incredible breakthrough for me to realize that it was about time for me to start putting faith in myself."

Lynn and Mark had one final blowout. It started in the car. They had gotten into an argument, and Mark began threatening Lynn. "Mark suddenly jumped out of the car, left it in the middle of the street, and ran into our apartment. I ran after him. Usually I'd be too afraid of him when he was in this state, but this time I thought, *What can he do to me that he hasn't already done?* In a moment of clarity, I suddenly knew that I wasn't afraid of him anymore. The door was locked. I shouted at him, 'Let me in!' In all the years we'd been married, he'd never seen me stand up to him. I'm not saying I wasn't scared. I was shaking. But I'd reached my limit. I said, 'If you're going to kill me, then kill me already, but stop threatening me!' He let me in, and I watched him run through the entire gamut of emotions that batterers go through, from

posturing and threatening me to instant remorse to crying, 'I need you! I love you! I'll never do it again!' to comforting me because *I* was crying. He even tried to put his
arms around me, but I pulled away, and I remember
thinking, *I will never again let the person who is causing my
pain try to comfort me!* I walked out of that apartment for
the last time, and I started my life."

In AA, Lynn met husband number two, Alan. As in
Barbara's second marriage, Alan was the flip-side of Mark.
Instead of exploding in anger, Alan sat on his, and for a
long time Lynn didn't see it. "At the time, his withdrawals
were a welcome relief, much better than hitting and
shouting! All I saw was that Alan was kind and he didn't
hit me, so I thought everything was fine. We had a baby
girl. My life settled down enough so that for once I had
some energy left over to think about work. I was tired of
dead-end, low-self-esteem jobs. I'd become enough to
aspire to more."

One day a man in AA who was in the real estate business asked Lynn if she wanted to do some typing for him
at home. She said yes. After that, he asked her to assist
him in doing some market research. She said yes to that,
too. Then he needed some advertising done, and then a
brochure, and she did that, too. Over a number of years
this part-time work led to a full-time job doing market
research for a real estate agency. "All my skills from the
past—my writing, my quickness, my organizational skills—
came to the fore, and I was finally able to utilize them in
one place. Then one of the partners left, and I stepped in
as a partner, and we developed into a very successful market research company. Sitting on one of those bar stools
back in Brooklyn, I never thought I'd be doing that!"

Lynn was so busy getting her work life together that
she failed to notice that Alan was becoming increasingly
moody and withdrawn. "He wouldn't communicate about
it. He'd go into his shell, sit on his resentment, and refuse
to talk. Twice, without even bothering to tell me what he

was upset about, he just left. When I realized that that, too, was 'abuse,' I said no more and my daughter and I left. I started life over again one more time."

A Newfound Courage and a Newfound Love

In the work area, Lynn eventually went into the marketing research business for herself, working out of her house, and the business did well. "After all those years of sobriety, I discovered that I wasn't the coward I always thought I was. I was really courageous. All my life I'd assumed that courage meant the absence of fear. But courage isn't the absence of fear, it's the ability to act *in spite of* fear. AA people kept telling me, 'So you're afraid! Do it anyway!' Fear no longer held me up, and what *freedom* that was! When I had to talk to clients about money, somebody in AA suggested that I simply state my needs, so I'd go in and say, 'These are my needs, and I either get them met or I move on,' and I'd usually get them met. Another business secret I learned in AA was: Do your best work! If you do good work, your business will succeed. So I always turned out my best work, and my business succeeded. For years I was on a roll, until I brought in a partner. To make a long story short, he didn't have the kind of integrity I was used to dealing with, but by the time I caught on I had a disaster on my hands."

At this point Lynn waxes philosophical. "Everything bad that happens is an opportunity in disguise, and as it turned out, this was an opportunity for me to change direction. I was really ready to close up shop. My mother was dying and needed me, my daughter needed me, and I was bone tired from all those years of 14- and 15-hour days. I'm not saying I let go of my business easily. It was hard! My therapist had to practically *order* me to give up the business, and I'd keep thinking, 'I can't walk away from my own business! I can't even imagine such a thing.' But the truth is, I could walk away. It was time to walk away. And I did walk away."

Another reason Lynn decided to let go of her business was because she'd married again. She wanted to devote some time to her new relationship. As was the case with Alan, she met Ted in AA, too. "Only he's a keeper!" she says emphatically. "We knew each other for over a year before we started dating. It started out as a friendship, with mutual respect. Then he started writing me letters, then love letters, then we started dating, and finally we got to love and marriage. We've been married for over 10 years.

"I go to a number of women's meetings in AA and, just as you might suspect, they talk a lot about relationships. We AAs aren't exactly known for our great choices. Anyway, the other day I was at a women's discussion meeting and I heard a older woman say, 'I spent a lifetime seeking relationships with men who had that unpredictability and unreliability that you girls think of as *excitement*!' Of course, the whole room roared with the laughter of identification, and so did I, because we've all been there!"

But she's not there any longer. "Today, I'm happy to say, I am married to a man who is not only predictable and reliable, he's also able to communicate his feelings. One of the things I appreciate most about Ted is that we can sit down and talk about things. After my other marital experiences, I am continually amazed that I now have a man who is willing to talk, even if it's uncomfortable. With him, it seems so simple, but with others it was like pulling teeth."

With Ted's full approval and emotional support, and using some of her own savings, Lynn gave herself the gift of a year off to stay home and write a novel. "It was a secret wish, but something I thought I'd never do because it wasn't 'practical.' Plus I didn't think I 'deserved' such a present—how *dare* I do what I *wanted* to do? But being married to a man like Ted, who is kind and loving, has allowed me to think of myself as deserving instead of seeing myself as I always assumed my parents saw me, as 'never enough.'

"My husband knows what his priorities are, and our marriage is his priority. If handling a problem that comes up in our relationship means going through some discomfort, he'll do it gladly.

"There was a time in my life where I didn't think I deserved that kind of treatment. Now I couldn't live without it!"

SOBER LOVE TIPS LIST

1. The unwritten AA rule for newcomers is Don't get emotionally involved in your first year of sobriety.

2. Falling in love with somebody healthier, not sicker, than you are is the equivalent of "marrying up." Hold out for it!

3. People are what they do—and they're not what they don't do. In all your relationships, listen to the words, but only believe the deeds.

4. Rule of thumb: In a good relationship, you like yourself when you're around your partner. In a bad relationship, you don't.

5. Don't explain away the feelings that come up in your relationship. Like it or not, they're telling you something.

6. Unhappiness is *the* major clue that a relationship is bad. If you're uncomfortable or unhappy in your relationship, get out.

7. You have to know where you want your relationship to go. If you don't, you'll drift like a ship without a destination.

8. Don't let your relationship distract you from your number one priority, which is your sobriety. Keep going to meetings—no matter what.

9. Warning: Anytime you start a relationship with the phrase, "I can handle it," watch out.

10. Don't let a bad or dead-end relationship keep you off the market. For a woman especially, time is of the essence.

11. Heed the warning signs that pop up at the very beginning of every new relationship. They'll tell you everything you need to know.

12. Don't have a silent relationship. Speak out. Say how you feel, what you need, what you want, what you don't want. If your partner can't handle it, perhaps you shouldn't be there.

13. You cannot change another person. You can ask, but if the other person won't change, and you can't accept him for who he is or is not, you may have to leave.

14. It's important to get as much insight into your original family as you can, especially if it was dysfunctional, so you won't keep re-creating old patterns in your present life.

15. There are "safe" relationships and there are "intimate" relationships. Most recovering women start out wanting safe relationships, then graduate to wanting more intimate relationships, which are scarier and take more work.

16. Stay out of other people's heads. If you think somebody is mad at you, ask. Don't assume anything.

17. AA slogan: "When it hurts badly enough, you'll do something about it." Even if everyone else is telling you to get out of your relationship, you probably won't do it until you starting hurting badly enough. *Then* you'll take action.

18. When you start to take care of yourself in a relationship, be prepared for resistance from your partner.

19. Write this 100 times: Irresponsible, unpredictable, and unreliable men are not "exciting."

20. You can have a moment-of-clarity awakening in the area of relationships, just as you can in other areas, including addiction. So don't lose hope. Even if you're involved in the world's sickest, most obsessive relationship, you can still recover and be just fine.

21. Work your relationship "out loud" by talking about it with other people—with a sponsor, at meetings, with other recovering women. Keep getting feedback, even if you ignore it.

22. The most honest you are with yourself, the better your relationships with others will be.

23. This is ancient advice, but still valid: When a potential partner tells you bad things about himself, listen up! It could save you a lot of heartache.

5

SOBER FAMILY

I had people telling me, "It's okay if
you don't forgive your mother,
because what she did to you was
unforgivable." But the truth is, I
can't live with resentment, so I had
to find a way to forgive her.

—Ellen, sober 14 years

The great rallying cry of every alcoholic is, "I'm only hurting myself." But, of course, that's not true. We are all interactive, social creatures, and we affect one another in both obvious and subtle ways. Each woman who uses or drinks has an impact on everybody around her—spouse, kids, parents, siblings, friends, co-workers, neighbors, community. Sometimes the person who ingests a mind-altering substance becomes noticeably different within minutes. Many just withdraw, while others become nasty, cruel, even abusive. Their claim that they are only hurting *themselves* is patently ridiculous.

A few years ago I caught part of a TV documentary about the impact of mothers' moods on their babies. A film showed a mother playing with her child, laughing, hugging, fully interacting, and the baby was responding with smiles and gurgles. In another scene, the same mother suddenly withdrew. She stopped smiling and simply stared at her child with a blank expression on her face. Within seconds, the baby stopped laughing, looked scared, and began to cry. You'd have to be pretty dense not to conclude that people *do* affect one another.

HEALING THE FAMILY

When the alcoholic sobers up, there's a lot of repair work
to be done. If family relationships are going to survive, all
those hurts and resentments from past interactions have
to be healed. There's a lack of trust on both sides. In
some cases, there remain some severe neurotic connections between the alcoholic and family members, such as
co-dependency, that may require professional help,
maybe even psychotherapy.

In addiction recovery, the ideal is to reunite family
members in order to improve marriages, heal breaches
between parents and children, resolve tensions between
siblings, and so on. Sometimes it happens, sometimes it
doesn't. When it doesn't, it's not always the recovering
alcoholic's fault. As often as not, it's a family member who
tries to sabotage things. One scenario is the husband who
is all *for* his wife getting sober until she *does*, at which
point he turns around and makes it difficult for her to
maintain that sobriety. He may make her feel guilty for
going to meetings, or be jealous because of who she
might meet there, or feel neglected because she's out a
lot, or feel threatened by her newfound independence.
Children who've been getting away with murder when
their alcoholic parent was too drunk to discipline them
may resent it when that parent sobers up and gets tough
on them again. Sober people are harder to manipulate
than drunk people!

Each year there's more evidence that points to a
genetic link in the disease of alcoholism. Studies have
shown that children and grandchildren of alcoholics have
a four-times-greater chance of becoming alcoholic themselves. For this reason, it behooves parents who have alcoholism, or who know of alcoholism in their families, to

forewarn their children that they might also be suscepti-
ble to the illness. Our last interviewee in this chapter, Jill,
did this with her five children, one of whom is now in AA
himself.

The fact that two of the three interviewees in this
chapter happen to be twins (Jill is a fraternal twin, Mollie
an identical twin) is also interesting from a genetic point
of view. Studies show that in the case of identical twins,
when one twin is an alcoholic, the other is also likely to be
an alcoholic, even if the twins were raised apart. In alcoholic families, the chances of both fraternal twins being
alcoholic are the same as for siblings—one in four.

The process of healing families calls for recovering
alcoholics to take certain steps. First, they need to get in
touch with their memories and feelings. Second, they
need to learn to deal with those memories and feelings,
which might involve one-to-one confrontations with family members. Third, they need to honestly assess their own
character defects. Fourth, they need to make amends for
their wrongdoings. Fifth, they need to forgive the wrongdoings of others. In AA, forgiveness is seen as a very practical move: resentments threaten serenity, which in turn
threatens sobriety, so forgiveness is necessary in order to
better assure sobriety. Again, it's always sobriety first.

After they got sober, each of the three women in this
chapter had to go through these stages in dealing with
their own family members. Of the three, our first interviewee, Ellen, probably had the most horrendous family
situation to face. She came from a family of alcoholics
who not only inflicted physical and sexual abuse upon her
but also involved her in a cult, which included ritual
abuse. Our second interviewee, Mollie, is still struggling
with what she admits is an "unresolved co-dependent
relationship" with her identical twin sister, Sallie, who's a
pill addict. Jill, our third interviewee, had to deal with the
reactions of her five children to her sobriety. This meant
confronting the adaptive roles each child had been forced

to take on in order to cope with Jill's alcoholism, roles not always easily relinquished when the alcoholic family member finally gets sober. Jill also had to reconnect with the children's father, her exhusband. She made amends to him for her drinking and forgave him for the actions he'd committed under the influence of his own addiction, which was gambling—an addiction that had played a key role in the destruction of their marriage.

ELLEN, SOBER 14 YEARS

> *I realized that I can't afford the pain of being a victim anymore. I can't afford to believe that life is not on my side. Now, for the first time in my entire life, I feel whole.*
>
> —Ellen

"I've been in terror all my life. There was hardly a time when I wasn't afraid," says Ellen, a slim, sweet-faced, single young woman who works as a waitress. At 32, she is our youngest interviewee. She was only 16 when she got sober for the first time. After a brief slip, she sobered up again at 18, and now has been 14 years sober.

Ellen was born in Pasadena, California, to unmarried parents who were both practicing alcoholics. From infancy she was physically abused by her mother. "She'd do things like burn my palms with cigarettes as a way of teaching me not to eat the cigarette butts out of ashtrays." Her parents later married, then divorced. "My family was completely incestuous. My mother, father, grandmother, and uncle were all involved—my father least of all. There was incest with each other, and with me." When Ellen was

7, she and her mother moved in with her grandmother and her uncle Andy, both of whom were heavily involved in a cult. "My grandmother and Uncle Andy were both psychotic, and because of their involvement in the cult, from the age of 7 until I was 11 and my mother got married again and we moved, I experienced ritual abuse as well as physical and sexual abuse."

Ellen didn't even remember being abused until after she'd been sober for years. She admits it's still a very painful subject for her to talk about, and there were times during the interview when she was near tears. "I get scared and I go blank," she says: "I've talked about it in generalities before, but this is the first time I've verbalized some of the details outside of therapy."

A Turning Point

Ellen discovered, as do most alcoholics, that alcohol and drugs are useful in keeping painful memories at bay. "I drank and smoked pot every chance I got. It wasn't that those things made me feel *good*, it's that they helped me not to feel quite so *bad*."

By 13 Ellen was a full-blown alcoholic who had already tried suicide three times. "I guess you might say I didn't handle puberty very well!" she jokes. Her grades in school went from As down to Ds and Fs. By 14, she'd run away to Tijuana, Mexico. By 15, she was pregnant. By 16, she was on her own, with a baby, on welfare, doing whatever she had to do to get money for drugs, food, and alcohol. "I felt so empty inside that nothing in this universe could fill me up. I had that feeling so many alcoholics describe: a hole in my gut the size of the Grand Canyon, with the wind howling through it. Then, one Friday at 10 o'clock in the morning, I had a moment-of-clarity experience that changed my life. I was looking inside a friend's refrigerator, and all I saw was red wine,

which always made me deathly ill. I knew I *needed* something to fill up that empty space, but there was no food,
no money to buy any, and no men to sleep with, so I was
going to drink the red wine when all of a sudden I had
this thought: *Oh, God! You* need *this!* I knew enough about
addiction to know that when a person *needs* alcohol, it's
alcoholism. That's when I realized I was an alcoholic. I
went to AA, and for the first time in my life I had hope, a
vision of a better way to live."

Ellen discovered that it's not always easy for a young
person to make it in recovery. She experienced a lot of
pain. For one thing, just after she got sober she gave her
small son up for adoption. "It was something I felt I had
to do for his sake, but I miss him. I've always missed him. I
can hardly believe that he's a teenager now."

Young people in AA find themselves subjected to a
variety of conflicting pressures, from non-AA peers trying
to talk them into getting high again, to AA adults telling
them they're too young to be alcoholic. Ellen felt some of
these pressures, too. "I'd go to AA meetings, and I'd be
told stupid things like, 'Kid, I spilled more than you
drank!' or 'You haven't *hurt* enough yet.' I felt desperate. I
knew that if I didn't stay sober I'd die, so I worked hard to
prove that I had a right to be there, no matter how many
people told me I hadn't suffered enough. I knew I'd suffered enough. I hung on to the AA tradition that 'the only
requirement for AA membership is a desire to stop drinking,' because it said nothing about any minimum age for
sobriety."

After a year or so, Ellen began to feel better—so
much better, in fact, that she became less vigilant, less
attentive to her program. "I thought I was fine now and
that everything was cool, so I didn't need to go to as many
meetings." The result was that after two years, she slipped.
"It proved to me that the *desire* to stay sober isn't enough.
Staying sober also takes maintenance work on a daily
basis, like working the steps and reading the AA Big

Book." Fortunately, her slip didn't last long. She returned to AA and tried again.

Now 18 and back in AA, Ellen supported herself in a "low-self-worth way," she says. "Sober, I did things that some people only do when they're drinking, and most not even then. I lived on Hollywood Boulevard and I panhandled, sold drugs, and sold my body. When I could hold a job, I worked in a B & D [bondage and discipline] house. After that, I got a job as a topless dancer. Each thing I did was the best I could do at the time and, for me, a step up from what I'd done previously."

In the area of relationships, Ellen had already come out the first time she got sober. "Being gay was the first thing I found out about myself in AA that didn't fit with the image I had of marriage—you know, a white picket fence, 2.3 children. In fact, I'd always been phobic about gays. I was living with a man when I got sober, but that turned out *not* to be who I am. My personal philosophy about gays is that it's biological, not psychological. I blame nobody for my sexuality. It's just the way I am. I don't think the sexual abuse had a thing to do with it, especially since I was abused by two men and two women, so that doesn't prove a thing. I also think that I've been sober long enough and healed enough, so that if my sexuality was due to the abuse, that fact would have surfaced by now, but it hasn't. Gay is just the way I am." For the past six months, Ellen has been in a comfortable relationship with a sober woman she met in AA. "It just works," she says.

Opening the Floodgates of Memory

While other recovering alcoholics she knew seemed to be improving their lives by thawing out and dealing with their feelings, Ellen sensed that something was holding her back. "Here I was, working my butt off in AA, and yet I was still being self-destructive," she explains. "One day I was

burning myself with a cigarette, something I did on a regular basis, but I didn't even feel any pain. It was the largest
burn I'd ever given myself, and I was dead inside. I had no
feeling. The next day I was driving on the freeway, and
suddenly a very low voice came out of me, like Linda Blair
in *The Exorcist*, and it said, 'You have to die now!' I started
to black out. I lost sensation in my arms and legs, and I
screamed at the top of my lungs, 'God help me!' Then,
slowly, I started to come to, to see again and feel again,
and I drove the rest of the way home repeating to myself,
'Red light is for stop. Green light is for go,' and I made it.

"It opened up the floodgates," Ellen continues. "After
that, all sorts of suppressed memories and emotions about
the incest and the ritual abuse came pouring out. It was a
nightmare. Every minute of every day I'd have physical
memories, and then emotional memories. I'd have a
movie switch on in my mind, and I'd see myself doing x, y,
or z, and then I'd get the feelings or hear the sounds that
went along with the movie, like the soundtrack. It was
awful. I couldn't stand my thoughts. I became very suicidal. But I just hung on to AA with both hands and let it
run its course. Today, I know that that's what it took for
me to get honest with my feelings. Facing the nightmare
of my own childhood was the price I had to pay for getting my sanity back."

What Ellen remembers about the sexual abuse at
the hands of her mother horrifies her. "My mother would
get drunk, and she'd fondle me and kiss me in inappropriate places, and make me touch her." Ellen remembers
similar abuse at the hands of her uncle Andy and her
grandmother when she was living at her grandmother's
for a six-month period without her mother. "My uncle
Andy became a multiple personality. At the time all I
knew was that there were these different Uncle Andys. In
the daytime, he was sweet and kind and would never let
anybody hurt me. That Uncle Andy was the one good, loving force in my life. But at night, when my grandmother

was there, he was her whipping boy, her slave, the antithesis of what he was in the daytime. Whatever my grandmother told him to do to me, he'd do, including sodomy."

The ritual cult abuse has been even harder for Ellen to remember and deal with. She defines the abuse as systematic, deliberate brainwashing, similar to what happens to prisoners of war. "What I've remembered feels very surreal," she says, "but I was drugged part of the time it was going on, so it's no wonder it felt surreal. It's *supposed* to feel surreal.

"In ritual abuse, various tactics are used, including forms of physical pain, instilling fear, and even animal sacrifices. The purpose is to break the reality barrier and force a person to lose touch with their own sense of what's real and what's right. You lose touch with your feelings and your basic instincts." She gave a graphic example. "One time when I was seven or eight, I was drugged and told I had remarkable powers. As proof, there was this naked woman, and they were masturbating her, and at the same time they were also masturbating me. They told me that I was so powerful that I could feel what she felt, and be her. In other words, what I was seeing I was also feeling. But of course, I *wasn't* that woman, and after a while I'd get all mixed up and not know what was real and what was not real. I remember they also did heinous things with blood and bugs, and on a regular basis they put me in a coffin. First they made me think I'd died, and then, because they were so powerful, of course, they brought me back to life. To top it off, I was told it was all a nightmare, and that I'd wake up in my own bed."

Asked what she thinks the attraction of cults is, Ellen answered in one word: "Power! Cults are definitely about power. Wanting power is part of the human ego. People feel powerless in their lives, but they don't like to feel powerless, so they reach out for something that will make them feel like they're on top of things. That's what cults offer, a sense of power, which just gets reconfirmed by what they do with children and animals. I was told that the more souls you can claim, the more powerful you are. It's an illusion, of course—an illusion that very powerless people tend to fall for."

Ellen augmented her AA work with psychotherapy. "For me, coming out of my family, where I'd been told that black was white and white was black and that I didn't feel what I did feel, living sober was very confusing. I'd ask my therapist things like, 'How do you know when the truth is the truth, and when a lie is a lie?' and she'd say, 'You feel love right in here,' and she'd point to her chest, 'and you feel anger right in here,' and she'd point to her stomach. That helped me a lot. I began noticing what parts of my body were being affected by what emotions. I learned that it's important for me not to deny what I feel inside. Today I say, 'Okay, I might be wrong, but this is how I feel.'"

Forgiving the Unforgivable

When Ellen dug up all the memories about her past, she was left with a lot of anger to deal with. For her, anger has always been a tricky, slippery emotion. "I was punished for having anger, so I started denying I had it. Even today, if I don't stay on top of my anger, it starts disappearing on me again. If somebody asks, 'Are you angry?' I'll usually say, 'I don't know. I just feel funny.' Just this year I've discovered that when I say, 'I feel funny,' it usually means there's anger there, only I don't want to acknowledge it. The other day my lover said to me, 'You seem angry,' and I said, 'No, no, I just feel *funny*.' Then I stopped myself because I knew it was more than that. I had to say to her, 'Yeah, I'm angry.'"

In healing childhood abuse, it's often recommended that the victim confront the perpetrator. Ellen knew it was important for her to face her mother, who was by then herself sober in AA. "She was the only person left to confront. My father had committed suicide. My grandmother had been dead for years. And my uncle Andy had become a drunk on Hollywood Boulevard, and nobody had heard from him in years."

The setting for Ellen's confrontation with her mother was her therapist's office. "I had written down every abuse I remembered on a sheet of paper so I wouldn't forget, and I read the list to my mother in front of my therapist. I said, 'I remember you doing this, this, and this, and I also remember you doing this, this, and this.' My mother started crying, and then her own denial system broke down, and she admitted everything and more. She said, 'Yes, I did those things, and I *also* did this, this, and this, and I did this, this, and this.' One thing she told me she did that really shocked me was that she used to French kiss my grandmother—her own mother—right in front of me. To this day, I *still* don't remember that! Anyway, after that session I couldn't even talk to my mother for a whole year. She went into therapy and started to deal with her own childhood abuse at the hands of her mother, my grandmother. She went through a period of being suicidal herself, but she hung in there, and because she did, she was instrumental in my own healing and I'm grateful to her."

After that confrontation, Ellen's relationship with her mother slowly began healing. "From AA, I had the *concept* of forgiveness, but I still couldn't forgive. People kept telling me it was okay *not* to forgive my mother because what she'd done to me was unforgivable. But because I'm an alcoholic, I knew I couldn't afford the luxury of hanging on to my resentments without running the risk of drinking again, so I just kept praying for a way to forgive her. Of course, AA doesn't just tell you to sit around and *hope* for things to get better. You have to do the footwork. The footwork I did was I got in contact with my mother and I told her I wanted to have a relationship with her,

but only on my terms. She agreed. At first we just wrote
letters. Then we had phone calls. And then I saw her. But
it was all real slow, and at any point I could move back a
step. If we were on the phone and I got uncomfortable
with her, we'd move back to writing letters again.

"Slowly, we built a new relationship on a foundation
of honesty," Ellen says. "You see, my whole childhood had
been about lies and about putting my mom's feelings first,
so the biggest part of the new relationship with her was to
put my own feelings first, to always take care of myself no
matter how selfish that felt. Anytime I got the least bit
uneasy, I'd stop right then and there and tell her the
truth about how I felt. That way, every day we started with
a clean slate. Even when she was ill with cancer, we handled the relationship the same way. I saw her just a few
times during the whole year she was dying because I
couldn't handle seeing her any more than that. But the
times we did see each other were good."

In AA it's commonplace to hear people express gratitude for having been alcoholic, because it led them to
sobriety and to a much better life. Ellen is one such person. "Until AA, I never knew I could be so loved. AA people have just basically held me in their arms through all
I've had to go through. There was always somebody who
had hope when I didn't. Aside from my sobriety, of
course, the best thing AA did for me was teach me that I
have a choice. I can either be a victim in life, or I can be a
winner. I have chosen to be a winner."

MOLLIE, SOBER 10 YEARS

> *My family had lost trust in me, so it*
> *took a while after I got sober to get*
> *close to them again. They had*
> *resentments, and so did I. By the*
> *time my father died, my relationship*
> *with him was wonderful, but my*
> *relationship with my twin sister is*
> *still unresolved.*
>
> —Mollie

Mollie, 49, a delicately boned woman with silky, light-brown hair, is single and works as a legal secretary. Born in Los Angeles, California, she has an identical twin, Sallie, who is older than Mollie by seven minutes. There were no other children. According to Mollie, her twin is also an alcoholic, which is further evidence supporting the genetic theory of the disease. Her parents, however, did not drink, although her mother did use a lot of medications. In addition to alcoholism, the twins share a food addiction. Mollie's is manifested in overeating, while her sister's is manifested in bulimia—two sides of the same coin.

Mollie and Sallie were 15 when they got drunk for the first time. "Our parents had gone away for the weekend, and within a half hour after they left we headed for the liquor cabinet, drank, and got drunk. Our grandmother, who was baby-sitting, didn't notice a thing."

A Struggle for Identity

"I've always hated being a twin," Mollie admits frankly. "Some twins are fine with it, but I wasn't. To me, there's nothing magical about it. I don't think twins can read each other's minds or do any of that nonsense. I never knew what my sister was thinking or how she felt. We always got stared at and got a lot of attention, and at times I felt special because of it, and at other times I felt like a freak, like we belonged on the front page of the *National Enquirer.* People kept comparing us. Sallie looked like me and acted like me, but she was so much angrier that she frightened me. But I was stuck with her. I couldn't get away from her. As a result, we fought constantly. Being a twin felt like a rip-off. Whatever needs I had coming to me in life were being cut in half.

"My family believed it was wrong to treat us differently, so they treated us the same, no matter who did what. But I *wanted* to be different. I did outrageous things just to be different. I pleaded with my mother not to dress us alike, but to no avail. It wasn't until I went to college that I started to use the word *I* instead of *we.* Psychologically, I'm still trying to separate myself from my sister, still trying to individuate myself and be whole on my own."

Growing up, Mollie's relationship with her father was also painful. "He was the put-down artist of all time. He never missed an opportunity to zap us with his sarcasm. It was like having Don Rickles living in the house. Yet I adored him and kept gravitating to him because he was so much more intelligent than my mother, and I could talk to him about books and about what I was learning in school. Once, when Sallie and I were teenagers and we'd done something to displease him, he turned to my mother at the dinner table and said, 'I know what's wrong with these girls. Whatever it takes to make up a whole human being had to be divided, so neither of them got what it takes to be whole.' At other times, he'd single me out. Once he told me, 'Mollie, if you never get married you'll be making some man very happy—maybe *all* of them!' My mother also put us down verbally a lot.

Mollie's tense relationship with her father colored her relationships with men and made her wary. "With some exceptions, I've avoided men. I've never been married, never lived with anybody, never even come close. I'm still too angry at them and too afraid of getting zapped, just like I got zapped by my father. Even in sobriety, I've had only one relationship, and that lasted only a month. Recently I went on a vacation and had a two-week affair, but that's about it. I never learned dating skills or learned how to flirt. Back when I was drinking, I didn't need to. All I had to do was put on a long, slinky dress and walk down the street at midnight, and the men just sort of drifted to me. Now that I'm sober and older, I can't do things like that."

Sallie, on the other hand, did marry and have a child, but she is now divorced.

As Mollie and Sallie got older, they tried individuating by going to different places and doing different things. "When my sister decided she wanted to work in the medical field, I remember thinking, 'Well, if she's doing that, then I can't.' So I went away to college in Arizona to become a French teacher. I learned to speak French, then changed my major to German and learned to speak German. I learned Spanish as well. Languages were easy for me. Even though I was drinking, I could still get As in French and German. At night, I'd take a cab to a bar and get drunk. I'd outdrink everybody. It was no longer just college drinking, it was serious drinking. If anybody who knew me then had known about alcoholism, they'd have recognized that I was an alcoholic. I got totally crazed behind alcohol and amphetamines, and so paranoid that I often barricaded my door."

Eventually, the drinking forced Mollie to drop out of school, which meant dropping her plans for a teaching career. Meanwhile, at home, her sister had her own troubles. "She'd made four suicide attempts and had ended up in a psychiatric hospital. Because of that, the whole family got into counseling. I was lucky, because my psychiatrist was wonderful, but my sister's psychiatrist asked her to perform oral sex on him on a regular basis, so she didn't benefit too much from her treatment."

However, it was Sallie who got sober first. "I didn't know she'd gone to AA until I called her up one night after I'd been fired from a job for drinking. She came over with AA literature and took me to a meeting. I've been sober ever since."

During those first couple of years when the twins were both sober, their relationship started to improve. But all that changed when Sallie slipped, started taking Valium and other pills, and got deeper into her bulimia. "When I heard that my sister was no longer sober, it was as though I'd been stabbed in the heart. I was devastated. Today she's sicker than ever. She's down to 85 pounds and throws up several times a day. She's dying from her bulimia, and she's in total denial about it, and in denial about being addicted to pills, so we've had to go our separate ways."

Coping with Co-dependency

The fact that Mollie has been getting better while her twin has been getting worse has created a lot of turmoil within Mollie. "I'm unable to get rid of the feeling that it's not okay for me to do better than Sallie. I'm still having trouble separating myself from her! I'm co-dependent. When she's doing okay, I feel better. When she's not doing okay, I feel terrible. I think about her so much it qualifies as an obsession. I refer to her constantly when I view the world: 'What would Sallie think about this or that?' I worry about her pain to the point where it prevents me from dealing with my own. I can't shake the feeling that I'm somehow responsible for her. My deeply held belief is that I'm not allowed to be happy, or successful, until she is, and that if I move on, I'll be doing something terrible to her by leaving her behind and she won't have company."

The struggle to break the neurotic, co-dependent bond with her twin continues to be painful for Mollie. "I want so much to go to France and speak French again, but I feel guilty for even thinking of living it up like that because Sallie's going downhill. My heart is back there with her. Until I save her, I can't move on."

But since AA teaches recovering alcoholics to take personal responsibility for their own lives and stop blaming others for holding them back, Mollie knows she has to stop playing victim and has to get herself unstuck. "Maybe the truth is that I'm hiding behind my sister, using her as an excuse not to deal with my own fear, laziness, and lack of direction. Instead of taking risks, I can point to her and say, 'If it wasn't for *her*, I'd be successful. If it wasn't for her, I'd be happy. If it wasn't for her, I wouldn't be stuck.' But in reality, how could my being successful possibly harm my sister? It could only be an inspiration to her, something to shoot for. Maybe *my* being stuck is what's keeping *her* stuck instead of the other way around. Maybe if I get off the dime it will give Sallie permission to do the same. I simply can't go on blaming her for holding me back. *I'm* holding me back.

"I used to disparage family as being unimportant, but it has become very important to me to have good relationships with them," Mollie says. While her relationship with her sister remains tenuous, the longer she's sober, the more her dealings with other relatives keeps improving. "But it took a while. Because of my drinking, many of them had lost trust in me and I had to prove myself first. In fact, I had one aunt who died before she could ever speak to me again. But now, with the exception of my sister, I've got them all back—aunts, uncles, cousins—and they all think I'm doing wonderfully."

Making Amends

To get to this point, Mollie has had to walk through all the steps in the family healing process that AA recommends, which have included dealing with hurts and resentments, having one-on-one confrontations, making amends, and being able to forgive. "I made amends to different family members for different things, and I did it in different ways," Mollie says. "I made amends to my aunt—for crawling in through her dog door and eating and drinking everything in her house—by simply telling her what I'd done and saying I was sorry. I made amends to my mother, who's now dead, by visiting the mausoleum where she's buried and, on several occasions, having long conversations with her. I made amends to my father by writing out a list of all the positive things he'd done for me and thanking him."

When it came time to expressing some of her hurt and resentment to her father, however, it was hard. "Even though my relationship with him had improved immensely, and I'd grown to adore him, I still didn't trust him. Until the day he died he kept right on zapping me, only I learned how to handle it better, how not to take it so personally. I sat him down and, *not* in a heavy or confrontive way, I told him about some of the things he'd said and done that had hurt me, like his crack about how I'd make some man very happy if I didn't marry him. I realized that at 79 years old, he wasn't going to change, but I needed to tell him for myself. His response was, 'Well, I didn't mean those things, I was joking.' But I said, 'Still, it hurt me.' Today I know that his lashing out at me was more about *his* fear of intimacy than it was about me. It was *his* limitation, not mine. I think he'd be really upset if he knew just how much those things he said really stung."

Where her sister is concerned, dealing with hurts and resentments has been even harder. In fact, Mollie entered therapy with the specific goal of dealing with this still very painful family relationship. "My sister has been so angry all her life and I have a lifetime of hurt where she's concerned. When our father died, just the way she told me was terrible. Instead of telling me, she screamed at me in this unbelievably angry voice, 'Don't you *know*?! He *died*!' It was awful. But whenever I try to tell her that I don't like the way she treats me, she won't hear it. She walks away. And when I try to talk to her about her pill-taking and her bulimia, she gets defensive, evasive, and mad. She's starving herself to death, and she's in massive denial about it. She looks like a skeleton. She can't work. And she lies. She insists the reason she's so thin is because she's on Weight Watchers! Last time I busted her on that lie, she blew up at me and ran out of the room."

Mollie's plan is to write her sister a letter in which she'll discuss her own hurts and resentments, as well as her concerns about Sallie's bulimia and pill addiction. "I'm afraid she's dying, and if I don't say something I'll never be able to live with myself, and then I'll never be able to get on with my life."

No Story Ever Ends

Just because you're in recovery doesn't mean you're finished, complete, or that there's nothing more to do. There's always more to do, more to explore, more to work on. No story ever ends.

In spite of the fact that her relationship with her twin is incomplete, Mollie is nonetheless deeply grateful for her sobriety and for her life. She shows this by working with other recovering alcoholics and doing what AA calls "service."

"My home was so nuts that until I got to AA, I didn't know there existed a world where people are thoughtful and rational, and where they help one another. Now more than ever, I feel privileged to have 10 years in AA. There's something about a decade of sobriety that challenges me to live up to it. I feel a personal responsibility now to carry the message of recovery to other women alcoholics. They need to know that 10 years of sobriety is wonderful, and it can be theirs if they want it. All they have to do is ask."

JILL, SOBER 22 YEARS

> *As a family, what we do now that we never did before is hug a lot and say "I love you." I think it's a gift of sobriety to be able to see how important that is, and to actually be able to do it.*
>
> —Jill

"I am totally convinced of the genetic aspect of alcoholism," says Jill, 69, a warm, gray-haired, slightly overweight, divorced mother of five grown children (including twin sons), who for the past 20 years has been working in the chemical-dependency field as a counselor.

Jill was born in New York City of Irish Catholic background. She had a twin brother who died of a heart attack 10 years ago, and a sister, two years older. "I think to one degree or another, the whole family was alcoholic," Jill states. Her father drank. Her brother took pills. And today her sister has a problem with pills.

According to Jill, the family didn't want for anything except for the mental presence of her father, whose drinking always kept him away from the house. "He didn't drive, so he hired a driver to take him to his drinking spots. It was the driver who would call home and give my mother reports from the field: 'We're now at such-and-such a hotel, and we'll stay here for the evening.' On

Friday nights, after the driver brought my father home, we'd have a physician come to the house and do what we know today as 'detox' my father over the weekend so he could go back to work on Monday morning. This went on for years." At the time Jill did what most children of alcoholics did: she swore to herself, 'It will never happen to me.'"

The fact that her father's drinking went on for years without anybody doing anything about it makes Jill sad today. "Back in those days nobody knew that what was wrong with him was alcoholism. *He* certainly didn't know it. He finally stopped drinking five years before he died, but it was bite-the-bullet sobriety, not AA sobriety. After I got sober myself, I used to wish I could go back in time and tell my father about AA."

A Late Bloomer

Jill didn't drink in high school or college; in fact, her alcoholism didn't show up until after she was married. "I was a late bloomer," she states. "By the time I graduated from Barnard College in New York, we were in World War II, so I joined up with the Red Cross and was assigned to a club-mobile unit that was attached to the famous New York 42nd Infantry Division. A club mobile is something like a catering truck, and a real innovation for the Red Cross. Three women staffed it, and inside we had a stove, a doughnut machine, and all kinds of supplies, including toothbrushes. If our division got orders to move, we'd pack up and go with them, like camp followers. What the club mobiles did for morale was wonderful. Sometimes we were the only women the men had talked to in months. If we saw men in their gun turrets, we'd go right up to them and give them doughnuts. The club mobiles were right behind the firing lines most of the time, and some of the women who staffed them got killed. We were always on the move, and over two years I ended up seeing the whole European theater. I landed in England, then went on to France, Germany, and Italy. Also, we had time off, so I traveled to Ireland and Switzerland. It was an incredible adventure. The only thing that absolutely terrified me was the buzz bombs in London. You were safe as long as you could still hear them, but the moment the motor stopped, the bomb would drop. I'd lie there in bed and say, 'Oh, my God, where is it going to land?' The anxiety drove me crazy!"

It was in Europe during the height of the war that Jill met her husband, Paul. Their romance was a kind of Hemingway short story brought to life. "Paul's sister was working in the club mobile with me, so I met him when he came to visit her. He was in the Air Force and flew many missions over Germany, so we wouldn't see him for a month or two, and then one morning we'd open up and he'd be standing there. When he'd leave again, I'd worry."

Jill and Paul both made it safely through the war and returned to America. Jill got a job in the guest relations department at the then-new ABC-TV studio in New York but quit after she and Paul eloped. She became a full-time housewife and had five children.

A few years into the marriage, Jill started to drink. "I became an alcoholic instantly, hidden bottles and all," she states. "It's as though alcoholism was just sitting there in my body, waiting to happen. I never went to bars. I did all my drinking in the house and no one knew. I definitely had the phenomenon called the obsession to drink. I, who had been such a disciplined person all my life, was totally powerless over my drinking. I finally understood what my father had gone through. I was what they call a functioning drunk. I made sure that I always did Little League and the PTA. I managed to fool some of my closest friends. When I went to AA some of them said, 'But why, Jill? You don't even drink!' "

Jill's husband turned out to have his own addiction, compulsive gambling. It was very painful and difficult for her. "I'd always been a frugal person, super-responsible with money, uncomfortable if a bill wasn't paid. And here I was, married to this man who was totally irresponsible and ended up gambling away everything we had. I'd received an inheritance from my father, and Paul went through that, too, and kept right on going."

But since Jill was drinking at the time, she didn't notice that the money was disappearing. "I simply wasn't paying attention. One day Paul came home and said, 'We've lost everything. We have to move.' So the seven of us got into the car and drove to a lesser neighborhood. We rented a lesser house and moved in. The move accelerated my drinking. I'd left friends and neighbors behind, but of course I didn't let on to anybody that I was hurting or lonely. I stuffed it all inside and tried to keep the happy family facade going."

Paul gambled more and Jill drank more. "He handled my drinking by avoiding it. He'd leave early in the morning and come home late at night. He'd call home and ask one of the girls, 'How's your mother?' and if they said, 'She's had a few drinks,' he wouldn't come home."

Casting Roles in an Alcoholic Drama

Jill relinquished more and more of her parental responsibilities and allowed her children to take over. "I stopped cooking. I even stopped driving. I'd wait for my oldest daughter to get home—she'd just gotten her driver's license—and I'd say, 'Oh, by the way, I haven't had time to go to the market, so could you go and pick up these things?' I'd already have a list for her. She always knew exactly what I was doing. After dinner I'd let the kids clean up, and I'd pour myself another drink and head off to my bedroom to watch TV, making a sort of slurred statement on the way like, 'Don't forget your homework.' Amazingly, there wasn't a lot of fighting or arguing in the house. It was almost like there was a conspiracy of silence. The less I did, the more they did to make up for it, and to take care of me and protect me."

Although Jill wasn't aware of it at the time, her drinking had a negative impact on all five of her children. "In an alcoholic family, each child takes on a specific role," Jill says. "For example, in our family our second oldest daughter became the family caretaker and controller. Whenever anything happened, she was the one everybody went to. She was the sensitive one who could always sniff out how everybody else in the family was feeling. She'd know it when I'd had even one drink! She was also the perfectionist and the superachiever—good at sports, straight As in school. It was her way of saying, 'See, we're *not* a dysfunctional family, because anybody who gets straight As can't possibly come from a dysfunctional family!'

"My oldest daughter, on the other hand, protected herself by becoming an avoider, just like her father. She was wary and slow to trust. She detached herself and stayed away from the house as much as possible. She'd do her homework over at a friend's house and only come home for meals. The twins were avoiders, too. They didn't like to bring their friends home after school for fear I'd be plastered and embarrass them. My youngest son took on both the comedian role and the scapegoat role. He was always full of humor and jokes, a great way to avoid feelings, and he was also the person who kept bringing attention to himself by getting on everybody's nerves. The purpose of the scapegoat is to take the spotlight off the drinker. Instead of getting angry at *me* for drinking, they'd get angry at *him* for being a jerk."

Another trait typical of children of alcoholics is guilt, and Jill's kids had it, too. "They all felt guilty that somehow *they* must have been the cause of my alcoholism, that it must have been something they said, or something they did, that made me drink. So they tried so hard to please me and not upset me."

Jill's Moment of Clarity

Although Jill finally went to AA, her moment of clarity didn't happen right away,, in fact, it took six months. "For my first six months, I simply couldn't stay sober, but I kept returning to meetings just the way they tell you to do. Finally one day I was at a woman's meeting and suddenly this feeling came over me—a feeling of hope. In that one instant, I knew deep inside that I was going to be all right, and that was *it*."

Though 47 when she got sober, Jill still had to go through the same learning process that everybody else has to go through in recovery. She had to start getting in touch with her feelings. "I'd always stuffed my feelings but good. Trapped inside my body were feelings dating back to my childhood, especially the pain over my father's drinking. Until I got sober, I had no idea that those feelings were even there. One day I was sitting in a women's AA discussion group, and I started thinking about my father, and I started to sob. I sobbed as though I'd never stop. The women in the group were so kind and supportive. Some of them came over and hugged me. It was the start of my being able to heal all that unfinished father business."

Jill discovered that one of the best way to identify her own feelings was by listening to other people talk about *their* feelings. I'd sit in meetings and listen to people talk about anger, grief, guilt, and I'd say, 'Wow, yes, I've felt that, too. I understand that!' When they'd label a feeling, it would help me to identify that same feeling in myself.' When Jill was able to pinpoint anger, she realized she had a lot of it. "I was astounded at how much anger I had inside of me, much of it at my father for his drinking, and the rest of it at people who'd manipulated me and taken advantage of me when I was drinking. I also had anger at myself for letting myself be taken advantage of. I'd been such a people-pleaser all my life that it was horrifying to me to see how mad I really was."

A Painful Readjustment

Jill's sobriety really upset the applecart where her marriage was concerned. As she got better, her husband's gambling got worse. For years, they'd played the tit-for-tat game: he got to gamble, and she got to drink. But once she was sober, that old game didn't work anymore. "Even though I still loved him, I knew I couldn't live with a compulsive gambler. He was gone most of the time. He wasn't bringing any money home. He lied and broke promises. Finally one day I packed his bags and threw him out.

"It was hard," Jill continues. "There I was, newly sober, with five children, no job, and no money. It was quite a challenge. I had no choice but to keep the faith and press on. My sponsor ordered me to apply for welfare. Welfare! Never in all my life did I ever think I'd be applying for welfare! She said to me, 'Look at the situation you're in. That is what welfare is.' I swallowed my pride, went and stood in line, got my food stamps, and that's how my kids and I survived for nearly a year."

After a year on welfare, Jill decided to go back to school to get the credentials needed to become an addiction counselor. "No sooner had I finished my training when somebody offered me a job in the chemical-dependency field, and I've been in it ever since." Currently she's a counselor in a hospital treatment program. She is still very active in AA. "I believe it's crucial to keep doing daily practices to maintain sobriety. In addition, I do spiritual practices. I read prayer books. I meditate. I do service, meaning I work with newcomer alcoholics. It's all part of staying sober."

To move past her hurt and resentment, Jill had to approach her ex-husband, who'd ultimately abandoned the family, and not only tell him that he'd hurt her, but also make amends to him for her drinking. She also had to forgive both him and herself. By the time she'd done that, "we were able to sit and have long talks together about how we were two dysfunctional people, doing the best we could under the circumstances. When he died eight years ago, I wasn't left with a lot of unfinished business. Our relationship was complete."

Jill has chosen not to marry again. "I didn't feel the need to. I have my AA friends and my non-AA friends. I don't limit myself to a recovering-alcoholic universe. I'd go mad if all I talked about was alcoholism. There *is* a world out there! I do other things. I go to the theater. I take trips. Ten years ago I bought a condo. My daughter said, 'It's good you got a small one, Mother, otherwise some of us might move back in with you!' "

Nearing 70 doesn't scare her. "I don't dwell on it. I don't feel old, I feel young. When I hear people talk about how frightened they are of aging, I think it's sad. I don't feel that way. The only change I've noticed is that I don't accept every invitation anymore!"

Jill admits she has more work to do on herself. "I'm still a very oral person, an overeater and a sugar addict. I always have to have something in my mouth. The minute I stopped drinking, my craving for candy bars increased. I wanted sugar every day, but I know I don't have diabetes because I've been tested for it many times. What I have is the typical recovering alcoholic's sugar madness. When I first got sober and my kids were still at home, I'd buy huge Hershey bars and put them in the refrigerator because I like them cold, but my kids would find them, so I started hiding them in the very same places that I used to hide my booze. I still love those Hershey bars, but now I don't have to hide them anymore!"

Family Ties

The people who benefited the most when Jill got sober were her five children. At that time their ages were 16, 14, 12 (the twins), and 10. "None of my kids ever blamed me or said anything like 'You were never there for us.' In fact, in the beginning they even made excuses for me by blaming my drinking on their father's gambling." But Jill, who was practicing the AA principles of honesty and integrity, knew she couldn't pin her drinking on anyone but herself. "Even if your father had been a saint," she told her kids, "I'd *still* have taken those drinks because I'm an alcoholic."

When she made her amends to her children for her alcoholic behavior with them, they told her she was crazy for worrying that her drinking had hurt them. They said, "Oh, Mom, we don't know what you're so uptight about. You were always home and dinner was always on the table, so don't be so guilty!"

Jill remains honest, however. "True, I wasn't a bar drinker. I didn't make scenes or abuse anybody. But I'm convinced nonetheless that my drinking *did* have a negative effect on their lives. You just can't be a loving parent if you're a practicing alcoholic. You're too self-centered. Alcohol creates distance, like a wall of ice between people. How could I possibly have loved them properly when I was so busy hating myself for what I was doing to myself? That kind of self-loathing *always* takes its toll."

After Jill had been sober for a year, she decided to sit down with all five of her children and discuss addiction with them in depth. "I discussed the different adaptive roles that children of alcoholics automatically take on, and pointed out how these roles had affected them and might still be affecting them. When we talked about it openly, they could really see it. I also discussed the genetics of alcoholism with them and the possibility that they were each predisposed to the disease, and how important it was that they be aware of it. I also told them that if I had my druthers, I would hope that they would *never* experiment with alcohol, never give it a chance to take hold, but I realize they'd have to decide that for themselves when they got older. During the whole conversation the kids couldn't have been more receptive and loving. They took it in and accepted it."

Sobriety, and time, heals most wounds. "Today my five children are proud of me for being sober in AA for 22 years. They're open about it and there's no shame or stigma about my alcoholism in their eyes. They've even recruited people to talk to me. They tell their friends, 'Oh, you just *have* to talk to my mother. She'll help you!' I think half the students in their classes in high school and college have called me at one time or another about an addiction problem somewhere in their lives.

"And every year, my entire family, including the grandkids, comes to my regular AA meeting just to see me blow out the candles on another AA birthday cake and help me celebrate another year of sobriety. When I see them all sitting there, applauding like crazy, it makes me feel absolutely wonderful."

SOBER FAMILY TIPS LIST

1. "I'm only hurting myself" is the alcoholic's Big Lie. In families where there's addiction, everybody gets hurt.

2. Whenever sobriety strikes a family, there's always a lot of repair work to do, so don't expect to walk off into the sunset right away.

3. For survival's sake, children in alcoholic families take on different adaptive roles: Caretaker, scapegoat, rebel. If you're from an alcoholic family, which role(s) did you play? If you have kids, which roles do they play? Share your knowledge of family roles with your kids to help them heal.

4. Sobriety upsets the family applecart. Family members who have taken on adaptive roles may be reluctant to give them up, even though they are no longer appropriate.

5. Everyone in an alcoholic family has his or her own pain, and each person's healing process will take place on his or her own time and in his or her own way.

6. Encourage family members to deal with their resentments, hurt, guilt, and distrust, as well as their enabling and co-dependency issues, in their own recovery groups (Al-Anon, CocAnon, Alateen, Co-dependents Anonymous, ACA/ACoA). Some families need extra healing help, such as individual or group psychotherapy.

7. Evidence points to a genetic link in alcoholism. Draw an alcoholism "family tree." Who's alcoholic in your family? If you have kids, warn them that they may be predisposed.

8. AA says, "More will be revealed." The longer you're sober, the more you'll remember and understand, and the better equipped you'll be to handle what you discover.

9. Remember, recovery is a "selfish" program. Even when trying to heal your family, *your sobriety comes first.*

10. "Doing service" by helping another alcoholic can be done anywhere, even in the family. Keep looking out for what you can do to help another alcoholic or potential alcoholic.

11. Forgiveness is the goal of any family's recovery process, but it can only occur as the result of walking yourself bravely through the steps that come before it.

12. Staying sober is the best amend you can ever make to your family

6

SOBER FINANCES

My AA sponsor kept telling me that if I didn't do something about my compulsive spending, I'd drink again.

—Jessie, sober 15 years

Money itself is neither good nor bad, it just *is*. However, how a person views money, makes money, spends money, saves money, and handles money often says a lot about who they are. Through money, we expose our character, maturity level, and the health of our self-esteem.

For many, not just those in chemical-dependency recovery, there's a certain shame attached to the subject of money. In this culture, we get mixed messages. Money is considered filthy lucre on the one hand, yet highly desirable on the other. Even in Alcoholics Anonymous there are some who consider it somewhat tacky to focus on "money, property, and prestige," rather than on more spiritual matters. Women especially are often brought up to think that it's "not nice" to discuss money because money is associated with power, which makes it something that only *men* should tangle with. "I think I'd rather talk about sex!" says one interviewee who was raised with this notion that nice girls don't talk money. Another interviewee admits that in her early years of sobriety she'd go on job interviews and be too embarrassed to ask what the jobs paid. "I didn't want them to think that money was actually important to me," she says.

Some women can't talk about money for reasons of low self-worth. In Chapter 3, for example, we saw how the actress Deanne didn't think she "deserved" to be successful and make lots of money. Even though she was the star of a TV show, if she'd been asked to set her own salary, she probably would have given herself poverty wages! One of the signs of increasing self-esteem in a recovering alcoholic is his or her capacity to comfortably accept abundance.

For some women in recovery, money is a nonissue, but for others it's a huge issue, one unrelated to current economic trends. Many who have money-handling problems today turn out to have had them for years. A client of mine once told me that she'd been in debt from the age of seven. "I took advances on my allowance, so when it came due it was all owed. Twenty years later I'm still doing the same thing, only now it's my paycheck that's all owed."

When such a woman gets sober, she may be willing to shape up in the other areas of life—work, relationships, health—but out of embarrassment over her fiscal fumbling, she'll leave the money area for last.

AN ADDICTION IS AN ADDICTION IS AN ADDICTION

A number of women interviewed for this book are admitted compulsive spenders. There are striking parallels between chemical dependency and compulsive spending. Like alcoholism, compulsive spending is a progressive disorder that gets worse over time. And, like other addictions, the spending behavior anesthetizes feelings and deadens intuition. It provides a temporary fix. Until the behavior is stopped, the feelings stay buried. Spenders, like alcoholics, suffer from denial. Many can't admit that their spending style is "different." They put the blame elsewhere—the economy is always a handy target. They refuse to recognize their own part in their debting, or their poverty, or their chronic underearning, or their general money mismanagement.

Our three interviewees for this chapter, Shirley, Hope, and Jessie, who have 25, 17, and 15 years of sobriety, respectively, have each had problems around money. For Shirley, who grew up in wartime London and whose mother became impoverished after her divorce, money meant security and self-worth. Shirley's husband, on the other hand, saw money as *power*. He controlled Shirley with money, particularly by withholding it. For Hope, money, along with lofty job titles, was a way of impressing other people, which she hoped would make her feel more worthy. For Jessie, money was spent compulsively to distract herself from her feelings.

In sobriety, each woman has had to struggle with her own unique money style, determine what money (or the lack of it) means to her, and come to terms with it. Of the three, Jessie is the true compulsive spender. What finally got her to start dealing with her addictive spending was inheriting the proverbial one million dollars! She says, "When I saw that I was pissing it away at an alarming rate, I turned myself in to Debtors Anonymous."

Debtors Anonymous (DA) is yet another 12-step recovery group based on Alcoholics Anonymous but instead focusing on money. The organization is not just for debtors but for anyone who considers themselves "funny with money."

Sooner or later, the recovering woman who has other addictions, such as compulsive spending or debting, will have to face them. It's a common story in AA that once a woman gets sober, she goes on to handle overeating, smoking, gambling, co-dependency, or whatever else ails her, as we've seen in the previous chapters. If she doesn't, it creates tension in her life and eventually will begin interfering with her sobriety. That's serious, because sobriety is her number one priority. Whenever she senses that her sobriety is threatened, she usually takes action.

Giving up one's destructive spending habits can be almost as painful as giving up alcohol and drugs. It is rarely done happily or gracefully, as Jessie will attest to. "I've been in DA for over a year and I'm still having a hard time admitting that I don't have this money thing nailed!"

Another parallel to chemical dependency is the fact that it's not as important for a woman to understand *why* she's funny with money as it is for her to *stop* the behavior. Once she stops the behavior, the feelings that the behavior is covering up will show through.

SHIRLEY, SOBER 25 YEARS

> *All my life the subject of money has been a constant source of anguish and agony. No matter how much money I have, there's always a part of me that feels like the "poor relation."*
>
> —Shirley

Shirley, 59, a married, sandy-haired, humorous, "still struggling" novelist, was born in London, England, an only child. She has a grown son and grown stepchildren.

When she was five, her parents separated over her father's adultery. "My mother and I walked out of the house one Christmas Eve and never went back. My father moved his girlfriend right in, and while my mother and I were living in a one-room flat with an outside toilet, the girlfriend's son was sleeping in my old bed." Shirley saw her father only a few times after the separation. One of those times was in court, "where he went to deny that he could pay child support."

Growing up, Shirley felt "absolutely responsible" for her parents' divorce because of a lie she'd told at the tender age of four. "I told my mother that while she'd been in the hospital having an operation, my father had brought his lover to the house. The reason I told the lie was to please her. I knew that's what she wanted to hear, and I thought she'd love me more if I gave her that information. The irony was that this *had* actually happened, but I didn't know, so from my point of view I was lying. When my mother finally left my father, I thought it was my fault. In reality, she left him because of his ongoing affair, but I perceived the reason to be because of what I'd told her. I carried the guilt on my shoulders for years."

World War II broke out when Shirley was seven, and during the German blitz of London she was evacuated to the English countryside for her safety. Her mother remained behind. "My cousins had been evacuated someplace else, together as a family. Because of that, I felt thrown away and abandoned—punished for my sins."

It wasn't until Shirley was an adult that she learned the *real* reason why she'd been evacuated to a different place: money. "My mother simply couldn't afford to send me to wherever it was that my cousins had be sent."

For five years, Shirley lived in the country with "strangers in emotionally abusive circumstances. I was allowed to wear only one white blouse a week, and I was always dirty. I felt like Cinderella *before* the prince."

"The Poor Relations"

After the war, Shirley returned to her mother in London. They lived in Shirley's aunt's flat. "We were the poor relations. My mother, grandmother, and I all shared one bed, while one of my cousins had a room of her own. This reinforced my belief that I was not as good as other folks because I didn't have money. I thought I deserved to live this way."

Shirley was bright and escaped into books—"my first addiction," she says. She practically lived at the library. "I started with the A's, and I read my way through to the Zs. I read the classics and I read trash, and I didn't know the difference." But at home, being bright wasn't the least bit appreciated. "I came from a background where they'd tell me things like, 'No man will ever want you because you're too smart, so you'd better hide your brains.' My grandmother was always saying, 'Don't argue with your uncles.'"

In school, however, her brightness was her ticket out of poverty. "I took an exam that decided my future. I got the highest grade in the county, and as a result I got a scholarship to an excellent school."

She did well in this school until the age of 15, when she began to experiment with alcohol. "Instantly it did something very special for me—it took that 'poor relations' feeling away."

After about three years, alcohol also made her flunk out of school just short of graduating. At 18, she went to work for a hotel chain in London. Though Shirley was still drinking, it hadn't progressed to the point where it seriously interfered with her work. At 22, she got a job transfer to the United States. By then the drinking was *starting* to get in the way of her daily functioning. After a few months in New York, she met a man who was "inadequate, immature, and did nothing after work except sit in front of the TV and read the paper—a man just like my father."

She married him. "All I knew was that I desperately wanted security, wanted somebody to take care of me, wanted to belong somewhere and be part of a couple." Shirley left the hotel job for a less demanding job as a secretary for an architect/contractor. After a year or so, as her marriage started to sour, Shirley and her employer, Paul, himself married and the father of five children, started an affair. "It destroyed both our marriages," Shirley says simply.

After bitter divorces, Shirley and Paul got married and had a son. The marriage, needless to say, was rocky. "*Why* I assumed that a man who could leave his wife and five children for his alcoholic secretary was good marriage material, I'll never know!" Amazingly enough, they are still together today, more than 30 years later.

Shirley's drinking progressed rapidly, and she and Paul fought constantly over her drinking, over one of Paul's sons, 15, who'd come to live with them, and over money. "I drank with drawn drapes. If someone knocked on the door, I'd hide. At times I was violent. Once I tried to kill my husband with a hammer. I knew I wasn't fit to be a mother, and I lived in fear that somebody would take my little boy, whom I adored, away from me.

"One night on TV I saw a public service spot for AA, and I called the number. It was one of those special moments that I've had three or four times in my life, moments of tremendous clarity, like something outside myself was showing me a clear path, showing me exactly what to do next."

The next day two women from AA came to see her. "I haven't had, nor have I even wanted, a drink since—and that was 25 years ago."

Shirley took to AA like a duck to water. "Since I'd always felt thrown away, felt that I never belonged anywhere, coming into AA was like coming home. I felt I'd found my family, my clan, my tribe. I belonged. We're all tribal creatures, and we need to belong to a tribe. AA was mine."

The War of the Finances

After Shirley's drinking was no longer an issue in the marriage, the couple's fights shifted to money. "Our marriage was the War of the Finances. Paul and I were locked in a power struggle, and money was our battleground. He tried to control me by withholding money, and I retaliated by nagging him to be an entrepreneur, even though that's not what he was. He wasn't capable of making big business deals. We never sat down and talked about our finances in a civil manner, never discussed what we could and couldn't afford."

It would be years before Shirley would gain enough insight into this aspect of her marriage to recognize that her "poor-relations" feeling from childhood had more than a little something to do with why she had picked a husband who turned out to be financially punitive and withholding. Even as an adult, her unconscious belief that she was "bad" allowed herself to play the money victim for years. She felt she didn't deserve any better.

Shirley says, "When I first got sober I wasn't working because I had this small son to take care of, so I had no money of my own, and Paul wouldn't give me any. He kept me totally without cash. I had charge accounts all over town, but no cash. It made me dependent on him. If we needed carrots, I'd have to call him up at work and say, 'We need carrots.' Even if I used a credit card, I'd never know what the limits were, so I was always terrified of spending too much. If we needed a dish towel, I'd charge four, bring them home, ask Paul which one to keep, and take the others back. More and more I felt like a child. And he was controlling in other ways. If I wanted to read in bed at night and he wanted to go to sleep, he'd rip the book out of my hands and say, 'You'll go to sleep when I tell you to go to sleep.' Meanwhile, my stepson would leave me little notes saying, 'You didn't clean under my bed.' I felt victimized and dominated, and I couldn't see a way out of it. But I kept going to AA and I listened and learned. One day I was scrubbing the floor when I had another of those moments of clarity. I suddenly thought to myself, 'I'm doing this for nothing. I've been sober for three years. I'm 37 years old. I have an 8-year-old son. It's time for me to have my own money.'"

When she asked Paul for housekeeping money, he became enraged, "but when he saw how determined I was, he consented to a small weekly allowance, out of which I also had to pay for my mother's yearly visits from England. But at least it was a start."

Asking for that money was the kind of action that AA encourages, the kind that helps build self-esteem. It was Shirley's way of letting both her husband and herself know, "I deserve."

Paul and Shirley's new financial arrangement worked for a while, until a crisis arose. Shirley and her stepson, now 18, had a run-in and Shirley hit him with a flyswatter. "He's got to go," she told Paul. "I cannot have him here any longer!" Paul agreed to send his son to Hawaii for the summer, but then he added, "And I'll be taking his plane fare out of your housekeeping money— $18 a week."

That was the last straw for Shirley. "I became so enraged I thought it would affect my sobriety, so to stay sober I decided to leave him. I really meant it. My bags were packed, my young son's bags were packed, and I was going to walk out of my home and never go back, just as my mother and I had walked out on my father so many years before. I felt psychologically destined to repeat my mother's story. Fortunately, before I did it I talked about it at an AA discussion meeting. After the meeting, one of the AA members, who also happened to be a well-known lawyer, came up to me and said, 'You've got legal rights, you know.' Well, I had no idea that I had rights. Then he said, "In this state, the wife and child get to maintain the home, and it's the husband who has to leave. Have your husband come and see me.'"

Shirley went home and told Paul about her conversation with the lawyer. "He said, 'You're going to divorce me over $18 a week?' and I said, 'Yes, if that's what you perceive it to be, then I'm going to divorce you over $18 a week.' Paul then made an appointment to talk to the lawyer himself. I don't know what was said between them, but when Paul came home, for the first time in our married life, he apologized to me. He said, 'Yes, you're right, and I'm wrong.' And we carried on from there."

Fiscal Disaster and a Major Life Change

If basic money attitude problems go untreated in a family, it's the same as if alcoholism goes untreated. It continues to do damage. Although Paul and Shirley didn't divorce, Shirley's insecurities were still intact, and the conflicts were far from over. In fact, one common money "style" they had in common was chronic vagueness. Neither of them ever kept track of where the money went. "Some years Paul made good money, but neither of us ever knew what we spent it on. It was just gone. Year after year, we were always playing catch-up. Our house was nice, but the drapes were rotting, and the walls and roof were falling apart. Then the economy took a dip, Paul couldn't get any new construction contracts, and we went broke. He keep saying, 'It can't last,' but it lasted. We owed everybody in town. I went to work, but what I made wasn't even enough to keep us going, let alone make a dent in our debts. I kept trying to jump-start Paul into pulling off a business deal to rescue us, and Paul's mission in life became resisting me. He'd leave me fuming and retreat into the garage to refurbish antique cars."

Ultimately, Paul had to close his construction office. Determined to pay off every last debt, he absolutely refused to declare bankruptcy. Instead, he accepted a job in Saudi Arabia as an architect in charge of residential development for a town just outside of Jidda, on the Red Sea. His integrity concerning their debts is something that Shirley appreciates now, but at the time she wasn't pleased. "I didn't really want to go to Saudi, but I didn't resist. I saw it as my duty. Besides, I thought it was going to be for only 18 months, and then we'd be home again. When I walked out my front door, it never occurred to me that I was seeing my home for the last time. Without even knowing it, I was re-creating that scene from my childhood after all. I felt like I was being punished again, just like I felt when I was sent away from London as a child during the war. Here I was, 16 years sober, our son was off at Georgetown University, and I'd been a good AA member. I thought I'd done everything right, so why this? Why was I now being asked to leave my home, leave my friends, leave my dogs, and move to a desert half a world away. It wasn't fair!"

The 18 months in Saudi became four years, which turned out to be a remarkable time for Shirley. "I wouldn't have missed that experience for the world," she beams. Her first surprise was that life in Saudi was a relief. "It was like taking off a tight corset. Nobody expected me to be anything other than my husband's wife. There was no achievement pressure. I didn't feel I had to be getting a Ph.D. while I had a baby in one hand and a job in the other." Since drinking is illegal there, the locations of AA meetings are kept secret, but Shirley managed to ferret one out by putting a notice up on the bulletin board in the local market: "Is anybody here a friend of Bill Wilson?" (AA's co-founder). It's a code that AA members use to find other AA members. The little local group Shirley uncovered, which was made up mostly of Westerners, got her through.

One truism about Alcoholics Anonymous is that what works during one phase of sobriety may not be the best course of action during another. Having spent her first 16 years in AA learning how to open up and talk about her problems, Shirley now had to learn to shut up and hold her mud. "When I first started attending AA meetings in Saudi, I'd share my anguish about losing my home in America, about leaving my friends, about missing my son. But I noticed that the others didn't seem to want to hear it. That wasn't at all what I was used to, so at first I was mad. I felt my lifeline was being cut off. But over time I began to see that all my life I'd been hanging on to things to cry "poor me" over. It was getting boring! In Saudi I learned that everybody's got things that hurt, and that anguish is relative. I learned that real recovery means focusing on what you have instead of what you lack. Happiness can't depend on having a house, or a husband who makes big business deals, or having a lot of money. I saw that my 'victim' stance was one of my main character defects. What a shock! I took a lot of long walks in the desert to mull over this one. In the end, Saudi was a time of real spiritual evaluation for me. I came out of this period believing in a universal spiritual power that I can tap into and get strength from anytime, no matter what my circumstances are, financial or otherwise."

Her eyes now opened, Shirley was better able to see how lucky she was. "All I had to do was compare my life to the life of a Saudi woman, and I felt very grateful. To be a woman in Saudi society is not an easy thing. Saudi girls have to put on long, black *gomduras* when they're 11 or 12 and be segregated from the boys, so they never get to know them as people. After that, the only men who ever see the women without their veils are their husbands, fathers, and sons. And since women—Western or Saudi— are not allowed to drive, we'd all have to go grocery shopping on our bicycles. We would peddle along in 100-degree heat, carrying the groceries in our baskets, while our menfolk would sail by in their air-conditioned company cars."

In Saudi, Shirley's next step was to determine what she wanted to do with her time. "I could have done what other Western wives did—help organize the library, or start a book group, but I felt I'd gone past that, and now I had to do something that was *me*. It was the first time in my life that I'd tried to define myself aside from my relationship to somebody else."

Ultimately, Shirley decided that she wanted to write. "I ended up writing two novels, neither of which are set in Saudi. In fact, I set one of them in the California wine country, which may seem like a rather strange thing for a recovering alcoholic writer to do!"

Shirley caught on right away that there's always a price to pay for following your dream. "Writing is isolating, and people kept trying to pull me away from it. I'd explain that I was writing a book, but they'd be put out anyway. It was one more time in my life where I ended up feeling like an outsider. Only this time there was a difference: it was *my* choice."

Coming Home

Shirley's four years in Saudi, which occurred just a few years before the Gulf War of 1991, ended when Paul had earned enough money to pay off all his debts. "We rented a house in England for a year to be near my mother, who was getting old and frail. Living there was wonderful. I continued to work on my novels, and Paul took up painting. Ironically, our son, who by then was out of college and working in real estate development, had emerged as the brilliant entrepreneur of the family, the very thing I'd always wanted Paul to be. Even when we were still in Saudi, he kept urging us to return to the United States, saying, 'It's the biggest boom ever,' but Paul wouldn't budge. He was reluctant to come back to where he'd had his balls in a vise. Unfortunately, by the time we did return to America, the boom was over." This put Shirley's new live-and-let-live philosophy where Paul's business dealings were concerned to the test, especially when she learned that their son had heeded his own advice and had invested heavily in real estate. As a result, he'd made millions. "When he picked us up at the airport, he said, 'Money will never be an issue with me again.'"

Still, the lessons Shirley learned in Saudi stuck with her. "I stopped moaning over lost opportunities and started taking more personal responsibility for the choices in my life. Maybe I was a victim of circumstance when I was a child, but I certainly wasn't a helpless victim as an adult, even though I pretended to be. Every business decision my husband ever made, *I* chose to go along with, so I had no right to blame him or punish him when those decisions turned out to be wrong. When we had to stay on in Saudi, and my husband decided to sell our house, it was just before the housing market skyrocketed. Had we hung on to it a while longer, we could have gotten four times what we did get. But *I* went along with Paul's decision to sell, so I can't blame him. I could have done something, said something, not signed the papers, insisted on renting it instead, something. But I didn't. So now I have to accept my responsibility in the matter and ask myself, 'If I knew better, then why did I stand by and let that happen? What was my payoff? Did it enable me to play victim one more time?' Well, that's the role Saudi taught me to stop playing."

Shirley's marriage has undergone many transformations, especially in the arena of money. "We still have problems with money, but today they're normal problems, not a financial battleground. Paul and I even have a joint checking account. Imagine! And this is the man who wouldn't even let me have housekeeping money! Today we're living comfortably, although not lavishly, off the proceeds of a single real estate deal that my son and my stepson—the one I had all those problems with!—engineered for us just after we got back from Saudi.

These days, Paul can usually be found in his workroom, building model aircrafts with 9-foot wingspans, while Shirley can be found at her desk, making the latest revisions to her novels. She has pulled off a real coup by getting an agent, who is sending her manuscripts around to publishers. "If I sell my books, I may only make tuppence-haypenny," Shirley says, "but at least it will be *my* tuppence-haypenny!"

HOPE, SOBER 17 YEARS

> *I was brought up to believe that you are your paycheck. But the times I was making the most money were also the times I was feeling the most miserable. I had to learn that impressing you isn't as important as making my dreams come true.*
>
> —Hope

"I was a working-class child with high-class ambitions," says Hope, 54, a tall, slender, brown-eyed blond divorcee with no children, who is currently in the midst of a major career change. She was born and raised in Brooklyn, New York, the last of six children (one died in infancy). "I was so much younger than my sister and brothers that by the time I came along they were almost out of the house," she says. "It was as though I was an only child."

The Need to Escape

According to Hope, her grandparents were uneducated immigrants, and her parents never even graduated from grade school. "I was the first one in the family to graduate from high school and go to college, and the first one who ever went to the opera, or to a museum, or to Carnegie Hall." As a child, she spent most of her free time on weekends going to these places alone. "My values and interests were so different from my family's that my mother used to tell me she thought she'd gotten the wrong baby. She said that as a put-down, but to me it was a great compliment. I didn't want to be a part of that family."

Hope's family had alcoholism on both sides. "Many relatives died of the disease. My father was an unadmitted alcoholic who kept drifting off and was a shadowy figure in my life. My mother's father, who also drank, owned a tavern until his wife made him get rid of it because she thought it was sinful that he took workingmen's paychecks for booze."

Growing up, Hope knew there were two things she wanted: an education and a glamorous life. "There again, my family didn't understand my wants. They felt that the only aspiration you should have in life is job security. Work had no purpose other than that. Nothing was ever said about taking joy in one's work. When I wanted to go to New York University, my family wouldn't help me, so I started working my way through by going nights. Unfortunately, at the time about the only thing you could take at night was accounting, so I quit. I knew there had to be a faster escape route out of my home. I signed up at a very respectable modeling academy on 5th Avenue in Manhattan, took their course, and graduated, but I was too shy to put together a portfolio and go out amongst the competition. Instead, I accepted a nice, safe job as a buyer's model at Lord and Taylor's department store in New York, and moved into an apartment with a roommate. Of course, my family didn't approve of either of these things."

Department-store modeling didn't turn out to be the glamorous work Hope thought it would be. "It was a lot of sitting around, worrying about the underpinnings for bridal gowns." She stuck it out for over a year, which turned out to be a bad idea because it resulted in Hope's first excursion into overspending. "I thought beautiful, expensive clothes would make me a beautiful, valuable person, so I went to all of Lord and Taylor's big sales. I ran up my credit cards way beyond what I was being paid. I so overextended myself that I had to move back in with my parents." This time, motivated by a strong desire to get away from her family once again, she quit the modeling work, curbed her spending, saved her money, and got another job as a secretary. On a bus going to work one day, she met a man named George. They began dating, and she ended up following him to Provo, Utah, where she married him. He turned out to be mentally ill.

A Diamond in the Rough?

"I could see that George wasn't wrapped too tight," Hope admits, "but all my life I'd been trained that it wasn't okay to trust your intuition, so when I felt those warnings, when my buzzers went off, I ignored them. Because he was smart and an avid Shakespearean scholar, I figured he was a diamond in the rough that I could polish up."

In Provo, George got a job working for an insurance company, and Hope got a job running an office for a contractor. She also signed up for classes at Brigham Young University. "I was still trying to get my degree and figure out what I wanted to be when I grew up."

Soon, Hope's intuitive feelings about George proved correct. Increasingly, he showed signs of paranoia. "He thought the CIA and his co-workers were spying on him and reporting to me. He had episodes of violence, and I was always frightened, always on edge, but because of my miserable self-esteem I put up with him for nearly two years. Meanwhile, in an attempt to anesthetize my feelings, I started to drink. I was one of those people who lost control of it immediately. Every day I'd wake up determined *not* to drink, and every day I'd end up drinking within a half hour of when my feet hit the floor. I also began overspending again, mostly on furniture and cars." When her husband ended up in the psychiatric unit of the VA hospital, Hope ended up with the bills. At first she tried to negotiate with the stores and the lenders, but in the end they repossessed everything and wrote off the debts. "It was horrifying in terms of my pride, but in terms of the debts being written off, it was a relief."

On the advice of her husband's psychiatrist, Hope filed for divorce. "The doctor told me that my husband was not only very ill but also potentially dangerous, and that if I wanted to save myself and not wind up dead, I'd better make myself scarce."

By the time she was divorced, Hope's alcoholism was in full bloom. She began a period of what AA calls "doing geographics." She kept moving from one place to another, changing jobs, signing up for new classes, dating one man after the other, hoping that each new move would make her feel better. "Every time I made a change I'd tell myself, 'I'm getting a fresh start,' and then nothing would change. I'd already lived in a dozen apartments, been to nine universities, and changed my major four times." Even when she finally finished college and got her BA degree, it didn't make her feel better about herself. "It didn't fix it," she says. She signed up for graduate school. "I figured maybe getting a master's degree would fix it."

Meanwhile, she kept drinking and working at unchallenging jobs that made her unhappy. "I hit bottom with a job that I hated so much I couldn't understand how I got there. I was working as a counselor in a group home for delinquent adolescent girls. The hours were crazy, the pay lousy, and I had no social life. All I did was work, go home, and drink. By now, my drinking had increased to the point where it took precedence over everything. One night I had a drunken episode during which I tore all the wallpaper off the dining-room wall of my latest apartment. When I woke up later and saw what I'd done, I felt so hopeless I didn't want to live anymore. Figuring I'd have nothing to lose, I called Alcoholics Anonymous."

Zapped Sober

By now accustomed to failure, it never occurred to Hope that AA could actually help her. Fortunately, faith in AA isn't a requirement for the program to work. "I walked into a meeting and the most amazing thing happened—I was zapped sober at the door. I mean that literally. The instant I walked through the door, the obsession to drink that I'd felt on a daily basis for 10 years just left me. It was simply removed. On one side of the doorway I was a hopeless alcoholic, and on the other side I was in recovery. I don't know how, or what, or why that happened, but it happened."

One of the first things Hope had to do after she got sober was stop running—stop doing geographics, and stay put. She admits it wasn't easy. "My impulse to run remained strong. My paternal grandfather was a sea captain, so I think it's in my genes! Sailing away whenever things get rough is a survival technique I learned back when I was that little girl who wanted to check out of my family, and I've been doing it ever since."

Another thing Hope had to deal with was her unhealthy attitude toward money. It took her years to get a sense of what her own values were. "I'd been so busy trying to look good and impress others that I'd never taken the time to find out if money, property, and prestige was what *I* wanted."

To determine once and for all whether money was her destiny, Hope decided that she'd do everything in her power to succeed, and then step back and see how success felt. It meant starting at the bottom again, which she was willing to do. "One positive thing about growing up in my family, where there was so much emphasis on job security, is that it never occurred to me that I *wouldn't* always have to work hard to earn a living and take care of myself. Even during periods of transition and overspending, I've worked and earned money. Either I had a part-time job, or I was in real estate or something. I've never been without income."

Her first job in sobriety was a temporary position in the accounting department of an insurance company. "It was for very little money, and I hated it. Every morning I'd pray for the willingness to show up and put in a day's work. Then one day when I was a year and a half sober, by a fluke, I ran into a man who turned out to be the CEO of the company I was working for. Unlike most corporate people I've met, he wanted employees to better themselves, go as far as they could go, so within a few weeks of meeting me he asked me to be his assistant. From there I went on to become the editor of the company's trade publication.

"This turn of events gave me tremendous confidence," Hope says. "For the first time in my life, I felt capable. The editorial job led to a bigger job as vice president of career consulting in a public relations and marketing firm, which in turn led to an even bigger job as a director of administration at a law firm. After two and a half years there, I left to go work in a larger, more prestigious law firm, where I made all kinds of money and had lots of perks. On paper I was making $60,000, plus they bought me a car, paid my insurance, paid mileage, gave me expense money, and all kinds of other things. I kept making money and I kept spending it. I bought very expensive furniture and I had a closet full of expensive designer clothes. There was a lot of 'image' involved in the job, and a lot of people looked up to me, envied me, but instead of being happy about it, I started to feel like a phony."

Hope also had a lot of stress. "I felt I'd advanced beyond my capacities, like the Peter Principle, and it was very stressful. I began to dread Monday morning. To combat stress, I'd go away on spiritual weekend retreats to commune with nature and animals. This led to my getting in touch with myself for the first time in my life. At the time it was scary. Today, of course, I'm no longer afraid of the inner journey because I feel I have a friend inside of me instead of an enemy, but back then I only saw the surface of everything. I had to learn that what's important in life is what's *under* the surface. In fact, and as far as I'm concerned, the whole process of learning what's *under* the surface is what the sobriety journey is all about."

When Hope's employer began to woo her with yet another promotion, this time with a transfer to a different city and a house thrown in to sweeten the deal, Hope pulled back. "I realized that if I went ahead with the move and accepted the house, and then bought more expensive furniture to fill it up, I'd be so bound to that job that it would end up being my prison!"

She eventually quit the job. "That was the end of that particular cycle for me. I'd gone as far as I could go with the money thing, and I'd finally seen that money wasn't it."

Honoring the Inner Self

The experience taught Hope to honor her instincts. "If I were to look back over all the mistakes I made, both before and after sobriety, and ask myself if there were times when I knew *before* I started down a certain path that the path was going to be a dead end, I think the answer in every instance is yes. I always knew it beforehand. My instincts were working for me, but I'd always let my intellect talk me out of it. My head would tell me, 'Hope, you *should* want this job, it'll make you look good,' or even, 'You *should* want that man.' I'd let my head win and do something that wasn't right for me in terms of my integrity or deep sense of who I am. I was always more concerned about winning over and impressing others than I was about doing something out of love or commitment."

Today if Hope does something that goes against the grain, she's in pain almost immediately. "If I'm on the wrong path, my whole body rebels," she says. "I get physically sick. I get migraines, spend weekends in bed, have no zest for life, feel depressed, and get pre-ulcer symptoms. But as soon as I walk away from whatever it is, I feel better."

The Road to Financial Sobriety

As soon as Hope no longer felt the pressure to take jobs because of how much they paid, her financial situation improved. "I read a lot of books on money, and I've actually become very shrewd with it," she says. "Today I get a lot of mileage out of what I have. I've learned to do with a dollar what Christ did with the fish. My secret isn't anything very sophisticated. I just don't fritter money away anymore. I don't use credit cards. I make investments. And I save. My one major rule is: Never touch savings. I live on whatever I make without touching reserves. But even though I've become conservative in my spending, even frugal, I don't deprive myself of anything I need. I have a decent car, a nice apartment, beautiful furniture, and nice clothes—even some designer clothes."

Having realized that she's not a "big-city corporate gal" after all, Hope has now decided that her dream for the near future is to move away from the city, buy a house, surround herself with her animals, and start a home-based business. "That dream has been the incentive that keeps me tucking my money away." Meanwhile, she supports herself with the proceeds of some wise investments and free-lance work.

Most alcoholics say they're loners, which is usually a defense that changes once they get sober. Hope seems to be a loner to the core, however. Sobriety hasn't changed her in that sense, nor should it. "I'm most comfortable alone. I've had some nice love relationships in sobriety, but I'd rather be alone than with the wrong person. Thanks to AA, I've been able to create a full, rich life for myself. I love my home, my plants, my animals. These are my priorities right now. At my age I'm realistic enough to know that a relationship probably won't happen, and if it doesn't I won't feel terribly cheated." She has no regrets about not having had children. "It's taken me this long to raise *me!*" she says, laughing.

She continues, "After all my years of focusing on money, property, and prestige, what I need to do now is focus on making my dream of a house in the country come true—a dream that's not meant to impress *you*, but express *me*."

Hope had a startling realization that resulted in a major shift in her life. "I realized that I have a right to my own life. Now this might sound obvious to anybody else, but it took me years to really 'get' it! All of a sudden I understood that I could create my life the way *I* want it to be. It doesn't have to have anything to do with my family's messages about how my life should be, nor does it have to incorporate their limitations. Even though for years I could *say* that my life was mine, now it's in my gut. Now I really *believe* it."

JESSIE, SOBER 15 YEARS

> *I love money, but I've never understood*
> *its limits. After 15 years of sobriety, I*
> *finally had to admit that I'm a compul-*
> *sive spender. Three years ago I inherited a*
> *million dollars, and with horror I've been*
> *watching myself piss it away. So unless I*
> *want to end up very broke, very fast, I'd*
> *better do something about the way I*
> *handle money!*
>
> —Jessie

"I was raised to be a princess," says Jessie, 49, who is tall and good-looking, with thick, shoulder-length dark hair. Born in San Diego, California, she was an only child who arrived late into her parents' marriage. "I was the extended family's 'designated child,' the apple of every-body's eye, and spoiled rotten. My father was constantly saying to me, 'If I gave you the moon, you'd want the stars.' Once I asked my mother why she'd had me, and she said in a rather fey way, 'Oh, I don't know, dear. All my friends were having babies.'"

Jessie played her spoiled-child role to the hilt. She thrived on all the attention and the perks. "I was thoroughly self-centered and never did anything for myself, let alone for anybody else. Not once did I do something thoughtful, like bring my mother breakfast in bed. Why should I when they were all so busy doing things for me?"

She remained the apple of everybody's eye until puberty, "when I became a geek, and my parents had to go on geek patrol. We went to the dermatologist. We got contact lenses for the eyes. We got braces for the buck teeth. We signed me up for auxiliaries and sent me to cotillions. As soon as we put out one fire, another would flare up." Fortunately, Jessie was bright, did well in school, and went on to college. "There I discovered the cure for social awkwardness—beer. On a fraternity hayride somebody put a beer in my hand, and it was like a dream come true. I was instantly beautiful, graceful, polished, and popular. No more geek!"

The first real consequence of drinking this magic elixir came when Jessie's parents discovered her drinking gin right out of the bottle. "They'd planned to send me to Europe for my junior year, but that idea was trashed." Instead of curtailing her drinking, Jessie experimented further. "I tried amphetamines and was addicted to them immediately. They became my first love."

She drank all through college and started having relationships compulsively. "I just couldn't be without a boyfriend. The minute I'd end one relationship I'd immediately go looking for someone else. It was like an addiction in itself."

For a while Jessie was able to function well despite her drinking and pill taking. She studied and graduated, then got a job as a sales clerk at I. Magnin, a department store. It was there that she realized that her looks, style, energy, creativity and brightness all made her highly "promotable." In fact, the company wanted to groom her for better things, but it wasn't what Jessie wanted, so she left and went to work for an ad agency. That *was* what she wanted. She got a chance to do copywriting and was eventually promoted to copywriter. Although she did well, the booze and pills inevitably caught up with her, and her job performance began to suffer. She became increasingly unpredictable and erratic. "I was 25, drinking on the job, and so hooked on pills that I couldn't write without them. In one week I had two overdoses." The second overdose landed her in a psychiatric hospital for a long stay.

Doing the Circuit

Hospitalization sent Jessie off into a new direction. She discovered that being "crazy" was a lot easier than working. "I liked being in the nut ward. It gave me a chance to withdraw from responsibility and go back to being a princess," she admits. "I became institutionalized immediately. I didn't have to work. I barely had to make my bed, just like when I was a kid. And I loved those cozy times around the old dayroom TV."

After her discharge from the hospital, Jessie overdosed again. "This time my father's social connections got me into the UCLA Neuropsychiatric Institute, where they supposedly dealt only with rare cases, and here I was, your garden-variety drunk!" Her next stop was further north, up the California coast to Camarillo State (Mental) Hospital. There she met her husband-to-be, Carl, a fellow patient. "He was an alcoholic and a drug abuser, and when I first laid eyes on him it was his first day, and he was having a seizure in the medication line. I said to myself, 'He's for me.'"

After being discharged from Camarillo, Jessie and Carl married and began "doing the circuit" of mental hospitals and chemical dependency units together. "We'd go to Long Beach Psychiatric Hospital in the winter, and to County General in the summer."

Between hospitalizations, Carl worked, but Jessie didn't. "Once I started on the rounds of those hospitals, I never worked again until after I got sober." To take up the financial slack, Jessie went to her parents for money—"the Bank of Mom and Dad," as she puts it. But by now her parents were beginning to catch on that throwing money at Jessie's addiction problem wasn't helping. "They were in the process of disengaging themselves from me when I got arrested for possession of marijuana and was thrown in jail. That did it. When I called Daddy for help, he hung up on me. Santa Claus hung up on me!"

Even that didn't stop Jessie's drinking and drug use, which was to continue for a few more years. "By the age of 29 I was incontinent, had a blind spot in one eye, my teeth were a mess, and I had polyneuritis in my hands and feet. I also had hypoglycemia. I was put on Antabuse, drank on top of Antabuse, and nearly died. I got the DTs and hallucinated for four days straight."

A Struggle for Sobriety—and Survival

One day Jessie called her husband at work to take her to yet another hospital. This time she was deathly ill. "The last thing I remember was Carl opening the car door, and a liquor bottle fell out and went *tink-tink-tink* across the hospital parking lot. Then I passed out. My vital signs were fading. I woke up in the emergency room, and I knew instantly, in a moment of great clarity, that I'd just had a very close call, and that if I didn't quit drinking I'd die."

Jessie decided to try AA, but Carl wouldn't go with her. "We'd always laugh at people who went to AA. We said they were like sheep following the herd. Now I was a sheep. Carl just couldn't handle my going to meetings. It threw him over the top, and he just stepped up his drinking. As I got better, he got worse."

Although Jessie did manage to stop drinking alcohol, she continued taking tranquilizers, and she began experimenting with cocaine. By AA standards ("no mind-altering chemicals"), she certainly wasn't sober. "I was starting to get into stuff I'd never even touched before," she says. "But at least I'd stopped the dying process."

When she'd been off alcohol for three months, Carl went on a drinking binge—and died. To keep from drinking over his death, Jessie threw herself into her AA meetings and allowed herself to be guided by her sponsor and her network of AA friends. After a year and a half, during which time she still took drugs, she had another revelation. "I said to my sponsor, 'Gee, if I'd quit using tranquilizers four months ago, I'd have four months of sobriety right now!' Lightbulb! I finally got it! I've been sober ever since."

Clean and sober at last, and by now recovered from the shock of her husband's death, Jessie started making some practical decisions about her life. It was then that she got a good look at her hot-potato style of handling money. "Carl's life insurance left me with about $40,000, and knowing how I ran through money, I got nervous, so I handed over half of it to a friend to invest. I told him, 'Quick, get this out of my face!' which is just like an addict handing over his drugs to somebody and saying, 'Don't let me have this!' and then calling up at four in the morning demanding them back. Anyway, this friend did get the money out of my face. He invested it in Mexico, and then the peso was devalued, and I lost half my investment! I ran down to Mexico and yanked out the other half. I should have continued working and kept this money in reserve, but I didn't. I proceeded to spend it down to my last cent. I quit my job, and until the money was all gone I didn't even begin looking for another one. Then, and only then, did I get up off my ass and move. That's the spending style I've been cursed with to this day."

Jessie went into psychotherapy to help her get in touch with those feelings that she'd kept buried under booze, pills, and of course, overspending. She also worked on utilizing her intuition. "My intellect and my intuition were entirely separate when I got sober. I'd listen to my intellect, which would give me good reasons why I should enter a certain relationship or buy something I wanted, and I'd totally ignore my intuition, which might be telling me the opposite. After I got sober I discovered that if I exercise regularly, especially if I do aerobics and yoga, my intellect and my intuition get integrated. But any time I stop exercising, they get separated again."

When Jessie tried to delay returning to work by applying to the Bank of Mom and Dad for another loan, her AA sponsor stopped her. "She told me that until I stopped taking money from my parents and started to become self-supporting, I wouldn't grow up. I hated hearing that, but I knew she was right."

In Search of a Dream Job

It was time to find work. Jessie decided to get not just any old job, but the job of her dreams. "Maybe it's because I grew up in Southern California, but ever since I was a little girl of seven, I'd dreamed of working at NBC. Now that I was sober and my life was no longer built on quicksand, I felt I had a crack at it. So one day I drove up to Los Angeles from San Diego, marched myself into NBC, and applied for work. I was turned down. For some reason, it didn't faze me. I had a kind of confidence inside I can't even explain. All I know is I had this feeling that I was meant to work there, so I kept hounding them, and I wouldn't take no for an answer. Finally they broke down and hired me in the engineering department as an engineering trainee. Luckily for me, it was the seventies and still in the early days of affirmative action, so the fact that I was a woman helped. I was their first woman engineer."

Jessie was also a quick study and willing to work hard. "I always had phone numbers handy of people who could help me, and books in my desk, and notes in my pocket, so I was able to muddle through." She became "promotable" again. "I got promotion after promotion and started making more money than I'd ever seen. I even wound up supervising people who knew more about the work than I did!"

What the NBC job gave Jessie, among other things, was the financial independence from her parents that she'd been seeking. "I was able to cut the cord. It gave me an enormous sense of self-worth."

After five years at NBC, Jessie quit in order to follow a man she'd fallen in love with to Houston, Texas. Even though the relationship ended after only a year and they never married, she stayed in Houston and has been there ever since.

When Jessie first arrived in Texas, she needed money while she looked for work. She decided to cash in her NBC retirement fund early. She got a lump sum of $8,000. Not surprisingly, getting the money triggered her old spend-to-the-end behavior. "I still hadn't worked on my spending pattern, so when I got this money, my compulsive spending kicked in again. Once more, I stopped looking for work until I was down to zero. Then I dug out my old portfolio from my drunken copywriting days, and luckily was able to get myself a job as a copywriter at an ad agency, but being down to nothing was hairy."

A few years later, she met another man and married him. "My husband was 10 years younger, and I thought I'd found myself a real fixer-upper, but he was devotedly stuck in his little-boy ways. When I couldn't change him, I began to deal with my feelings by overspending again. He used to call me the Great Liquidator. As long as I was spending, I didn't have to look at our marriage. When I got laid off during an economic slump, I *did* have to look at our marriage, and that's when I ended it."

Million-Dollar Princess

Jessie's parents died only a year apart, just a few years after Jessie's divorce. Their deaths were closely followed by the death of a favorite aunt. As a result of the three deaths, Jessie ended up with an inheritance totaling a million dollars!

While this would be a dream opportunity for most folks, for Jessie it was scary. She knew exactly what she was going to do with the money—she was going to spend it.

"When I saw all those zeros behind the first number and realized it was a million bucks, I panicked. It did strange things to me. First of all, it sapped me of all motivation. Again, I quit the job I had at the time and refused to work. In the beginning, I didn't know if my lack of ambition was due to grieving or to having all that money. As time passed, it became clear to me that it was due to the money. Spending the money just gave me a renewed opportunity to cover my feelings—feelings of grief, sadness, loss—not just about my parents and aunt, but also about my marriage. As long as I spent, I didn't have to feel the feelings. So I'd buy a hairband here, a facelift there. It's hard to pass up a $10 headband, or even a $10,000 facelift, when you've got a million bucks in the bank. I'd say to myself, 'Why shouldn't I have this?' or, 'Why shouldn't I travel now before I get sick and old?' So one more time, I started pissing my money away. In three years I went through more than $300,000. Now, having been clean and sober for over 15 years, I knew enough about addictive, compulsive patterns to see the writing on the wall. It was unnerving to realize that in spite of my so-called recovery, I was still out of control with money.

"When my AA sponsor in Houston said, 'If you don't hurry up and do something about your spending, Jessie, you're going to end up drinking again,' she got my attention. I was really scared."

Turning to Debtors Anonymous

With the support of her close AA friends and her therapist, Jessie took two actions. She got herself an accountant, and she turned herself in to Debtors Anonymous. "People thought it was pretty funny seeing a millionaire walk into Debtors Anonymous! It was like seeing a really skinny person walk into an Overeaters Anonymous meeting. But each person's addiction is always lurking within them, and even if they're not currently doing the addictive behavior, if they don't get help it could start up again. I'll always be an alcoholic even if I don't drink, and I'll always be a compulsive spender even if I have money in the bank. I know that if I don't keep going to AA, I'll be drunk again. And if I don't keep going to DA, I'll be broke again. My money sickness, for whatever low-self-esteem reasons, is to spend until it's all gone and I can 'get back to normal' again, so to speak. So I had to take drastic action and go to DA, because I don't *want* to 'get back to normal' again. For me, normal is being broke!"

Jessie admits that being in DA is hard. "I hate being new in an anonymous group. I'm uncomfortable talking about money. I squirm when I have to discuss my spending with my DA sponsor. I didn't like having to cut up my credit cards, or give her my checkbook because I can't control myself. I don't like having to ask her if I can buy something! What if she says no? After all, I'm a princess, remember? So I rebel. We're supposed to write a money autobiography, and we're also supposed to write down every cent we earn and every cent we spend, every day, whether it's 10 cents for a parking meter or $38 for food. Well, I start out recording my money, but then I say, 'Oh, screw it!' The next day I have to start all over again."

In spite of her resistance, following DA rules has started to pay off. "Last week I went to see my accountant, and even though I'm still over budget, I was *less* over budget than the last time I checked in with him, so I became encouraged. He was mad at me, but *I* felt really good about myself because I know from 15 years in Alcoholics Anonymous that it's 'progress, not perfection,' and I'm satisfied with that."

The task, whether it's in the area of money, health, love, or work, is always the same: to find balance. As Jessie describes it, "Where money is concerned, I know the goal is to have more *income* than *out-go*. It couldn't be simpler.

But for someone like me, it's hard. I get it backward."

People can have life-changing moments of clarity in any area of life, including the money area. Jessie recently had such a moment in the form of a simple observation: "One day I said to myself, 'Jessie, you don't *have* to spend it all!' Another lightbulb! What a revelation!"

Since then, Jessie has not only managed to curb her spending, but she has also gone back to work in the advertising field. "I still don't have more income than out-go, but I've got it in sight. Besides, I like being back at work. I was starting to get saturated with leisure and uncomfortable about not being productive. Those AA sayings about being self-supporting and about doing service in the world kept ringing in my ear. Too much leisure is like eating too much cotton candy at the circus—it all tastes the same. It can even make you sick.

"Every alcoholic I've ever known, myself included, has low self-esteem. I don't know what causes it. Maybe it's inherited along with the drunk gene. But in order to build up that self-esteem, I think it's important to work and feel useful. I enjoy people. I enjoy the schmoozing that goes on at work. I like getting feedback on the projects I turn out. I enjoy the prestige attached to a job well done. It's fun."

Jessie is also dating again. "After my parents died, I knew enough not to use a man as a Band-aid for my grief. The compulsive overspending was distraction enough." When she felt ready, she joined a video dating service. "My self-esteem used to be so low that I didn't think a really 'together' man would be interested in me. But once I was willing to go the video dating route, grown-up men started coming out of the woodwork, men my own age or older who had their own work and their own money, so I didn't have to feel that they wanted to suck on my strength or go after my bank account."

Ironically, after shelling out money for the video dating service, Jessie took an adult education class, and met a

man there—for free. His name is Joe and he is turning
out to be special. "I think I'm in love," Jessie says. "How
do you like them apples?" Recently, they've been talking
about getting married. Joe is divorced and his children
are grown. Is Jessie sorry that *she* never had children? Like
Hope, her answer is no. "In AA, I've had to look honestly
at myself, without romanticizing things, and what I've
realized is that I'm still too self-centered to have children.
I lack the patience it takes to be with them. Recently I got
a puppy, and even that's almost more than I can handle.
Those puppies are eye-openers! And, oh yes, a lot less
expensive!"

Altruism: A New Emotion

Looking back on the past 15 years, Jessie feels that one of
the most profound moments of her recovery happened
the day she discovered that she is capable of unselfish
compassion. "For a self-centered princess, that's really a
stretch!" she jokes. "I was in a drugstore one day, and I
saw a little old lady trying to get a prescription filled, but
she didn't have enough money to pay for it. I overheard
her talking to the pharmacist, whom I knew, and I felt my
heart go right out to her. I took the pharmacist aside and
said, 'I would like to pay for that lady's medication without her knowing it, so whatever you need to do, do it.' I
gave him the money and left. Now this was before I'd
received the insurance from Carl's death, so I didn't have
a whole lot of money myself, but I felt compelled to do it.

"When I got into my car, this strange feeling came
over me, and I didn't know what it was. I cried all the way
home. I called my therapist and told her what happened.
'What was that *strange* feeling I had?' I asked her. And she
said, 'That's compassion, Jessie. You've developed compassion.' I thought, *Wow, what a profound thing!* It was the first
time I'd ever felt that emotion and the first time I'd ever

given money to anybody anonymously when there was no chance I'd get something in return. I'd loaned money before, but I always had strings attached—you'd better spend it my way or else. But this money was different. This money was a pure gift, and it felt absolutely wonderful."

SOBER FINANCES TIPS LIST

1. Compulsive spending is an addiction. It achieves many of the same ends as alcoholism. It will anesthetize your feelings, and it will interfere with sobriety. It needs to be dealt with.

2. Keep a spending record. Every day, write down every cent you spend and every cent you earn.

3. Write a money history or autobiography to get a clearer picture of where your money attitudes came from and how your spending habits developed.

4. If you think you're "funny with money," check out Debtors Anonymous. If there's no DA in your area, use AA and substitute the words "compulsive spending" for "alcoholism."

5. Some of the tools of Debtors Anonymous include not incurring compulsive unsecured debt one day at a time, writing down daily every cent received and spent, writing a money autobiography, attending DA (or AA) meetings, not borrowing or lending, making out a spending plan, making out a debt repayment plan, doing service.

6. Untreated compulsive spending is like untreated compulsive drinking or drug using: it has a negative impact on every area of life, and it progresses over time and gets worse.

7. Family members who enable compulsive spenders (by lending them money, for example) help to make things worse.

8. Educate yourself about money. Read books. Attend seminars. Buy money magazines. Take classes. Read the business news.

9. You don't need to know why you overspend in order to stop doing it. Stop the behavior first. Insight comes later.

10. The goal of AA is sobriety, not happiness, although happiness may come along the way. The goal of DA is solvency, not prosperity, although prosperity may happen along the way.

11. "Abundance" means different things to different people. It's important for you to define it for yourself. To one person, it may mean material things; to another, a large family; to another, creativity; to another, travel. Write down what an abundant life looks like to you, and begin to make it real.

12. Intuition and gut feelings play a part in money management. Sometimes your insides will tell you when to stop spending, even though your head is saying, "Buy! Buy!"

13. Become "self-supporting by your own contributions."

14. In DA, declaring bankruptcy is a no-no, so start making arrangements to pay off your debts, even if it's at a rate of only $5 a month. You'll like yourself better.

15. Keep going to DA meetings, working the DA steps, talking with DA members, reading DA literature, and educating yourself about money, because sooner or later one of these things may well trigger that "Aha!" or moment-of-clarity experience that can help heal your money-spending addiction.

16. Seek balance in all areas of life, including the financial. Wanting financial abundance is fine, but strive to be a whole person first, then you'll enjoy your money more.

SOBER

TROUBLES

I was terrified. I sat there in my doctor's office and I said, "I'm going to die." And he said, "No, you're not." And I said, "Everyone who has ovarian cancer dies." And he said, "That's not true."

—Lanie, sober 21 years

In AA, the term comes up again and again, like a mantra: "We don't drink or use—no matter what." It's a phrase the recovering alcoholic can grab on to when she thinks she has a good reason to drink again.

The phrase springs from the fact that in times of great stress, it's normal for alcoholics and addicts to have thoughts, if not outright urges, to drink or use again, no matter how many years they've been clean and sober. The addiction is still alive and well within themselves, and stress brings it out. "Thinking drinking" is a natural reaction. Some recovering alcoholics even have drinking dreams in response to stress—and are relieved when they wake up and realize they're still sober!

The "no matter what" phrase really comes in handy during times of trouble. If AA allowed exceptions to the rule, then most alcoholics, being alcoholics, would probably end up taking advantage of it. They'd drink *not* just over crises, but over every frivolous annoyance that came along, and that would throw them right back into the dreadful vicious circle of addiction all over again.

For an AA member, relapsing means much more than just getting drunk or stoned. For one thing, it means losing one's AA seniority. And for those who slip and then disappear from the program (meaning they stop going to meetings and stop calling people), it also means losing one's support group, one's sponsor, and one's AA family. In some cases where an alcoholic's marriage or employment is dependent on the maintenance of sobriety, a slip may even mean losing a spouse or job.

Clearly, then, it behooves the recovering alcoholic to strictly attend to this "no matter what" rule. Still, at one time or another even a woman with long-term sobriety is bound to ask herself, Is there anything out there that could drive me back to the bottle? What if this or that happened? What if my child were killed? What if I learned I had a terminal illness? What if I remembered being molested as a child? What if AA went out of business?

In this chapter, we're going to meet three women who got through some awful "what ifs" and stayed sober. Lanie, sober 21 years, not only had to confront the issue of childhood molestation but also had to deal with ovarian cancer. Monika, sober 11 years, lost her husband to lymphoma. And Elizabeth, sober 15 years, had a daughter who murdered her husband and then committed suicide in prison.

AA's view is that nothing, absolutely nothing, can be made better by returning to alcohol or drugs. Drinking and using will only make things worse.

CLOSING RANKS AND FINDING STRENGTH

If the recovering alcoholic works the program effectively, there's no crisis that he or she can't handle. The main thing the person has to remember is to keep on going to those AA meetings in order to fortify himself or herself against the anticipated onslaught of emotional pain. Nearly 60 years of AA history has shown that going to meetings, rubbing shoulders with other alcoholics, and sharing "experience, strength and hope" with those who've "been there" is the secret of sobriety. The AA member with troubles is also encouraged to step up every other aspect of the program: to do more journal writing than usual, to do more service than usual, and to make more phone calls than usual to sponsors and friends in order to take advantage of one's already well-established support network.

AA members in crisis are also encouraged to use whatever outside help is available, in addition to AA. That's just what the three interviewees in this chapter did by attending workshops and classes, seeking outside psychotherapy, participating in cancer groups, incest survivor groups, and grief groups, all of which provided some much-needed support. Each of the three women came out of her particular ordeal with the feeling that she had learned some valuable lessons about living, although none would have gone out of her way to court these troubles. One important lesson for each woman was the recognition that despite her pain, she'd been able to keep her commitments to her loved ones, to her ideals, and especially to her sobriety.

LANIE, SOBER 21 YEARS

I have no idea why I survived cancer and some others I know didn't. But I don't have to understand it to be grateful for it. AA has certainly taught me that.

—Lanie

Lanie, 54, who has short-cropped brown hair and a marvelously impish smile, is the older of two sisters. She was born in Chicago of a dysfunctional family that included incest as well as physical and emotional abuse. "My father was the perpetrator. My mother *must* have known, but she did nothing. And I never mentioned it to her. Instead of being able to talk to my mother about it, I ended up her confidant, listening to her tell me about *her* troubles, among them the fact that my father was having an affair with her best friend.

"I was 7½ when my sister was born. I adored her. She was my baby. I even picked her name. I was thrilled that I was no longer alone in that family. My sister later said to me, "I was never sure if *they* loved me, but I was always sure *you* loved me."

In grade school Lanie's response to the family craziness was to become a people-pleasing "good" girl. "I thought if I was good, they'd love me," she says ruefully, "but no matter what I did, it wasn't good enough. They made fun of everything I tried."

Eventually, Lanie's father left the family and married the woman he'd been having the affair with. "What that taught me was if you have a fight with somebody, they'll leave you, so I made a conscious decision to stuff my feelings and never fight," Lanie admits. "I didn't want my feelings. I didn't want to feel good, bad, or indifferent. I just didn't want to feel."

From Diet Pills to Alcohol…to Cancer and Sobriety

Lanie's substance abuse career started with diet pills at 15. "I was pudgy and unhappy about it, so my mother took me to the diet doctor. When the doctor said to take one pill, I'd secretly take two. In high school, I became more of a rebel. When the other rebels started to drink, so did I. In the beginning it wasn't wild, it was fun. It didn't worry anybody. I always had a boyfriend. Some evenings I'd have two or three dates, so it was no surprise that by 21 I was married."

Right after her marriage, Lanie's mother who'd been sick for five years, died of cancer. "I made a deathbed promise to her that I'd take care of my sister, who was only 14, but after my mother died, I couldn't cope with the stress of being caregiver to my sister, so I sent her to live with my father and stepmother in Arizona, and the guilt about breaking my promise just about killed me."

Before long, Lanie began to see that her marriage was a mistake. She had picked a man who, like her parents, offered her no emotional support. "When I was in the hospital having my first baby and in the throes of labor, my husband said, 'I think I'll go home and take a nap.' After I had my second child, I stayed loaded all the time so his behavior didn't bother me as much. For the next few years I walked around the house wearing a bathrobe with marijuana cigarette burns in it, and drinking and taking pills. My daughter got so used to seeing me pop pills that one day she imitated me and swallowed two bottles of baby aspirin. I was stoned and wasn't even paying attention. All I remember is her sitting in front of me, swaying, saying, 'I'm so tired, Mommy. I just want to go to sleep.' Fortunately, I had enough sense left to send my little son for help. Our neighbor, who was a male nurse, rushed over, picked my daughter up, held her over the kitchen sink, stuck his finger down her throat, and made her throw up. Then he looked at me. 'What about you?' he said. 'Do *you* need help?' At that I bristled. 'No, I'm fine, I can take care of myself.'"

At the age of 30, Lanie was diagnosed with breast cancer. It blew her world apart. "I had two mastectomies, and that was the beginning of the end of my marriage. My husband absolutely could not cope with it. He acted as though it had happened to *him.* He wanted to commit suicide. *I* had to keep reassuring *him* that I'd be okay. My father and stepmother were no better. They were so "upset" that it took them five days to make it into the hospital to see me. I realized that I had all these people around me who were totally unsupportive. I felt alone."

Following the surgery, Lanie felt a desperate need to "belong" someplace. First she joined the Friends of the Black Panthers. Then she got into Buddhist chanting. After that, it was something else. Every step of her "search" was aided by pills and booze. One day, loaded on pills, she went to pick up her kids from nursery school. "My last friend on Earth, Jane, was there picking up her kids, and when she saw me she yelled and screamed at me, 'You can't keep doing this, Lanie, you have to stop!' The next Sunday, which was Mother's Day, I called AA."

After Lanie's first meeting, some of the members took her to a coffee shop. "I opened up my wallet and a Valium fell out. Right away a couple of them took bets that I wouldn't be able to stay sober. Suddenly I felt challenged. I was going to prove them wrong! I think I ended up staying sober out of pure spite!"

Right after Lanie got sober, her husband left her "to go write the Great American novel," he said. It was a difficult time for Lanie—one where she might have had a slip—but it was then that she was told, "We don't drink and we don't use—no matter what." She got through it.

Dealing with Rage: A Childhood Trauma Revealed

Once grounded in her sobriety, which took a number of years, Lanie began to feel the need to get some professional help in dealing with feelings she was having that she didn't understand—anger, tenseness around men. She started psychotherapy. "After I'd been in treatment for a while, my therapist asked me, 'Did your father molest you when you were a child?' At that time I had no memory of being molested, so her question sounded ridiculous. I replied, 'Of course not!' Shortly after that, on a lark, I went to see a psychic and she said, unequivocally, 'Your father molested you when you were a child.' She said it as if it were an established fact. That's when I said to myself, 'Hmm. Maybe there's something here I should look at.'

"So I started off by writing about my early years, as AA tells you to do, trying to jiggle loose memories. I also read books on incest, talked to people, went to incest survivors' workshops, and eventually I remembered what had happened, and I was horrified. Starting at about 18 months of age and continuing until I was four or five, my father used to take me into the bathroom in the middle of the night, and under the guise of potty-training me, he molested me. When these memories began coming through, I was filled with rage. I didn't know what to do with them. I shared these memories at meetings, and I wrote in my journal about them, and I went out to the cemetery where my mother is buried, and I yelled at her grave, 'How could you let him do that to me? Why didn't you protect me?' I couldn't confront my father directly because he had died a few years earlier, but I took a photograph of him off my wall, and I screamed at it. Then I took a chisel and started hacking away at his picture until it was a pulp. Somebody had suggested that I beat a telephone book with a rubber hose to get my anger out, so I did that, too. I wrote some more, read some more, talked some more, and took some more workshops, until one weekend I was in a workshop on anger, and I realized I wasn't angry anymore. It was gone."

Getting in touch with her own anger made Lanie realize that she had to make it safe for her children to express their feelings. She hadn't been allowing that. "When I was first sober, my kids' anger scared me. But when I saw the consequences of suppressing anger, I changed my mind. I was determined to let them have their feelings. I remember one time standing by the kitchen sink and letting my son, who was then in his early teens, yell at me. I remember hanging on, thinking I was going to pass out, but I didn't stop him. And then he came over to me and rubbed my back, and it was over."

The Second Cancer Diagnosis

Twenty-two years after her mastectomies, Lanie was hit with cancer a second time.

"I was diagnosed with ovarian cancer. I was terrified. My doctor told me, 'We caught it early at stage 1, and the recovery rate for stage 1 is 95 percent.' How did I deal with it? It was terrible, absolutely terrible. I cried for a year. I had two surgeries. I was in a lot of pain. I had a year of chemotherapy. I was very sick physically. My hair fell out."

Lanie was again forced to use the tools she'd learned in AA over the years to help her through. "I kept going to AA meetings, mostly because the fear and anxiety made me so antsy I couldn't stay put. I'd jump up and run to a meeting. I kept talking to people about how I felt, and when that didn't work, I'd call up somebody I knew who was in worse shape than I was, and I'd talk to them about how *they* felt. I got Shirley MacLaine's video on meditation and learned to meditate. I meditated for an hour a day, and it was the only time I felt at peace. AA teaches us to put one foot in front of the other, and that's what I did. The thought of taking a drink never even occurred to me."

She also started going to the Wellness Community, a nationwide group for people with cancer. "It's a very committed, tight-knit group, and it was just like another AA meeting for me," she explains. "I'd call people and talk to them, and I knew they understood because they'd experienced what I'd experienced. They'd been there. I went for over a year. One day as I was sitting in a meeting,

I caught myself fretting about the fact that I'd gained weight. I said to myself, 'They're dealing with life-and-death issues, and I'm dealing with *fat!*' That's when I knew I was getting better."

Although now she doesn't go to the Wellness Community as often as she once did, Lanie is still connected to them. And, as she also does in AA, she expresses her gratitude by doing service. "I speak and do volunteer work for them. I think it's helpful for people to see that people survive."

A New Perspective, a New Determination

From her battles with cancer, Lanie learned how important it is to bring the right people into your life. "Today, the only people I keep in my life are those who can be there for me when I need them. I've let the others go. I lost a friendship over this issue. When I was in the hospital with ovarian cancer, I had a friend who was so scared of cancer she couldn't even bring herself to call me to see if I was dead or alive. My feelings were hurt. And since AA teaches us to be honest about these things, I had to tell her she'd hurt me. I said, 'I can no longer have people in my life who are not supportive. I'm not asking for a whole lot. I'm not asking for you to take care of me. I'm just asking for a phone call or a card, something to show that you care, that you're a friend. I see that as basic.' I even had to strong-arm my daughter, who lives in Boston, to come and see me. At first she refused. She said, 'If I don't see you, it means it's not real.' And I said, 'Bullshit! Get on a plane and come out here now!' And she did. A while back I fell in love with an ex-Vietnam vet. He was fine until the Gulf War started, then something snapped. He wasn't whole enough for me, and I had to let him go. I simply cannot do that to myself anymore."

Lanie is determined to be there emotionally for her own children. "I've seen the consequences of not being on hand for your kids," she says. "For a while I was seeing it in my sister who had not only developed alcoholism herself, but also seemed to carry on the family tradition of abandoning people, just as our father abandoned us. When she'd just gotten into her fifth marriage and couldn't handle her child, she asked me to take her. I told her, 'If you abandon your child you'll never be able to forgive yourself. You need to raise your own child.' She didn't listen. She put her daughter in a group home. But now she's sober herself in AA and seems to be getting her life together. She's finally reaching out and trying to be a part of this family again. I feel like I've gotten a sister back."

MONIKA, SOBER 11 YEARS

For the first time in my life, I was able to put myself totally aside and be there for somebody else. It was like there was a wind under my wings, and it carried me. No physical or emotional effort seemed too much for me. You'd have to be a mean-spirited person not to fall in love with the action of giving to another human being.

—Monika

Monika, 48, is a tall, good-looking, brown-eyed blond who has been sober for 11 years. The youngest of four, she has a brother and two sisters. Having been born in the eastern part of Germany shortly before the end of World War II, her life started off on a dramatic note. Bombings, fear, and hunger were a part of everyday life. In addition, her father was an alcoholic, a man who intimidated his wife and terrified his four children.

When the war was over, the Russians overtook East Germany, and Monika's family lost everything. "They took away my father's business, and then they appeared at our home and said, 'This house now belongs to the state. You can live here, but it's no longer yours.'"

Years after the war ended, Monika's father remained a staunch anti-Communist. "Even when he was in the hospital dying of alcoholism, he'd buy up all the newspapers containing Communist propaganda so other people couldn't read them," Monika says.

An Escape to the West

After his death, Monika's mother began plotting the family's escape from East Germany. "At the time my mother was 49, and now that I'm an adult, I realize what a sacrifice she made. She left her family and friends, and she left all her possessions down to the last napkin, just so we kids could have a better future. At 14, I thought escaping was exciting, but it was dangerous. It meant getting people on both sides of the Berlin Wall to help us. People took chances. And because my brother had already escaped, we were under constant surveillance. I told my best friend in school we were leaving, which was crazy. Imagine if she'd said something! We would have been shot! The night we left, we walked to our grandmother's house and told her we were going to a birthday party. We couldn't tell her we were leaving forever. We said, 'Good night. We'll see you tomorrow.' She was well into her seventies and, looking back, I try to imagine her shock when she learned that her daughter and grandchildren had left the country, leaving her behind.

"My mother and sisters and I were driven across the border to West Germany in a convoy of cars behind a limousine. Somebody up front had a passport, and they obviously had some cash, or clout, too, because the guards let the whole convoy through. We spent two weeks in a camp. We had bunk beds, and tin cups for food. My brother, who'd escaped earlier, vouched for us, got us out of the camp, and we began our new lives."

They settled in Frankenthal, west of Heidelberg, "45 minutes from the Black Forest." Over the next few years, Monika's mother worked and supported the family. Monika finished school and went on to pharmacology school to became a druggist. "I didn't *take* the drugs then, I just sold them!" she says, laughing. While still in school, she met her first husband. It was at best a mediocre match. "The day I got married, I said to my mother, 'Am I doing the right thing?' and she said, 'Well, you're dressed!' That was her idea of a good reason to go through with the wedding."

Passage to America

The couple got an apartment, and Monika got a job. Then came the fateful postcard from America, where one of Monika's sisters had recently moved. "The postcard was from California," Monika remembers. "There was a picture of oranges hanging from a tree, and a blue sky, and the card said, 'How would you like to live here?' I said to myself, 'I would.' Then I said to my husband, 'Listen, do you want to go to America with me? If you don't, I'm going anyway.' He said okay. Within a month we'd quit our jobs, sold everything, and had our tickets and off we went. Once you've left everything behind once, it's easy to do it again. When we arrived in California and I got one look at Beverly Hills, I said to myself, 'This is the lifestyle for me.' I just gravitated to materialism."

When her husband showed no interest in pursuing the lifestyle Monika was interested in, they divorced. "I hired myself out as a governess to a family in Beverly Hills. Of course, I knew nothing about kids. I thought nothing of locking them in the bathroom when they irritated me."

Fortunately Monika's striking good looks caught the eye of a Beverly Hills businessman, and they fell in love and got married. Monika quit her governess job. Things went relatively smoothly for a while, and then Monika decided she needed to get a job to occupy herself. "I started off in the L.A. fashion mart as a model, but I soon realized that there was more money in sales. I got hired by a man in the surplus piece-goods business. The day I started, I realized I wasn't making enough money, so I asked him for a raise. He said, 'Anybody who'd ask for a raise the day they start must have a lot of guts, so you've got your raise. Now prove yourself.' I did. I got more and more raises, and I finally figured out I'd make more money going out on my own, so I did that, and I got to be very successful. One day I got a call from Catalina Swimwear, one of my clients, and they said, 'We'd like to set you up but big,' and that was it. That was my success ceiling, my cut-off point. I'd gotten this far on raw nerve, but my low self-esteem finally caught up with me. That was too much to give me at that point in my life, and I couldn't handle it, so I quit, ran back to my house on the hill, and began to drink, rather than look at what had scared me away."

The Cocaine "Cure"

"After a while, I discovered pep pills and then cocaine," Monika continues. I thought cocaine would cure my drinking. What it did was bring me to my knees. My best friend's daughter was a celebrity, with easy access to cocaine, so I'd go to her house and stay for three or four days at a time. When I'd finally go home and my husband would say, 'Where the hell were you?' I'd get indignant. 'How dare you ask me that! Don't you trust me?'" I'd shoot back.

The more Monika used cocaine, the more paranoid she became. "I thought my husband wanted to deport me back to Germany. Come to think of it, that idea may well have occurred to him!" she jokes. "Anyway, I thought people were taping my phone calls. When I went out, I thought people's gardeners were spying on me. Some days I wouldn't take my car because I thought it was wired to blow up, so I took cabs instead. Once I called a cab after doing a lot of cocaine, and when the cab driver said, 'Boy, aren't we effervescent,' I thought, *Aha! He's been hired to watch me, too,* so I made him let me out, and I walked the rest of the way into Beverly Hills in my platform heels.

"Three times a week I'd go to my psychiatrist, tell him about my hallucinations, pay him a lot of money, and listen to him tell me I was doing fine. I was surrounded by enablers. It was only after we separated that my husband said to me, 'You know what? You have a problem. I think you should call AA.' But what finally did it was when he told me, 'Monika, it's beginning to show. You don't look so good anymore.' I went home, sat under my dining-room table, and, for the next four days, I drank. I was still coherent when my husband called to check on me. 'I'm doing fine,' I lied. 'I haven't touched a drop, and I'm really going to that place you told me about.' I hung up, and everything started to blur. I knew I had an inch of booze left in one of the bottles. I also knew that if I drank it, I'd die. It was my moment of clarity. Instead, I picked up the phone and called a friend for help."

Hospitalization was the result. "I walked into a chemical dependency treatment unit with a suitcase full of dirty towels and one high-heel shoe, and I demanded a room with a carpet and a TV. When they wouldn't give in to me, with a carpet and a TV. When they wouldn't give in to me, I started hollering. They slapped a 72-hour hold on me for observation."

Monika went on to complete the chemical dependency program, but even though she stopped drinking alcohol and using cocaine, she kept on taking her little "pep-up" pills for another two years. "I took them rarely, but even one meant I was still into my addiction. It kept distance between me and the real work of sobriety." It also contributed to her getting a divorce. When she finally stopped taking pills, her sobriety began.

The AA Cure

Monika threw herself into the AA program as well as into work and school. She'd decided to become an addiction therapist, and she got herself a staff job in a chemical dependency treatment center while she was still in school. Then she met and married her third husband, Jerry, an older man with grown children. Over a 10-year period, their relationship shifted from a chaotic, mutual obsession to a mature, committed partnership. What triggered the sea change in their explosive union was Jerry's terminal illness.

"In many ways, Jerry gave me the things I never got in my childhood—emotional attention and total acceptance for who I was, warts and all. But it was too intense at times, and we'd have to break away from each other in order to individuate again. We were one of those couples who couldn't live with each other and couldn't live without each other. We tried every possible arrangement—living together without being married, living apart while being married, and everything in between. Finally, we divorced."

A Struggle with Cancer

Less than a year later, Jerry was diagnosed with cancer of the lymph nodes. By then, Monika had started dating other men. When Jerry told her he was sick, Monika assumed it was another of his obsessive ploys to get her back. "I thought, *How tacky! This is just like him, having no shame, even lying to me to get me back!* I told him, 'Think of something different, Jerry!' But it was the truth. He had lymphoma, and it changed everything."

They decided to remarry.

"In the beginning, I was in denial about his illness. I didn't even want to talk about it. When we remarried, I told the priest, 'Don't say "until death do us part." I don't want Jerry to even *hear* the word "death."' We ran away to Palm Springs to live. When Jerry started to get sick and had to have chemotherapy, I got into a high state of anxiety about losing him."

Yet the experience of caring for her dying husband began to transform Monika into a mature woman.

"I had the same kind of moment of clarity about my relationship with Jerry as I had about my addiction. In one quick moment, I became aware of the preciousness of what he and I had together. It was a moment of commitment, and he sensed it. One day as I was tending him, he looked at me and said, just as if he'd never realized it before, 'You must really love me.'"

The danger for any recovering alcoholic who, like Monika, becomes deeply involved in something outside of AA is that she can forget that she, too, still has an illness that needs attention.

"I was so involved in Jerry's illness that it got harder and harder for me to go to AA meetings. I'd drop in like a visitor, and then resent it when people would talk about what I considered *trivia* when my husband was dying. I stopped going to AA altogether."

It's a natural reaction, but a dangerous one. What snapped Monika back to her senses was a conversation with Jerry's sister on the phone.

"Her own husband had died just six months earlier, so whenever I'd tell her about my pain, she'd always say to me in her thick New York accent, 'Yeah, but I had it woise!' She was serious. She kept insisting that I couldn't possibly understand her because she had it 'woise.' I realized that that's exactly what I was doing in AA—sitting there, listening to AA people talk, and saying to myself, 'Yeah, but I've got it woise.'"

Monika returned to AA in time to prevent a slip. "What allowed me to get away with avoiding AA for so long without drinking again was the fact that for years I'd been doing all the right things. I'd gone to meetings. I'd talked to people. I'd worked the steps. I'd made the phone calls. I'd helped people. So I had a little cushion. But now what I needed was the affection and the love I'd always found there. Maybe they couldn't help Jerry, but they could certainly help me."

As Jerry's illness got worse, Monika found herself drawing more and more on AA's one-day-at-a-time philosophy. "It wasn't just one day at a time with Jerry, it was one morning at a time, one moment at a time. We tried to enjoy the moment. We laughed a lot and talked a lot. I'd let him take the lead. If he wanted to talk about dying, I'd talk about dying. If he didn't, we didn't. We tried to complete unfinished business. We made our amends to each other. We made a big deal out of birthdays and holidays and anniversaries. On his last Christmas, I had the family over, including his kids. I dressed him up—he could no longer dress himself—and we made a video."

Monika tells a touching story of their last night out together. "We had tickets to *Phantom of the Opera,* and Jerry was really looking forward to it. But he was so ill. He was in a wheelchair and had periods of mental confusion where he wouldn't know where he was. It looked as though he might not make it to the theater. My friends said, 'Monika, take a night off. Go see *Phantom* with somebody else.' But I wanted Jerry to see it. On the day of the show, it took me three hours to get him dressed, and two and a half hours to drive into Los Angeles from Palm

Springs. All the while I kept telling him, 'Jerry, we're going to go see *Phantom of the Opera.*' When we got to the theater, there was nobody around to help us, so I put my arm around him—I don't know where I got the strength—and I practically carried him inside. I put him in his seat. He was still very confused. The curtain went up, and when the chandelier was lowered down, Jerry looked up and he said, 'Oh! Look! *Phantom of the Opera!*' And he was *there* for the whole show. He was like a child at Disneyland. The minute it was over, he slipped back into his confused state and we drove home. But there had been that window, and the memory of that night has been so important to me."

A few weeks later, Jerry was admitted into the hospital for the last time.

"On a February morning he woke up and said, 'Monika, it's our anniversary.' A few days later, on Valentine's Day, he came out of his confused state again, raised himself up on his elbow, and said, 'I love you.' Then he slipped into a coma again. How's that for love in the human spirit!

"At noon on his last day, I climbed up into his hospital bed and held him. At five o'clock, he died."

The hardest part of the whole ordeal, Monika says, was picking up his ashes after his cremation. "When they handed over the box of ashes to me, and I knew that this, this box, was Jerry, I was overwhelmed. I sat down on a couch in the funeral home and put my head between my legs, and I never wanted to get up from that seat ever again. But then the thought came through me that his soul was already back home at the house, and now he needed to be reunited with his ashes. That one thought enabled me to get up and move."

Staying Sober Through Grief

Following her husband's death, Monika has been through many of the stages of grief. She took advantage of utilizing the increasing number of bereavement groups and therapists. She is still involved in the grieving process and now hopes to turn around and learn how to help others through similar ordeals. She has also thrown herself back into her AA program because she knows that AA is where she'll find comfort and support for her pain. AA is also where she'll get the strength to avoid drinking as a way of dealing with that pain.

"When you're going through the grieving process, the feelings aren't all tidy, the way they're described in grief textbooks," she says. "At times I've been so depressed, I didn't care to go on. Sometimes I wonder, Where does pain like that *come* from? It hurts *something*, but what? What organ? We don't know, so we call it the soul. And I've been so angry. Here I am, finally grown up and able to have a good relationship with this man, and he's taken away. What do I do with my need now? Where do I put this grown-up-ness and capacity for love? I've even caught myself resenting other couples, although I tell myself I shouldn't. When it comes to acceptance, I have moments where I'm resigned to the fact that Jerry is dead, and I have other moments where I'm not resigned at all, and I go back to being angry again. And so it goes."

But the one thing Monika has not done is take a drink!

"At least now I'm doing things again, socializing, beginning to give my phone number out." She made plans to go to Germany to visit her mother, "to celebrate the fact that the Berlin Wall, that awful wall she once risked her life to sneak her children through to freedom, has been torn down."

Where her husband is concerned, by doing the loving thing, the unselfish thing, the right thing, Monika has built up her self-respect. She no longer has to be ashamed of her behavior back in the days of drinking and drugging and early sobriety. She has redeemed herself in her own eyes. "When Jerry couldn't talk anymore, I felt as though I could read his mind. I knew what it was that he wanted to say. At the very end, one of the things I know he wanted to say to me was, 'I'm dying, Monika. Thank you for being with me.'"

ELIZABETH, SOBER 15 YEARS

> *When my daughter was young, I had her evaluated by a number of psychiatrists, and they all said the same thing: "Oh, she'll be fine." Well, she wasn't fine! She was never fine. Now my task is to forgive myself, and convince myself that the problems of my children are not all my fault.*
>
> —Elizabeth

Elizabeth, 64, a tall, sporty, strikingly attractive woman with short, dark hair and cornflower-blue eyes, was born into a medical family in San Francisco. She has one brother. She grew up on the campus of Stanford University, "as did my mother before me, and my children after me, generation after generation in the same house." Both her parents were physicians. Her father was a professor of medicine; her grandfather had been a professor of chemistry. "Obviously, I grew up in a family with high intellectual expectations, and I conformed to their every wish. I was smart, musical, mechanical, well-coordinated, and intellectually competent."

Elizabeth states that the way her family dealt with unpleasantness was by not talking about it. She never saw her parents angry. "I remember my father was once short with a telephone operator, and I was shocked. Later in life, after I started drinking, I'd have blackouts and I'd do impolite things, like drive into my mother's flower beds, or end up nude on the bathroom floor where my father would find me. And nobody ever said anything. It was just not mentioned."

Elizabeth went to medical school, not out of any great passion to be a physician, but "because my father thought it would be good life insurance. He said, 'What if you have lots of children and your husband dies or leaves you? How are you going to support yourself?' She married a medical school classmate and did have lots of children—two daughters and three sons. "My husband was a man of my parents' choosing. I was not in love with him and he knew it, but he wanted to marry me anyway. He believed that what was important was the fact that our values were the same, and we were intellectually compatible. He figured that I'd learn to love him. He was right. We are still married today, 42 years later. He is a wonderful, kind man whom I've come to love very much."

One of the pluses that came from growing up in Elizabeth's family was the lack of male chauvinism. "My father always treated me as if I were a peer, so I grew up thinking of myself as totally equal. I didn't expect to be treated differently from men. When I become a physician and went out into the working world, it used to amaze me when male doctors would address my husband but treat me as if I were invisible. It still surprises me when that happens."

After graduating from medical school, Elizabeth and her husband interned in Philadelphia. For two years after that, they were stationed in Guam during the Korean War. They returned to the States and went to Boston, where Elizabeth's husband became an instructor at Harvard.

Prescription for Depression

"No one in the family drank, except for my brother, one cousin, and of course, me." What did seem to run genetically in the family was depression. Elizabeth's mother committed suicide at 70, soon after her eyes started to go bad. "Like me, she was a fiercely independent woman who was never able to let anyone do anything for her, so when she started to go blind, she figured life wasn't worth living if she couldn't take care of herself. So she went up into the hills behind Stanford University, overlooking where she'd grown up and spent her life, and gave herself a lethal injection of Demerol." Elizabeth goes on, "I myself began to have depression by the age of 19. My mother treated it with Dexedrine, which I took in small doses, and I kept right on taking it for the next 25 years." After a while, she added alcohol. "From the beginning, I knew I was an alcoholic. I was never in denial about it. I drank after dinner until I fell asleep. If I woke up during the night—which is one thing that happens when you start to go into minor withdrawal—I'd go downstairs and have another drink, unless it was after 4 A.M., in which case I'd tough it out because I had to go to work. I drank and used amphetamines during all five of my pregnancies."

Elizabeth managed to control her drinking so that it didn't seriously interfere with her work. She worked as a physician after her children were half-grown. Then her brother committed suicide. "His death, combined with my mother's suicide, convinced me to find out why people kill themselves. I also wanted to find out what was wrong with *me*—why I was so depressed and why I drank. I applied for a hospital psychiatric residency and was accepted immediately."

A Moment of Awakening

Upon the successful completion of her residency, Elizabeth went to work as a psychiatrist. Though she enjoyed the work, her training hadn't brought her to any understanding of her alcoholism. "It was getting so that I couldn't stand myself anymore. I felt as if I were going down in a whirlpool, and there was no way out." Her desperation forced her into a moment of clarity. "I woke up out of an alcoholic blackout one night with a strong feeling that my husband had had enough, that he wasn't going to stand for my drinking anymore. He'd never said anything to me about my drinking, except for 'Elizabeth, this is no answer.' Still, I knew that I had to do something. I called AA and went to a meeting. I sat in the back of the room. When I looked up at the podium, I saw that one of my own patients was leading the meeting, and I almost left, but I didn't. I sat on my pride and stayed. I never saw my patient again, but I've been sober ever since."

Sobriety had an immediate impact on Elizabeth's family. "It was a tremendous relief for me to be able to tell my children what had been the matter with me, that it was alcoholism. One of my daughters said, 'Well, Mom, I didn't know whether it was you or the alcohol I didn't like. I'm glad to know it was the alcohol.' My husband, who's a great denier, never did think I was a 'real' alcoholic. He just thinks I have great will power. I just say nothing because I know that's not true."

Elizabeth's early years of sobriety have turned out to be easier than her more recent years have been, marked by ongoing family problems. "For the first few years things went smoothly and I thought, *We're home free.* When all five of my children got married, I said to myself, 'Maybe we're all going to get to walk off into the sunset after all!' Well, it didn't turn out that way."

Dealing with Family Trauma and Parental Guilt

The first big problem was Elizabeth's oldest son. "I'd known for many years that he had mental problems, but when he went off to graduate school he had a paranoid psychotic episode. He thought people were broadcasting thoughts to his brain. It was a very trying time for all of us, and I'm grateful that I had the support of other women in AA or I'd have taken it even harder than I did. But they'd listen and not judge, which was what I desperately needed."

Her son improved—for a while. "He and his wife had two children, and I thought things were finally settling down. But recently he's had another flare-up, and he takes it out on his wife." Again, Elizabeth depends heavily on AA to help her deal with this ongoing situation.

An even bigger problem for Elizabeth was her younger daughter, who had suffered from chronic depression all her life. She'd already made one suicide attempt. One summer, she made another attempt by swallowing pills. This time, before passing out, she took a gun, walked into the bedroom where her husband was sleeping, and shot him dead.

"Before it happened, I knew something was brewing," Elizabeth explains. "My daughter had spent the last few years signing over all her property to her husband, making sure that he'd be happy after she died, and then she went and *killed* him! The night she did it, I sensed that something was wrong. I called 911 and they rushed over to my daughter's house, and they got to her before she died, but my son-in-law was already dead. It's still so hard for me to accept his death. I adored my son-in-law. We all adored him. He was a wonderful man, a man who never used or abused drugs or alcohol, and he shouldn't have died. I'm still grieving for his loss. Even my daughter knew how wonderful he was. I suspect she also knew he'd probably about *had* it with her suicidal behavior, with her constant abuse of him, and with her endless self-preoccupation. He wasn't going to divorce her right away, but he was planning on letting her down slowly. My guess is that on the level on which she operated, she couldn't tolerate the thought of him being with anyone else. She knew *she* wasn't capable of being what he needed, and the thought of his moving on was unacceptable. If she couldn't have him, nobody else could have him either, so she shot him. I don't know for sure if that's what really happened, but that's what I think happened."

After months of waiting for her daughter's murder-trial date to be set, a date which the judge kept putting off, Elizabeth's worst fear came true. One night in her cell her daughter made one more suicide attempt by hanging herself. This time she succeeded. "It was quite clear from the way she went about it that she meant business," Elizabeth says.

Elizabeth admits that the guilt she experienced over her daughter's death, as well as her son's mental illness, has been horrendous. "During the day when I'm awake and busy I'm okay. But at three o'clock, four o'clock in the morning, I start going back over the past, and asking myself, 'Did I do this to my children? Is this genetic noise from both sides of the family? How much is nature? How much is nurture?' Either I feel guilty that I must have damaged my son and daughter when I was pregnant by using alcohol and drugs, or I feel guilty that I was not an adequate mother to them because I was drinking. When my daughter was a baby, she was this pretty, sweet little thing who spent hours and hours rocking. But there was always this big black cloud hanging over her head, which makes me think that she was born with it.

"I don't have a hard time acknowledging that I'm powerless over my alcoholism, but I do have a hard time acknowledging that I'm powerless over my children's lives, especially when they're in trouble. No matter how old they get, they're still my children."

Utilizing the AA Tools

Elizabeth has had to utilize all her AA tools to help herself through this awful period. "I go to AA meetings, and I seek out people to talk to who are wise and insightful, and I call my sponsor. I also pay a lot of attention to my health, as I have from the beginning of my sobriety. I eat proper- ly, and three times a week I get up at six and go to the gym and work out. I go off on trips with my husband, and I spend time with my grandchildren. I also renew my serenity by taking wilderness trips. After a few days of hik- ing cross-country, my spirits are lifted."

Elizabeth goes on. "In a strange way, my daughter's death is a relief. For the past 15 years, I'd been waiting for the phone to ring and to hear somebody tell me that she finally managed to kill herself. And for 15 years, each time I heard that phone, my heart would leap into my mouth: Is this it? Is this the time she's finally done it? I didn't even realize that I'd been waiting for that call, until the waiting *stopped.* For a few months, while my daughter was in prison awaiting trail, I let myself relax a bit, thinking, *Well, at least she's in a safe place.* But as any psychiatrist will tell you, if somebody wants to kill themselves, they'll find a way and nobody can stop them.

"Killing herself is what my daughter has been wanting to do for nearly half her life. This is what she's been hell- bent on doing, and now she's done it. I will miss her terri- bly, but I am glad for her that she's finally free. The dreadful waiting is over. At least now when the telephone rings, I'll know that's not it."

SOBER TROUBLES TIPS LIST

1. When it comes to troubles in sobriety, we don't drink and we don't use—no matter what.

2. In times of trouble, step up your AA meeting atten- dance.

3. Make a list of troubles you're afraid might send you over the top and threaten your sobriety. Putting them down on paper makes them easier to confront and guard against.

4. AA philosophy holds that "we don't get more than we can handle." Whatever it is, you *will* get through it.

5. Educate yourself about your particular problem by talking to people, reading, and attending workshops and seminars.

6. Join a support group that specializes in your trouble (the Wellness Community, incest survivor groups, grief groups).

7. Learn techniques of coping with the feelings that crises bring. For fear, talk to others who've been there; get relaxation tapes. For grief about death, write letters to a loved one or relative who has died, or go to the cemetery and "talk" to the grave. For anger, arrange a one-to-one confrontation; beat a leather cushion with a tennis racket to get the rage out; write a direct letter. For guilt in the present, do the right thing in your relationship with that person today. For guilt in the past, make amends for wrongs; remind yourself you did the best you were capable of doing at the time; forgive yourself.

8. Meditate. You can learn how by renting video- or audiotapes, or by reading books or taking classes.

9. Find physical ways to nourish yourself and lift your spirits: walking, hiking, aerobics, yoga, dance.

10. Think in terms of doing service. When your troubles have got you down, call up somebody in worse shape than you are and offer help.

11. Use AA's one-day-at-a-time philosophy. You may want to bring it down to one hour at a time or even one minute at a time.

12. People react to troubles in different ways. Some want attention, others want to be left alone. You must *ask* for what *you* want. Don't expect anyone to read your mind.

13. Once you ask people for what you want, you can weed out the ones who can't deliver. Eliminate them from your life.

14. Make an effort to be there in support of the important people in *your* life. "Hospitals scare me" is an unacceptable excuse for not visiting a sick friend. Do the right thing, the loving thing, and it will do wonders for your self-esteem.

15. Regarding physical illnesses, a lot has been written on moment-of-clarity healings (unexplained recoveries or spontaneous remissions). It's worth checking out.

8

SOBER CITIZEN

> *I joined AA before it was fashionable,*
> *when there was a stigma attached.*
> *And what the AA program has given*
> *me is everything—everything I ever*
> *needed, all the entertainment, all the*
> *love, all the spirituality, all the emo-*
> *tions, all the joy. AA is a program for*
> *life. AA teaches people how to live in*
> *this world, and that is just exactly*
> *what I've done!*
>
> —Annie, sober 50 years

The alcoholic woman moves through three basic phases: from unhealthy selfishness, to healthy selfishness, to healthy unselfishness. When she's still drinking and using, as well as when she first sobers up, she's selfish in the worst sense of the word. She's self-absorbed, self-centered, and self-indulgent, and she's hurting just about everyone in her life. Once she's been sober a while, things begin to change, and she moves to healthy selfishness. She is now *encouraged* to be selfish, but it's in a different way, a healthier way. She learns, for example, how to take care of herself in life so that she stays happy and doesn't have to drink again. She learns how to handle her feelings, how to say no, how to work, how to love, and how to ask for what she wants. Meanwhile, in her AA meetings, she gets all the loving support she could possibly need while she's in the process of learning.

From there, the woman moves into healthy unselfishness, where she takes what she's learned out into the world. It is during this third phase that the recovering woman begins to become that person that she was on her way to becoming when her life was interrupted by her addiction. She finally becomes a citizen. Like Rip Van Winkle, she may have lost a decade or two in between, but now she's back on track.

DOING SERVICE

In this chapter, we're going to focus on the "healthy unselfish" phase of recovery, which in AA is called service. It means helping other alcoholics get sober and stay sober. It can be done by talking to somebody face-to-face, or by speaking from an AA podium. It can be done by sharing one's "experience, strength and hope" with a practicing alcoholic at a cocktail party, or by doing church or volunteer work with alcoholics. It can be done by using one's profession to help alcoholics, as Karen, an interviewee in this chapter, does. It can be done through teaching, or through education, or through the written word. Anything that helps the "alcoholic who still suffers," as AA puts it, is "doing service."

The tradition of doing service, of course, is not just an AA concept. Nearly every great philosophy and religion has stressed service and encouraged giving back in kind the valuable gifts that one has received. In AA, service is built right into the steps. The twelfth and last step reads: "Having had a spiritual awakening as the result of these steps, we tried to carry this message to alcoholics, and to practice these principles in all our affairs."

If it weren't for doing service, AA would have died years ago. But because AA's co-founders, Bill Wilson and Dr. Bob Smith, were willing to go out into the community and share their recovery stories with other alcoholics, who in turn shared their stories with others, AA was able to grow into the two-million-member phenomenon that it is today. Whenever an alcoholic is hurting, there's a place to go for help. Service, then, is the very lifeblood of the organization. It's also a condition of maintaining sobriety. When AA says, "You can't keep it unless you give it away," it's not a threat, it's simply a statement of fact. Statistically, those who fail to do service have a greater chance of drinking or using again.

The newcomer into AA is usually a far cry from Mother Teresa. In fact, the recovering alcoholic's usual first response to the idea of doing service is, "No thanks, not me." They're all for getting their health back, their home back, their kids back, their man back, their job back, their money back, their self-respect back, but they don't want to have to do *service* to make it happen. But as we'll see when we meet the three interviewees in this chapter, service can be one of the most rewarding experiences of a woman's sobriety.

First we'll meet Louise, sober 17 years, who works unceasingly with newcomers. She takes traveling AA meetings to prisons, talks to patients in hospitals, and sponsors AA women all over the country. Our second interviewee, Karen, a psychotherapist, incorporates the principles of AA in her work with patients. Unlike so many mental health professionals who are sadly unfamiliar with the workings of Alcoholics Anonymous, Karen uses psychotherapy as a way of preparing a patient for the AA experience. Our third interviewee, Annie, has the longest AA sobriety of any living woman in the country—50 years! She attributes her AA longevity to "not drinking one day at a time," of course, and to doing service.

LOUISE, SOBER 17 YEARS

> *My life revolves around service and*
> *giving back the gift that was given*
> *to me. When I am of service, I feel*
> *transcended to another level of con-*
> *sciousness, as though I am being*
> *directed from another source. It's my*
> *fulfillment. It's not about getting*
> *any kind of reward; it is the reward.*
>
> —Louise

"If I had to write down my ideal life, the life I'm leading is my ideal life," says Louise, an attractive, high-energy, short-haired woman of 66, who owns her own office-cleaning business. Born in Atlanta, Georgia, Louise is the youngest of seven children. "I was a change-of-life baby, 10 years younger than the next youngest, so it was like being an only child. People used to assume that my parents were my grandparents."

Louise's father, a full-blooded Cherokee, was a businessman and designed jewelry. Her mother, a Georgia native, was black. Nobody in the family drank. And because Georgia was a dry state, "I never even saw drinking, never saw anyone drunk." She describes the family as loving but stern. "Basically, they were hard-nosed, no-nonsense Baptists. They were emotionally distant. There was no touching; we never embraced. Mealtimes were formal events. We'd all have to stand behind our chairs until my father sat down."

Louise states that by age five, she felt "restless, irritable, discontent, and afraid." By age six, "I could have used a drink—a little bourbon on the rocks with a water back."

By age eight, "I was stealing for no reason other than to get negative attention." She'd cut school, go to the movies, and fantasize about becoming a dancer. She was flatly told by her family that ladies don't dance.

As she got older, Louise began having a real problem with her anger. "A lot of it had to do with growing up in Atlanta under segregated conditions. I was angry about the segregation laws. I'd buck them and end up getting thrown off of streetcars and out of department stores. I also hated being in a school with 4,000 black kids because there I'd get in fights for being mulatto, for being too light."

Early on, Louise showed promise as an artist. A high school teacher suggested that she apply for an art scholarship, which she did. She was accepted at the Boston Museum School for Fine Arts. "I remember the relief I felt when I got on that segregated train from Atlanta to Boston. I was glad to get away from my family, and out of that town."

Alcoholics often think that moving will change how they feel. Such moves, as mentioned earlier, are called geographics in AA. Louise was disappointed to discover that she'd brought her old feelings to Boston with her. She was still angry, still afraid, and still lacked any sense of self-worth. She was convinced that winning her art scholarship was a mistake, and that sooner or later, she'd be found out. "In my classes, I'd take my easel to the back of the room so nobody could see my work. I shook with fear that I'd be criticized. My fear was so great that it kept me from painting. I had no social life. There was only one other black student at the college, and he wanted to date me, and I always said no. I was terrified of boys. I never shared my pain with a soul. All I could do was what I'd learned to do from an early age growing up in Atlanta, which was look good, keep the secrets, and nobody will ever know. That's how I lived my life."

The Magic Martini

Louise was a set-up for drinking. "One night in Boston I was walking down the street, and I heard this great jazz music coming out through the door of a jazz club. I can still remember the excitement I felt hearing it. I walked in, walked up to the bar, and sat on a barstool, and when the bartender asked me, 'What are you going to have?' I remembered a line I'd heard in a movie, and I replied, 'A martini, honey, and make it dry.' When I took the first sip of that first drink, it was the most incredible feeling I'd ever experienced in my life. I knew that I wanted to feel that way for the rest of my life. In the pursuit of that magic feeling, I was to develop alcoholism and drink on a daily basis for the next 27 years."

Drinking drastically changed Louise's life. "Once I drank, I started doing things that were not me. I lost contact with all the values I had growing up. My morals went down the tubes. For example, I had a friend, and whenever she'd go to New York to visit her parents, I'd sleep with her boyfriend. When she'd get back, I'd talk to her like nothing happened. I handled my feelings of guilt for deceiving her by taking a drink. My flip attitude was, 'Well, who'll know 100 years from today!' But that kind of behavior will catch up with you sooner or later."

Louise lost her art school scholarship and started hanging around the jazz clubs with what she came to call "the colorful people," which included pimps and whores, as well as the major stars of the day, people such as Billie Holiday. "I didn't know what I was getting into. All I knew was that I just loved the excitement of that environment. I had no goals of my own. I lived vicariously through others. I became a true star-kisser."

It was in one of those jazz clubs that Louise met her husband, also an alcoholic. They married and had three children. But even though she stayed married to him for 24 years, Louise didn't let marriage, or even motherhood, interfere with her lifestyle. "We were both selfish and immature and never took any kind of responsibility for our kids. We'd dump them on their grandparents and go off and play. We'd buy them off with new clothes and expensive summer camps. The look of disappointment in their eyes, over and over, when we failed to keep our promises to them just about killed me, and I'd go have another drink."

Mr. Wonderful

Louise admits that she was terribly promiscuous. One night she was drinking at a bar in Boston, when "this cool-looking white guy came in, a topcoat thrown over his shoulders. He sat down next to me, pulled out a roll of money, spread it out on the bar, and said to me, 'Spend it.' I knew I'd found Mr. Wonderful!"

Mr. Wonderful turned out to be Mafia, and even though she had a husband and three children at home, Louise started an affair with him that lasted for years. "My husband always knew what I was up to, but he never said anything." Louise and Mr. Wonderful went everywhere together. "I was driven around in his limousine with two bodyguards. He'd take me to New York, and up to Harlem to all the fancy jazz clubs."

But the guilt kept poking through. "One Sunday morning I was being driven home in the limo, hung over after being out all night. I looked out the window, and I saw families walking together to church. I can remember suddenly feeling so ashamed, because I had never done any of those family things with my children. I'd never taken them to a park. I'd never attended a PTA meeting. My children were strangers to me. They'd see me when I'd come home from a bar and pass out on my front lawn, my nose in the grass. I could always see my neighbor's curtains moving, and feel the dew on my back, and I couldn't move. One time my youngest son, who was 10, came out, shame in his eyes, and he said, 'Mother, what happened to you?' I tried to talk, but I couldn't move. Finally, he just turned around, went back into the house, and closed the door. There were other mornings when I'd come to before dawn, and I'd need a drink bad. I'd put on my red wig, my sapphire earrings that hung down to my shoulders, my dark glasses, and my gold fuzzy house slippers, and I'd just slide on down to the liquor store for my day's supply. Sometimes I'd get there before 6 A.M., so I'd have to stand there outside the liquor store, waiting for the man to come open the door."

Yet Louise was in typical alcoholic denial. "I never could see that alcohol had anything to do with it. All I knew was that I just couldn't get it together. I'd start to go full speed ahead with some new life plan, and then the enthusiasm would be gone, and then I'd drop it."

Accompanied by her husband, Louise tried geographics, but moving to new places didn't help. Her alcoholism went with her. At one point, they started a house-cleaning business. It did well at first, but ultimatcly thcy lost the business "because we just couldn't show up anymore." They also lost the house, the car, and the kids. The two younger ones went to live with their grandparents, and the older one left home. "I will never forget the look of despair on my son's face when he said to me, 'I don't know who you are anymore. Good-bye,' and he walked out. The truth was, I didn't know who I was either."

But the biggest loss of all was when Louise's husband and drinking partner for all those years went and got sober. Once sober, he couldn't put up with her anymore. He, too, walked out. The final blow was when Louise's family refused to enable her drinking by sending her survival money, so they stopped. "I'm grateful to them for that now," she says, "because I know I *had* to hit bottom, and I did. I was living in a dirty little house in the ghetto, scrounging on welfare and food stamps. I'd spend my time in sleazy bars and get beaten up regularly. The irony was that each time I expected a different result! Instead of going to the last bar where I was beaten up, I'd go to another one, and the same thing would happen. And I never associated it with alcohol." One beating resulted in a concussion, a broken nose, and broken ribs. "The last thing I remember before passing out was the sound of my own ribs cracking, one at a time. I woke up in a hospital to find a nun leaning over me. She was about 23 years old and she had tears in her eyes, and she said, 'How did you ever let your life get into such a state?' I had such low self-esteem, I didn't think I even deserved to have anyone feel compassion for me. It was like a voice from my inner soul. I heard it so clear, it was like hearing a sound in a tunnel. Inside me, a light went on, and even though I didn't answer her, I never forgot her question."

Louise's Moment of Clarity

Although Louise did go out and drink again, she finally had her moment of clarity. "AA's co-founder, Bill Wilson, once said that God comforts some people slowly. Well, I was one of the slow ones. Whereas *his* moment of clarity was swift and profound, mine was so subtle that I almost missed it. I remember standing in the dark in my little ghetto house, 65 pounds overweight, bloated from Ripple wine, and I had this quiet awareness that if I didn't stop drinking, I would die. Then I did something that I, being an agnostic, said I'd never do. I prayed to God. I said, 'God, please, if you are there, help me. I don't want to die.' And it was like God kissed me gently and he said, 'You don't have to live like this anymore.'

"Without a second thought, I walked over to the phone, called the last friend I had left in the world, and for the first time in my life I told 'the secret,' which was that I couldn't stop drinking. She said, 'There's a group called Alcoholics Anonymous. I don't know what they do, but I hear that people go there and get sober.' I'd never heard of AA. She said, 'You could ask the operator.' I hung up and dialed the operator, and she said, 'Hold on, I'll put you right through.' She must have sensed my desperation. A voice answered, 'Alcoholics Anonymous,' and those two words changed the rest of my life. Immediately after that call, I dashed over to Woolworth's, stole a pair of false eyelashes, and went to my first meeting. I haven't taken a drink since."

A New Start

Without alcohol, Louise's feelings began to resurface. "At first, the only feeling I was in touch with was rage, that feeling I'd had from the time I was a little girl. In my first 90 days of sobriety, I simply couldn't control it. Every time I went out in what I used to call 'the common area,' meaning the world, I'd end up in a fight. Once I was in a supermarket checkout line, and I punched out the cashier because she was too slow with my change."

But as time passed, Louise got better, especially after her sponsor began to press her to get a job. "Some women focus on their love relationships when they first get sober, but my sponsor didn't think a relationship would be good for me, and I was relieved. Sober, my fear of men had returned. Each man I saw became the symbol of all the smiling faces of all the men I'd ever known, every man I'd ever let use me, use my body, and I didn't want anything to do with them!"

So, following AA's direction, Louise focused on work. "AA tells us to be self-supporting by our own contributions, so that meant I had to get off of welfare. I got a job as a waitress, and I hated it, but my sponsor made me stay on that job for two whole years as a form of discipline. I had to learn *how* to work. I had to learn how to be reliable, how to show up on time, how to be with other people with a good attitude, and how to get my ego out of the way. My ego really needed to be smashed, and, believe me, on that job it was. After all those years of hanging out with stars, riding in limos, and wearing fur coats, picking up nickels and dimes off of tables was not exactly what I had in mind! But I learned to accept it. I began to have some gratitude for the fact that I was sober, that I was alive. And I began to feel a feeling I'd never, ever felt before—self-worth."

Louise worked long hours, and saved her tips until she had enough for a down payment on a little house in a nice area. Her family, seeing that she was putting her life back together, co-signed the loan. Next, she got her first car. Finally, her two younger kids came back to live with her. "They could walk to a good school nearby, and we started living a normal life."

After two years of waitressing, Louise decided to go back into the housecleaning business that she and her husband had started years before. She bailed her equipment out of storage, had business cards printed, and on her day off from her waitressing job started ringing doorbells in Beverly Hills. "I'd give them my card and ask for work cleaning houses. Each time, I'd want to run, but I'd make myself stand there. Finally, a lady hired me, and I did such a good job that she recommended me to her friends, and the business started to grow. I got a second day off from my waitress job and took on more cleaning jobs. Then I cut down to part-time waitressing and part-time cleaning houses. Then I got so much business I had to hire somebody to help me. But in the beginning, I had such low self-esteem that I didn't charge enough for my services. I didn't know how to ask for more. I started feeling resentful. But in AA I learned that resentment kills alcoholics, so I was instructed to find a way to deal with it. It took me a long time, but in the end I dared to raise my fee. I'd ask—and hold my breath. Little by little, by taking the action of asking, the asking got easier. That's how I became a professional.

"Today I have a staff of 14 people, and I've gone from cleaning those little single houses to cleaning estates, office buildings, and the houses of movie stars. I have contracts. I also do construction clean-ups and new developments. I do honest work to the best of my ability. I don't cheat. I don't pad the bill. If I submit a bid and I'm turned down, I don't panic because I know that six months down the road, they may call me again." Because of her philosophy, the business continues to do well. "But it's not even the money that makes it so good," she says, "it's how I feel."

Sober Parenting

Louise spent years doing her best to repair the damage that her years of drinking had done to her three children. It was a painful time. For nine years after leaving home, her oldest son would have little to do with her. He traveled the world. He lived in India. He lived in Japan for three years, learned to speak Japanese fluently, and taught English conversation at the University of Tokyo. When he returned to the United States, however, he and Louise— thanks to her sobriety—reconnected. "Today our relationship is wonderful," she says. "For any parent, getting your children back in your life just has to be one of the greatest gifts of the AA program." She is also close to her other son, and to her daughter, a former professional ice-skater, who is now married with a child of her own.

"I realized that once I'd made my amends to my kids, as AA tells us to do, I couldn't keep beating myself up for the rest of my life over what I'd done wrong. I was always so sure that God had a rap sheet on me a mile long, and that for years, out of guilt, I'd let my kids manipulate me.

I finally had to learn how to say no. No matter how painful it was, no matter how much guilt I felt, I'd have to stand still and say no to them and let it hurt, and let it do whatever it had to do, and stand my ground. I realized that my job was just to be a living example of a sober woman. And by doing that, a funny thing began to happen—my kids began to seek me out. I can't explain exactly how that works, but when I stopped letting them manipulate me, and I started saying no, it got better. I don't mean to say that we became the Brady Bunch, but it got better."

The Highlight of Sobriety

Doing service wasn't something Louise took to easily—far from it. "All my life I'd been selfish, self-centered, and a liar and cheat, so my first response to the idea of doing service was to fight it. I was greedy enough to want to keep all the goodies I'd gotten in AA for myself. But I kept hearing AA people say, 'You can't keep it unless you give it away,' and I knew I wanted to keep it, so I figured I'd better start giving it away."

Ironically, helping others has turned out to be "the highlight of my sobriety," Louise says. "Service is my life." She does it all. She sponsors AA women. She speaks at meetings. She visits high-security prisons and talks about alcoholism to prisoners who are there for crimes committed under the influence of alcohol or drugs. She puts together panels of AA members and goes into hospitals, treatment centers, and correctional institutions to talk to the alcoholics. She's on the board of directors of a women's alcoholism recovery house. And for the past six years, every Saturday morning, she takes a traveling AA meeting down to one of the Skid Row missions. Not only does it give the Skid Row alcoholics a chance to see what sobriety is like, but it also helps Louise to stay sober. She says, "That's where I get to see what will happen to me if I don't stay sober. That's where I get to see the phenomenon of denial in action. Sometimes my heart sinks at what I see, because I *know* so well that there but for the grace of God go I. How many times did I sit on a barstool and drink myself into oblivion, and then wake up the next morning in some strange place, and say to myself, 'If only I could just have a second chance.' Well, AA gave me that second chance, and by doing service, maybe I can give somebody else that second chance."

Louise doesn't believe that doing service to the extent that she does is the path that every recovering alcoholic woman has to take. "However, I *do* think that we all need to be involved in *some* kind of service to our fellow man, even if it's not in AA. Unless we give of ourselves in an unselfish way through helping somebody else—it can be in the church, or in politics—we won't get to keep our sobriety. I sponsor a lot of women. I see them get sober, and they get back into the workplace, and they get involved in a relationship, and they stop paying attention to their AA program, stop going to meetings, and stop doing service, and eventually they drop out of AA and drink. It's sad."

Doing service takes Louise all over the United States and Canada—even back to Atlanta, Georgia, where it all began. "I find that service to people brings to me the kind of fulfillment that a lot of people find in relationships. I don't think a million dollars or any relationship with a man could give me that same feeling, so with me, service comes first. I'm willing to go anywhere if I can be guided to someone who needs help. The more I do it, the more I want to do it. When I come home from work and find a phone message from some alcoholic who may have heard me speak months before, telling me she's *made* it, that she's staying sober, that's the greatest reward I can get."

KAREN, SOBER 25 YEARS

> *I think being a recovering alcoholic myself is a definite asset in my work as a psychotherapist. I think you have to create a climate where the alcoholic patient can hear you, and trust you, and believe what you're saying. They have to have some faith in the messenger. They need to see that it's possible to change, that you can get there from here.*
>
> —Karen

Karen, 61, is a small, blond, blue-eyed, husky-voiced divorced mother of two adult daughters. For the past 20 years, she has worked as a psychotherapist and has done service in this capacity. She was born in Columbus, Ohio, and has one sister who drinks, as did their father. "Drinking was all around us growing up, so it seemed like a natural thing to do. I thought all sensitive, sharp, intelligent, creative people drank. I thought they had to because the world was so cruel, and something was needed to buffer the pain."

An Alcoholic in Denial

Karen's drinking started in high school, and she was alcoholic almost from the start. "If somebody said to me, 'You want to go out for a beer?' and they literally meant *a* beer, I wouldn't go. Never in my life did I want just *one* drink. Why would anybody want just one?"

She dropped out of Ohio State to marry. Her husband drank, too. When she got pregnant, it put a temporary stop to her drinking. "For some reason, even though we didn't know about fetal alcohol syndrome back then, I felt very protective of the life inside of me, and I didn't drink." But her pregnancy didn't put a stop to her husband's drinking or the behavior that went along with it. Soon after Karen's twin daughters were born, she left him and raised the children on her own. "I continued drinking, continued to surround myself with drinkers, so I never even noticed that my drinking had turned into alcoholism. I could see alcoholism happening in others, but not in myself. I'd say to friends, 'Isn't it a shame that so-and-so has an alcohol problem. She's such a mess when she drinks. God, I'm glad *I'm* not an alcoholic. Got any beer in the refrigerator?'"

At one point, Karen even drove one of her alcoholic friends to Alcoholics Anonymous meetings. "I was really impressed with AA," she says. "I remember thinking, *Why, anybody could identify with this stuff!* I also told my friends, 'Gee, I feel sort of guilty taking up space in AA when I'm not even an alcoholic.' Finally, somebody suggested that I might be more comfortable in AA meetings if I stopped drinking, too. At first I thought the suggestion was ridiculous, but then I said, 'Heck, why not?'"

That's when Karen found out that she was more hooked on booze than she'd thought, because stopping wasn't all that easy. "But I still wasn't convinced I was a 'real' alcoholic. Later, I came to find out that 75 percent of the people who go to AA don't initially see themselves as having a problem with alcohol!" To Karen's surprise, she not only experienced the physiological craving, which in itself is a symptom of addiction, but also the psychological craving. "I was one of those people who said that drinking wasn't my problem, it was my solution. It was honest self-deception. I truly believed this. It took me a long time to see that alcohol was my problem, and that *not* drinking was my solution."

Gliding Slowly into Sobriety

While Bill Wilson's moment of clarity may have been swift and dramatic, Karen's seemed to happen in little dribs and drabs over a period of months. "You might say I just sort of *glided* into permanent sobriety. For me, it wasn't so much one grand moment of clarity as it was a series of little moments that, one on top of the other, caused an *illumination* about the nature of my alcoholism, and what I'd need to do to heal it." Even though she wasn't drinking during those months, she didn't feel surrendered. "But I kept going to AA meetings, kept making friends, kept listening, and kept having this phrase go through my head, *I wish there was a way to live in this world without drinking, because drinking seems to cause so many problems.* I'd find myself repeating that phrase over and over like some sort of existential question I was asking my unconscious. The other recurring thought I had was, *Wouldn't it be wonderful to live in a world where there wasn't any drinking?* Obviously I thought the only way I'd be able to stop drinking was to make it disappear off the face of the earth!"

Karen continues, "I'd been going to AA meetings for three months, and I'd never raised my hand as an alcoholic. One day I *did* raise my hand. Mostly I did it to get people off my back," she admits. "And when my hand went up, people cheered." But what finally threw her over the line, she says, was the powerful practice of honesty in AA. "If you tell the truth, eventually it will take you places, to where *it* wants to go, not necessarily where *you* want to go. If you let it, the truth will set you free." Honesty took Karen to a point where she finally admitted her addiction. "I can't pinpoint the exact moment I capitulated, but it happened the day I realized that I'd been sober for 18 months, and that that was the longest period I'd been without a drink since I'd been a teenager. In that moment, I made a commitment to sobriety."

Once committed to sobriety, Karen jumped into the AA program and began to make some long-overdue changes in her life. With children to raise, Karen had a practical decision to make about work. "The fantasy I'd carried from childhood was that I'd work in the theater as an actress. I'd been in college on a theater arts scholarship, so I still assumed I wanted to be an actress. I even went to New York to some auditions. My head was all excited, saying, "An actor's life for me!' But when I got there, my intuition, which I'd never listened to in my whole life, started disagreeing with my head, saying, 'No, Karen, you can't be an actress because you're not willing to expend the energy it takes, or pay the price.' Now that was very irritating! I felt totally confused. Which was right, my head or my gut?

"But people in AA kept reassuring me that as long as I did the footwork and let myself simply notice my feelings, that eventually my feelings would *tell* me which way to go. So that's what I did. I did the footwork by going to the scheduled auditions, and I let part of me just stand back and observe how I was reacting to it all. Sure enough, my feelings started to tell me the truth. The first thing I noticed was that instead of feeling energized by the auditions, the way I usually feel when I'm enthusiastic about something, I felt lightheaded, even bored. I also noticed that I had this queasy feeling in my gut, a feeling that something was wrong. One night I went to see a Broadway musical with friends and I remember looking at the dancers and thinking, *I don't have the energy to hop around on a stage like that!* Finally, as I walked around New York, I began to realize, 'I don't want to be here. I don't want to live in New York City. I don't want to have to haul my kids here. Whatever was I thinking of?'" When all the information was in, Karen made the decision to go back home. "Happily, I gave up thoughts of Broadway forever."

She re-enrolled in college and switched her major from theater arts to psychology. Again, her feelings led the way. "When I switched to psychology, I had the feeling of 'I'm home! This is why I went through all that pain and all that difficulty in my life.'" After she finished college, she went on to graduate school, got licensed, and has been a psychotherapist ever since. "The things I viewed as draw-backs in my life—being over 35, being divorced, having two kids, starting a second career, going to school after everyone else had finished—all turned out to be assets in many ways. And I sure did know something about being an alcoholic!" Karen started out doing some consulting work for a women's alcoholism program, then she worked as a counselor in a chemical dependency treatment program, then as a chief therapist, and ultimately as a program director. "I learned a tremendous amount and found it surprisingly fulfilling." She is now in private practice.

Karen never remarried, but for the past 17 years she has been in a committed relationship with another sober alcoholic woman. "I don't feel 'gay.' I don't even identify with that word. I just feel like a person. We've both been married, both been attracted to men, but we simply *prefer* being with each other. Just as in any long-term marriage, our relationship has gone through many transitions. There are errors we all commit, but I think in most cases, if you stick it out, you can work through whatever comes up. In our social circle, our relationship is looked at by people, both gay and straight, as some kind of model."

Service Through Work

For every alcoholic in AA recovery, there are 99 others out there in the community still drinking and using. Some will wander into AA. Some will stop off and try psy-chotherapy first. Of those that try psychotherapy, most will have absolutely no idea that alcoholism is their prob-lem. Unfortunately, most of the therapists they pick will also have absolutely no idea that alcoholism is their problem.

That's where somebody like Karen can be of service. Not only is she a licensed psychotherapist, but she is also a recovering alcoholic with 25 years of AA experience. She can help where other mental health professionals often can't. And the alcoholic's life may depend on getting the right kind of help.

"If I think the patient I'm working with is an alcoholic in denial, I'll start off gently. First I'll introduce them to information about addiction, and then I'll introduce them to a little pain, by which I mean I'll suggest that they don't drink for a week just to see how it feels. Next, I'll suggest they not drink for another week. Usually an alcoholic will feel anxious, nervous, angry, and afraid, just as I did. They'll either rebel, or they'll 'get' it that they're not as in control of their drinking as they thought they were, which, of course, is *alcoholism*! Then I'll suggest going to AA. I'll be careful to pick out a specific meeting for them to attend, one that will most likely blast any stereotypes they have about who's an alcoholic and who's not. An upscale AA meeting, full of well-dressed, happy people, usually works. It sure blows the Skid Row bum idea to smithereens. If the patient rebels or cheats, that's valuable information, too. I do not cast people out of therapy because they won't go to an AA meeting. I think that's one time they need not to be abandoned. They need a place of safety to work it all out, just as I did. Sometimes it's even important for a person to drink again just to discover for themselves that they can't stay away from the stuff. It's all grist for the mill."

Because of her AA experience, Karen is basically a moment-of-clarity therapist. "People have a basic core of health within them, and they need to find a way to tap into that. A moment of clarity is just another way of describing the process of tapping into that healthy core." Unlike some therapists, who keep looking for the "reasons why" the alcoholic drinks, Karen knows that an instant healing can take place even if the alcoholic *never* finds out what caused the addiction. If the timing is right, and if the right "triggers" happen, then recovery happens. She's witnessed it hundreds of times.

"I purposely set up situations I hope will trigger the healing moment-of-clarity response," she says. "I know I can't force it to happen, but I can set things up to increase the chances of it happening. But to facilitate this, the patient has to be willing to take certain actions, like going to the AA meeting when I suggest it, just to see if going there triggers something within. If they don't go, they won't know. When they go, and it *does* trigger a moment of clarity, I'm so pleased, even if it means I end up losing a patient because they don't need me anymore! Sometimes they come back to me and say, 'It's amazing! I don't know what happened, but when I went to the meeting, one minute I was a hopeless drunk, and the next minute my obsession to drink was gone and I knew I was going to be okay!' I just love to see people get their minds blown like that! As a therapist, as well as an alcoholic, I'm thrilled to have been a part of that."

ANNIE, SOBER 50 YEARS

> *I've needed AA more than I've needed any medicine. Life can get rough, but it will get good again. Nothing lasts forever. We've got to believe that this program will work through death and disaster, and everything that goes along with it.*
>
> —Annie

An 83-year-old woman, holding tightly onto her husband's arm for support, walks into an AA meeting. The

couple tries to slip inconspicuously into their seats up
front, but they are spotted. A young woman speaking
from the podium stops in mid-sentence and points them
out. "Oh, good! My sponsor, Annie, is here. She's been
sober for 50 years." There is an audible gasp from the
audience, followed by applause. People begin rising to
their feet to give Annie a standing ovation. It goes on for
minutes.

Later, during the first coffee break, Annie is surrounded by people who want to greet her, talk to her,
even touch her. "Annie is basically a very humble lady, and
the fuss that's made over her mystifies her," says
Sam, her husband of 25 years, who is also a recovering
alcoholic. "But it's just human nature. After all, she's a
pioneer."

Annie is, indeed, a pioneer. She was the first woman
west of the Mississippi to get sober in AA, and today, as far
as anyone can determine, she's the only living woman in
the country to have 50 years of AA sobriety. Sam laughs at
the irony of Annie's celebrity status. "She's always been
the one to say that when you enter AA, you leave your
degrees, your pedigrees, your titles, and your bankbook
outside the door, because in AA everybody is equal—a
drunk is just a drunk."

Although Annie still attends AA meetings, often just
to give a woman she sponsors a cake for another year of
sobriety, lately she has been ill—too ill to speak or be
interviewed. When I set up my interview with Annie and
Sam, it was conditional: "Only if she's having a good day,"
Sam had said. When I arrived at the restaurant we'd
picked for the interview, Sam was alone. "Not a good day
for her," he said. I thanked him and turned to leave when
he added suddenly, "Why not interview me? I've known
Annie for 40 years, and I've been married to her for 25
years. I've heard her tell her story from the AA podium so
many times, I think that by now I probably know her better than she knows herself!"

So instead of interviewing Annie, I interviewed Sam, her clearly devoted and very loving husband. Here, it is Sam who is Annie's memory, and Sam who tells Annie's tale.

Annie's Early Years

Annie was born in 1908 in a storm cellar in Clovis, New Mexico, the last of four children. Her father had all kinds of jobs—beekeeper, farmer, horse groomer, streetcar driver, "boomtowner" in the oil fields. The family followed him around from job to job, state to state. "They'd travel in a covered wagon, and Annie's mother would walk ahead with a stick and beat away the rattlesnakes so they wouldn't scare the horses." As soon as each child was old enough, they were taken out of school to go to work, so Annie never got to finish her education.

Unhappy living at home, at 15 Annie escaped by marrying a 16-year-old neighbor. It was the first of her five marriages. Sam quotes her as saying, "In my generation, if you were in love with a guy, you married him, so I married a lot of good guys."

Annie went to work in an office as a typist. When her marriage broke up, she found typing lacked the excitement she was looking for, so she went to work in a bar. "She was a B-girl—the B stands for bar," explains her husband. "It started her off on a rather sordid life. She was the girl who would walk up to you and say, 'Want to buy me a drink, honey?' She was a hustler. A guy would buy her a beer and get charged an arm and a leg for it. In another place she was a taxi dancer, a 10-cents-a-dance girl. That's where she met her second husband. He was a wealthy guy, but bashful, which is why he went to dance halls to meet girls. When he met Annie, who looked like a social worker, he said, 'Let me take you away from all this. Let's get married and I'll support you,' and Annie said,

'Let's do.' And they did. He turned out to be a good husband to her for 17 years. He didn't drink, and he put up with all her alcoholic shenanigans.

"When she got pregnant, Annie thought, *I'll be a good mother and stop drinking.* Three weeks after her daughter was born, she was off drinking again. Her primary drinking partner was her alcoholic brother, Frank, who was 10 years older. She bailed Frank out of jail a total of 89 times. Each time, the minute he got into her car, he'd ask, 'Got a bottle with you?' But when *she* drank, Frank scolded her. 'Annie, you're a woman, and you shouldn't drink the way you drink, and do the things you do. You've got a husband and baby now, and you should go home and take care of the house." But that wasn't something Annie could do.

According to Sam, when Annie speaks at AA meetings, she sums up her drinking years in a few sentences: "I drank a lot. I got beaten up a lot. I was missing a lot. I couldn't be depended on. I made promises I didn't keep. I'd beg for forgiveness. I'd swear on the Bible. I'd say 'never again,' and then I'd do it again. I'd go out to a bar, lose my car, and have to walk home, or I'd crawl home on my knees and arrive with ripped stockings and bloody knees. Sometimes a cop would pick me up and say, 'You're too young for this kind of thing, so I'm going to take you home to your mother.' All the way home, I'd be racking my brain for some lie to tell my husband so he wouldn't give me thunder. Why he didn't leave me I'll never know. The sad part was that I didn't know what was wrong with me. I'd say, 'Well, it's my nerves, *that's* why I drink!'"

Discovering Alcoholics Anonymous

Annie hit bottom one night in 1941. She was 33. She'd been out drinking and was too drunk and too scared to go home and face her husband. Instead, she checked into an all-night Turkish bath, at the time a popular place for alcoholics to go and sober up. "You'd go there for the night and they'd massage you and bring you back to life." While Annie was being massaged, she picked up a copy of the *Saturday Evening Post* dated March 1, 1941. There was a cover story about Alcoholics Anonymous. According to Sam, Annie was too sick to read the article, but she looked at the pictures, and as a result, she made a decision that changed her life. "It wasn't a dramatic hot flash, it was just, 'Here's what I've been looking for. Here's what I need.' That was it." Even though she hadn't written a letter in years, Annie asked the Turkish bath attendant for a pen, paper, and a stamp, and she wrote a letter to AA in New York City, telling them that she was a desperate woman alcoholic and needed help. She got a letter back from Bill Wilson's secretary saying, "Fortunately for you, there's an AA meeting in your area," and giving her a phone number and an address.

Annie's first AA meeting was basically a comedy of errors. She got her nonalcoholic husband to take her. They arrived at the Elk's club and found 9 or 10 men in a banquet room sitting around a big table. When the meeting began, the leader stood up and asked the women to please leave, "but you may return *after* the meeting for coffee and doughnuts," he said. Since Annie, wearing a bright red turban, was the only woman there, she couldn't exactly hide, so she left. Her husband stayed behind.

Devastated at being thrown out, Annie paced up and down outside the meeting room, alternately swearing and sobbing. When the meeting was finally over and her husband came out, he was in shock. "You don't know what they put me through in there!" he said. "They assumed *I* was the alcoholic, and they refused to believe me when I told them I don't drink! They read things to me out of a book, and I couldn't make head or tails out of it. It put me in a terrible position. I'm never coming back here again!"

"But what did they say about *me*?" Annie asked.

"They don't even know you're alive!" he said. They went home. And as soon as her husband was asleep, Annie snuck out to a bar. She perched herself on a barstool, drink in her hand, and announced, "Nobody knows this, but I'm a member of Alcoholics Anonymous."

Fortunately, Annie's stubbornness wouldn't allow her to give up. A few days later, she called the AA number that was in the letter from New York, and complained. "They threw me out!" she said. The man who answered was horrified. "It's all a terrible mistake," he told her. "They've never had a woman show up before, and they naturally assumed it was your *husband* who was the alcoholic, not you. They thought you were the wife. If they'd known you were an alcoholic, they'd have been so pleased. AA needs you desperately, so *please* go back." Annie did go back, and she's been going back ever since—for nearly 51 years.

When Annie sobered up in AA, brother Frank, her drinking buddy, got upset. "Annie, you chump, you fall for everything," he told her. "AA is obviously a money-making scheme. But don't fear, I'm going to go down there and expose them all!" Annie begged him not to go. "You'll just screw it up for me. I had a hard enough time just getting in!" But Frank was determined. He marched down to AA fully intending to destroy them. He got sober instead, and stayed sober until the day he died.

A Woman Pioneer

In the early days of AA, there were so few people sober that if AA was even going to survive, everybody, even newcomers, had to do service. There was no such thing as waiting until you felt ready. Members with only hours or, at best, days of sobriety were sent out on 12-step calls to help drinking alcoholics, sometimes with predictably disastrous results. Instead of the AA getting the alcoholic sober, the alcoholic would get the AA member drunk.

When Annie had been going to AA meetings for only a few weeks, another AA member approached her with a stack of letters.

"Annie, you got to AA by writing a letter saying you needed help, right?"

"That's right," Annie said, "Well, these letters here are all from women alcoholics who need help, too. And since you're our only woman alcoholic, you're going to have to be the one to go calling on them. If you don't go, some of them might die."

Annie was unnerved. She resisted. "But I don't know what to say."

"You don't know anything yet, so just say very little," the AA man told her. "Just go there and bring the women in."

So Annie started doing service by making 12-step calls on women alcoholics. The person who drove her around from place to place was none other than her brother, Frank. "Let's go punch those doorbells," he said.

When each women opened her door, Annie was ready with her pitch: "I'm Annie, and I'm from AA. I wrote a letter asking for help, too. Last week I went down there to look those AA people over, and now they want me to tell you a little bit about them, and ask you if you'd like to go to a meeting Friday night, and find out for yourself. If you would, my brother and I would be happy to drive you."

Half the time, the women would agree to go to AA but changed their minds by the time Annie and Frank arrived to pick them up. Or they'd say, "Oh, my mother wrote that letter and I didn't know a thing about it. I don't need any help." To which Annie would reply, "Well, that's all right. If you ever do, here's our address and phone number." Month after month, Annie and Frank went out on 12-step calls, bringing dozens of women into AA. Even Frank was impressed. "I'll lay you eight to five that this thing is going to grow so fast that we won't just have *one* AA group in town, we'll have a whole bunch. Who knows how far this thing can go?" Later, Annie was to say, "Once it started, there was no way to stop it. No human being on the face of this earth could possibly have stopped it."

When AA grew enough to have a local office, Annie worked there for 12 years. Women continued to come in droves. Today, in some of the larger cities, half of all new members are women.

Doing service in AA also means speaking from the AA podium. For those with stage fright, like Annie, it's scary. When some of the AA old-timers asked Annie to speak for the first time, she pleaded with them, "Oh, please don't make me talk!" but they said, "You have to speak because you're not growing fast enough. You hide out in the back row. Besides, other women in the room need to hear a woman talk. So just stand at the podium and say something, anything. It doesn't matter so long as you take the action." Annie, tears in her eyes, stood at the AA podium, and opened her mouth. "My voice quivered, my hands shook, and I thought I'd die. I *wished* I'd die. I don't even remember what I said, and then I sat down. And do you know what happened? There was applause. The people there knew about my fear, and they applauded me. I thought, *Wow! I wasn't even good, and they love me anyway.* And it's always been like that for me in AA. AA takes the poor, sick alcoholic like me, and loves them well."

Annie's Choice

Sobriety upset the balance of Annie's marriage. This is a common phenomenon, which some marriages don't survive. While her husband had been able to tolerate 17 years of her drinking, he couldn't handle her sobriety. He felt left out. One night in 1942, when Annie got home from an AA meeting, her husband met her at the door. "I've made a decision," he said. "I've decided that I want you to go back to drinking, just like you did in the good old days, and then I'll be able to take care of you. So you just go ahead, and drink to your heart's content, and I'll be here to take care of you. You won't have to suffer at all."

Astounded, Annie just stood there and looked at him. Sam quotes her as saying, "I didn't blow my top, or cuss, or rant, or scream, or holler, even though I wanted to do all those things. I was stunned speechless. I couldn't believe what I'd heard. What he was saying was that it was okay with him if I died—because if I ever drank again, that's exactly what would happen!"

Annie turned and went upstairs, thinking to herself, *He's a good man, but I can't give up AA, not even for him. If I can't trust AA to work when the chips are down, then it's not worth a plug nickel.* She packed a suitcase, and walked back downstairs, out of the house, and out of her marriage. "I saw my new car sitting in the driveway, but then I thought, *Nope. Give yourself a clean break.* I took a streetcar to my daughter's house. Then I got a room in a rooming house for $7 a week and then a job."

Living in a single room wasn't much fun, but Annie did it. She went to AA meetings, practiced the 12 steps, and worked to support herself, and things began to get a little better. She fell in love again with a man she met in AA and married him. He turned out to be a gambler. "I knew about compulsive drinking, but not compulsive gambling. We lived in Reno for six months while he gambled away our entire savings." Ultimately he stopped gambling and founded Gamblers Anonymous, while Annie founded GamAnon (like Al-Anon) for the family members. Once again, she found herself in the role of pioneer. That marriage ended when her husband began to drink again and "took up with a pretty young blond. That I couldn't take." Annie married and divorced a fourth time. That husband also was unable to resist extramarital affairs.

"The first time I met Annie, it was in AA over 40 years ago," says Sam. "She was wearing a hat with a feather in it, and she looked like a Sunday School teacher." They were friends for 15 years before they began dating.

Theirs is a true AA marriage. Both have long-term sobriety, and both are actively involved in service. "For years we'd go down to the county hospital together and talk to the alcoholic patients. It was both a rewarding experience and a sad one because so many of those patients were in denial. One time Annie was talking to a young woman who'd been hospitalized for cirrhosis of the liver. Annie was telling her about AA, and suddenly the woman said, 'No, no, you don't understand. My problem isn't alcoholism. My problem is my *boyfriend.*' When we went back the following week, the woman was dead."

According to Sam, Annie has a definite philosophy when it comes to sponsoring other women alcoholics. "She sponsors very gently. She doesn't believe in telling anybody what to do. You can go to her with a problem, and she'll tell you what *she* or somebody else did in a similar situation, but she'll never tell you what you have to do. The only advice she'll ever give you is, 'Don't drink.' Anything else would be presumptuous."

Bill Wilson Remembered

One of the perks of being married to Annie, Sam says, is the fact that she knows so many fascinating people She knew AA's co-founder Bill Wilson well. "By virtue of being Annie's husband, I had the honor of being a guest at the home of Bill and his wife, Lois, in Bedford Hills, New York, on several occasions," Sam says. "I carry a number of little vignettes about Bill in my mind, like the time we were there on Christmas and I watched Bill, this man who was by now famous all over the world, as he washed out his socks and hung them on a string over the kitchen sink.

Another time Annie and I went with him to the AA General Service Office in New York, but because of this celebrity thing, this hero worship, he couldn't even walk into the lobby without being surrounded by people wanting to touch him. Later, we had to sneak out the back way by taking the freight elevator. The three of us ran across a street and into a little restaurant, where we got a table in the back, in the dark, and we sat there for the rest of the afternoon, talking. That's what Annie and I loved about Bill, that you could *do* that with him. Like Annie, Bill was the first to say, 'A man is just a man,' but it was hard for him when people kept treating him like God. Even Annie fell into that at times. We were with Bill in Toronto once to hear him speak at a meeting, and when he got off the podium, he turned to Annie and asked, 'How did I do, Annie?' Annie had laughed and said, 'But you're Bill! How can you do wrong?' To her, it was incomprehensible that he could be unsure. But the funny thing is, she'd do the same thing. She'd ask, 'Did I do okay?' and then people would find it incomprehensible that Annie could ever be unsure. That's the way it goes!"

Sam adds, "Bill Wilson was definitely a human being. Occasionally he even had a little outburst of temper. I remember a time when Annie and I were eating lunch with him, and he started telling us about some incident involving the AA trustees, something that got him spitting mad, and he pounded on the table, and he said, 'My God, Annie, I think I still have some clout around this organization! If those trustees don't do what I tell them to do, I'm going to take this show on the road!' Well, of course, he didn't do that because AA is still very much with us."

AA Celebrity

According to Sam, Annie's celebrity status has been a burden at times. "Annie still can't go to a meeting without creating a big stir. We've gone to AA conventions, and tried to go out to eat dinner at a restaurant, and before you know it we'd have people sitting down at our table, talking to her, or standing around her chair, leaning down, asking her to sign this, sign that.

"But there's been a plus side to all this," Sam goes on. "I'll never forget the time Annie addressed 70,000 people at the International AA Convention in Montreal. At the time she was 78 years old, and as she spoke, again and again she brought down the house. Over all those years that she'd be doing service in Alcoholics Anonymous, she had at one time or another personally touched the lives of thousands of men and women who were sitting in that hall that night, and they were appreciating her and thanking her en masse! It made for one hell of an AA evening!"

Clearly, Alcoholics Anonymous has given Annie a wonderful life, and for 50 years, Annie has been giving back to Alcoholics Anonymous—heart and soul.

SOBER CITIZEN TIPS LIST

1. Service is a tradition seen in most great philosophies and religions. It's spelled out in AA's Step 12: "Having had a spiritual awakening as the result of these steps, we tried to carry this message to alcoholics, and to practice these principles in all our affairs."

2. The AA paradox, "You can't keep it unless you give it away," means that your best chance of staying sober is by helping others to get sober. Be part of the chain.

3. Even simple things like shaking a hand or handing out your phone number is doing service. Such gestures might make the difference between a newcomer staying at an AA meeting or walking out and never coming back again.

4. Types of service include speaking at AA meetings or conventions; sponsoring other alcoholics; making "12-step" calls by going to wherever the alcoholic *is*; speaking to alcoholics anywhere about sobriety and AA—visiting hospitals, treatment centers, prisons, halfway houses, Skid Row missions; volunteering at an AA office; helping to set up the chairs at an AA meeting; serving as a meeting secretary, literature chairperson, treasurer; even making coffee.

5. Mental health, medical, educational, and religious professionals who know about alcoholism can do service by guiding the alcoholic who still suffers into appropriate treatment.

6. It's not unusual to resist doing service. But if you keep at it, it will pay huge benefits. You'll feel good about yourself, and you'll stay sober!

7. You can do service in areas other than addiction by doing volunteer work in your community, school, or profession, or by giving time to causes that are special to you.

8. AA says, "It's progress, not perfection." No one expects you to become a saint. If you're an alcoholic, the purpose of service is to remind you where you came from, and to help you stay sober so that you *never* have to go back there again.

9. When you work with others, remember two things: You cannot take credit for another person's sobriety, and you cannot accept blame for another person's drinking again.

10. In AA they say that sooner or later you'll hear *your* story from the podium. So whenever you get a chance at an AA meeting to take a chip, take a cake, or speak up, *do* so, because *your* story may be the story

that some newcomer needs to hear in order to commit to the program.

11. Service is often an attitude. Whenever you go someplace—home to visit the family, to a party, to a class—instead of focusing on expectations ("What am I going to get?") focus on what you think somebody else might need ("What can I give? How can I help out?"). *That's* service!

9

CONCLUSIONS

*If we are painstaking about this phase of our develop-
ment, we will be amazed before we are half way
through. We are going to know a new freedom and a
new happiness. We will not regret the past nor wish to
shut the door on it. We will comprehend the word serenity and we will know peace. No matter how far down
the scale we have gone, we will see how our experience
can benefit others. That feeling of uselessness and self-
pity will disappear. We will lose interest in selfish
things and gain interest in our fellows. Self-seeking
will slip away. Our whole attitude and outlook upon
life will change. Fear of people and of economic insecurity will leave us. We will intuitively know how to handle situations which used to baffle us. We will suddenly realize that God is doing for us what we could not do
for ourselves."*

—The Promises from Alcoholics Anonymous

An AA woman named Alice with 13 years of sobriety
attended a business convention. While there, she
befriended two other women from different parts of the
country, neither of whom were in AA. The three women
decided to go out to dinner together one night. At the
restaurant Alice ordered a soft drink while the others
ordered cocktails. Not knowing their views on alcoholism
or their attitudes about AA, Alice saw no reason to
explain.

The following night the three women went out to dinner again. As before, the women ordered cocktails and Alice ordered a soft drink. This time one of the women said to her, "I notice that you don't drink." Alice decided to be honest. "That's because I've been sober in AA for 13 years." Immediately the woman said, "Oh, I'm so relieved! My daughter has been in AA for three months, and I didn't know that sobriety *lasts*!"

If I've done one thing in this book, I hope it is to show that sobriety not only lasts, but lasts a long time— even 50 years. I think it's comforting to know that a person can be a "hopeless" addict or drunk, and then something can happen—some moment of clarity, some turning point, some soul shift—and in a flash they can change completely and forever, without ever having to know why they were addicted in the first place.

I also think it's comforting to know that there's such a thing as redemption after all. Literally, the word means "a buying back," and that's what the women in this book have done. They've paid the necessary price, and they've been given back the lives they were always meant to lead.

As the interviews show, the sobriety journey is a varied, ever-changing, and exciting one, making each year better than the year before. No area of life remains untouched.

What a relief to know that "sober" doesn't mean "somber," and that biting the bullet while dying for a drink isn't necessary because the obsession to drink or use, which *is* the addiction, goes away.

All 21 interviewees admitted that working the AA program was hard at times, even painful. "Sobriety isn't always the easiest way to go," says Julie (Chapter 2). "Sometimes it feels as if it might be easier to die drunk than to live sober. To stay sober really takes courage." However, none of these recovering women ever so much as hinted that she thought her sobriety wasn't worth the price she had to pay for it.

THE PROMISES REALIZED

My favorite section of the "Big Book" of Alcoholics Anonymous is reprinted at the beginning of this chapter.

Let's start with, "We will be amazed before we are half way through." As we've seen, nearly every recovering woman interviewed expressed amazement at how different her life had become because of sobriety. One said, "I thought I joined AA just to stop drinking. I had no idea that I was going to discover a whole new existence."

The next promise, "We are going to know a new freedom and a new happiness," is borne out again and again by the interviewees' stories. Addiction is a burden, a fact that is rarely appreciated until *after* the addicted person gets sober. It's like the old expression about not knowing how much beating your head against the wall hurts—until you stop. Once the alcoholic stops drinking, she begins to see how miserable she was.

The promise after that reads, "We will not regret the past nor wish to shut the door on it." Most of the interviewees came into sobriety full of denial, shame, and guilt, and much victimized by the stigma surrounding addiction. They soon learned that such negative emotions have no place in healthy sobriety. But by owning up to their illness, taking responsibility for their behavior, cleaning up their character defects, and making amends, the recovering alcoholics start to feel better. Respectable behavior, they find, has a remarkable side effect: self-respect. The recovering woman learns to hold her head up again.

Usually, when recovering alcoholics read the promise "We will comprehend the word serenity and we will know peace," they laugh. Coming from where they have come from, few can imagine feeling serene. For years they've known only drama and chaos. But the longer they're sober, the more they settle down. The roller-coaster ride flattens out to a road with occasional bumps and a few hills now and again, but that's it. They seek and find bal-

ance. One day they notice that they feel "at peace," just as
Frances did (Chapter 2) the day she was driving along
and became aware that she felt joy.

Next, there's the promise that "no matter how far
down the scale we have gone, we will see how our experience can benefit others." This comes as an enormous
relief. It may take a while, but the day finally comes when
the recovering woman realizes that her past, instead of
being something to hide and be ashamed of, is actually an
asset. Whenever she can share her secrets, whatever they
are—drug use, promiscuity, jail time, childhood traumas,
sexual abuse, incest, legal problems—with someone else,
it not only helps her, it helps them. Suddenly she feels
valuable and useful. It puts a brand-new spin on her past,
and she's grateful for it.

As a result, the promise "That feeling of uselessness
and self-pity will disappear" makes sense. Once the recovering woman can unload her secrets, free herself of guilt
and shame, and see that she's making an important con-
tribution, she feels more powerful and less of a victim.
Her self-pitying loser stance drops away.

Some of the women in this book have shown that victims stop being victims and start being powerful when
they take appropriate action. Shirley did this (Chapter 5)
when she took actions to end the "War of the Finances"
with her husband and stop feeling like a "poor relation"
in life. Annie did this (Chapter 8) when she gave up a
marriage that was becoming a threat to her sobriety.

The two promises, "We will lose interest in selfish
things and gain interest in our fellows" and "Self-seeking
will slip away," come about automatically. Initially, the
recovering woman is supremely self-centered. As she gets
more sobriety under her belt, her head clears. She starts
looking around. She notices that there are other people
out there who have needs and feelings, too. She begins to
respond to her family, her community, her world. She
picks up a newspaper and, perhaps for the first time in

years, she reads what's going on someplace else. She begins to care because she finally sees that everything is interrelated. She's not the isolated island she thought she was, but part of a larger context. When the larger context is healthy and happy, it trickles down and affects her, and vice versa. By giving of herself, she learns, and she gets back.

Many recovering alcoholics around the world have gone on to make contributions that have had an impact on scores, maybe thousands, of other people. In some cases, they've even become famous. One is the governor of a large state, another an Academy Award winner, another a Pulitzer Prize winner. Other recovering women are doctors, writers, journalists, therapists, teachers, lawyers, judges, entertainers, and law-enforcement people. I know an AA waitress in a coffee shop who regularly guides customers into AA, and a cashier at an auto-repair shop who has 12-stepped customers who were involved in alcohol-related accidents.

The next promise, "Our whole attitude and outlook upon life will change," is also borne out by the interviewees' stories. When you compare how the 21 women viewed life before sobriety to how they view life now, the result is staggering. "It's another person, another time, another life," said one. Louise (Chapter 8) went from being a selfish, immature, and amoral alcoholic to being a warm, generous, loving, and successful sober woman whose entire life today revolves around doing service. That's quite a switch.

For many of the interviewees, the promise "Fear of people and of economic insecurity will leave us" is especially important. Most started out as people-pleasers, terrified of any kind of confrontation. They couldn't stand up for themselves, couldn't tell people how they felt. By learning to become honest and communicate, they lost their fear. They went from being victims to being winners. Look how Ellen (Chapter 5) was able to confront her mother about the physical, sexual, and ritual abuse of her childhood. That took courage! But as Ellen herself says, what she got from doing it was her sanity.

As the recovering women learned to feel more powerful in their dealings with others, they felt less pressured to hide behind the questionable values of money, property, and prestige. Remember Hope (Chapter 6), who thought money and fancy job titles would make her happy? She discovered that she was wrong and changed her ways. In the same chapter, Shirley learned that money wasn't going to make her feel "safe" after all. Instead, her feelings of safety grew out of her sobriety, her integrity, and her creativity.

The promise I like best is the one that states, "We will intuitively know how to handle situations which used to baffle us." In my work as a therapist, I've heard dozens of recovering alcoholics say in utter amazement, "I don't know where the words came from, but I was standing there talking to my [husband/boss/friend/parent/child], and suddenly the right words just came tumbling out of my mouth!" Even if the recovering woman doesn't approach a specific problem consciously, if she merely stays clean and sober, something will click anyway, and she finds herself easily handling a situation that used to baffle her.

Finally, there is the promise, "We will suddenly realize that God is doing for us what we could not do for ourselves." In AA, *God* can be defined in any way that makes the AA member comfortable. God can mean Higher Power, or Nature, or Universal Consciousness, or it can mean the unconscious mind, or the inner self, or the life force. Whatever it is, it's enough to push that flower I talked about in Chapter 1 up through layers of asphalt in a driveway, and enough to get an alcoholic sober and keep her that way.

The Importance of Maintenance Work

Without belaboring the process again in detail, suffice it to say that the recovering women who have the best chance of staying sober are those who "work the program" by going to AA meetings, working the 12 steps, speaking and sharing, and helping newcomers. These are the basics of sobriety maintenance. Those who don't do the basics may end up paying the price. Sometimes the price is drinking again.

Louise tells a chilling story about an AA woman who stopped doing the maintenance work. To quote her, "As part of my service, I went to speak at an AA meeting in a women's prison. When I looked out into the audience, I saw a woman prisoner sitting there, and I recognized her as someone I'd met in meetings on the outside. When I'd last seen her, she had had 10 years of sobriety.

"Now, I knew we weren't supposed to talk to the prisoners, so after the meeting, as we were all walking out of the meeting hall, I scooted up next to her and, keeping my eyes straight ahead, I asked, 'What happened to you?' and she answered, simply, 'I stopped going to meetings.' When she said that, a chill went up and down my spine. It reminded me one more time that this disease of alcoholism is cunning, baffling, and powerful, just as AA says it is. As recovering alcoholics, we need to remain ever vigilant. We need to do whatever it takes to hang on to our sobriety because it's the greatest gift we'll ever have."

Nobody is immune. Anybody can slip. Ellen and Deanne slipped, and Barbara came close. Racking up years of sobriety is no protection. The woman Louise saw at the prison slipped at 10 years. Many women slip with even more time. What happens is, life gets good again and the recovering alcoholic gets complacent, which is the worst thing she can do. When she starts thinking, *Maybe my drinking wasn't really all* that *bad,* she's in trouble. That's when she needs to get herself to an AA meeting fast, to help bring her to her senses.

THE FUTURE OF ALCOHOLICS ANONYMOUS

"One of the things that worries me most about the future of AA is its astounding success," says Annie's husband, Sam, who, as you'll recall, has 30 years of sobriety himself. "People are flocking to AA these days in record numbers, and I'm afraid that if it's turned into a social club, they'll stop taking it seriously. Some of the new people coming in have just spent three weeks in a chemical dependency treatment center. They think they know more about AA than people who've been there for years. I heard a guy stand up to take an AA chip to celebrate 30 days of sobriety, and he gave a longer talk than I gave when I stood up to take a birthday cake for 30 years! What worries me most of all is that the people listening won't even know the difference!"

Others, like Louise, worry that AA's rapid growth means that newcomers into the program won't get enough attention or won't get the right kind of sponsor because there aren't enough service-oriented old-timers to go around. "I travel all over the country speaking on behalf of recovery, and I meet newcomers all the time," Louise has said. "I know they need to be hovered over. They need old-timers around to make sure they get to meetings, to help them start working the 12 steps, and to teach them about service. If newcomers don't get this, they'll just slip away and disappear. They'll go back to drinking and nobody will even know they're missing!" As most seasoned AA members will tell you, in the old days if somebody was missing from a meeting, 10 people would call them up to find out what happened.

Louise goes on: "It makes me afraid that future generations of AA will be getting just a watered-down version of what the AA program is all about." Then she adds, "Then I have to remind myself that I'm powerless over the future of Alcoholics Anonymous. I can't *make* anybody get sober and I can't *make* anybody get drunk. That's basically up to each person. All I can do is work my own AA program to the best of my ability, share my 'experience, strength and hope' with the alcoholic who still suffers, and make sure that *I* don't get drunk!" Then she adds, "Besides, I do believe that AA will survive."

THE FUTURE OF ADDICTION

At this moment in history, it looks as though the addiction problem is going to get worse before it gets better. As Jill, who still works in the chemical dependency field, says, "I wish I was an optimist and could tell you that I think addiction will lessen, but I don't think it will. However, at the same time, some things are definitely better. For example, today there's more acceptance of alcoholism as a disease. People are more aware of it, more educated, especially about the impact that addiction has on families. And there's much less stigma, especially where women are concerned. People like the former first lady, Betty Ford, have done wonders. Thanks to her and others like her who have been so open and honest about their own addiction problems, women who would never have asked for help before are doing so now. The attitude shift about alcoholism is remarkable." Says Julie, "I can remember when we were *all* closet cases."

There are changes, too, in the treatment side of the chemical dependency field. To quote Jill again, "Many chemical dependency treatment centers are only half full today because tight money has made insurance companies less willing to pay for addiction treatment, especially since so many people slip and have to return to treatment again and again. It gets expensive for them, and they're cutting way back. Some will cover only 10-day programs, others only outpatient treatment, others only detox." Louise speculates that more and more, we'll begin to see chemical dependency units closing, and AIDS units opening in their place. In some hospitals, this has happened already.

The impact of this down the road is that things will have come full circle. Alcoholics will once again be coming into AA cold, without stopping off for treatment first, like it was back in Annie's day. Then again, maybe something will come of the current research into a possible genetic involvement in alcoholism, which could send the field off into a whole new direction. We'll just have to wait and see.

FORGING THE CHAIN

One of the most remarkable aspects of addiction recovery is its impact on a recovering woman's relationships, especially if she has children. For the first time in generations, perhaps she gets a chance to break the tragic family chain of both addiction and dysfunction.

Seventeen years ago an alcoholic named Val, a divorcee with a five-year-old little girl named Leslie, turned herself in to Alcoholics Anonymous. She got a sponsor, and the first thing the sponsor told her was, "If you want to stay sober, you'll have to go to a meeting four or five nights a week." Val had reached the point where she was willing to do anything to keep her precious sobriety, so when she could get a sitter for her child, she did, and when she couldn't, she'd take Leslie to AA meetings with her. She'd pack a toy bag with storybooks, coloring books, crayons, maybe a doll or two, and Leslie would keep herself occupied while Val listened to the meeting as best she could. At least she was there. The other AA members gave Leslie a lot of loving attention, lots of hugs, and even cookies, which Leslie seemed to enjoy. Val was never quite sure how much Leslie understood what was going on, or whether she was listening. Sometimes Leslie would even fall asleep in her mother's arms. "Poor kid," Val would say. "She's probably bored out of her mind." But Val knew that her number one job was to stay clean and sober, for Leslie's sake as well as for her own, and this is what she had to do. It wasn't an ideal arrangement, but it was necessary.

By the time Val was a year sober, Leslie had already been to more than a hundred AA meetings, and as the years went on, she'd attend hundreds more. Val used to laugh to her friends, "Well, at least if Leslie ever becomes an alcoholic when she grows up, she'll know where to go for help!"

Fortunately, Leslie didn't become an alcoholic. She grew up into a healthy, outgoing, friendly, beautiful young woman. She went to college, and when she graduated she got a wonderful graduation present from her aunt, a woman who loved to travel but had recently been grounded with cancer. The present was enough money for a six-month European backpacking trip. "Send postcards and bring back lots of pictures so I can enjoy the trip vicariously through you," her aunt told her.

So Leslie went off on her trip. She sent cards and took pictures of all her aunt's favorite places. In mid-December, only a week before Christmas and just before Leslie was to return home, her aunt died. Val had to break the news to Leslie on the phone when Leslie called from the crowded lobby of a youth hostel in Belgium. Leslie was devastated. She wept openly on the phone. Val was concerned.

"Honey, is there anybody around you can talk to?" Val asked.

"No. Everybody here speaks either German or French."

"I wish I could be with you," Val said. Even at 21, Leslie was still her baby. "I wish I could slide right through the phone line and give you a hug and let you cry on my shoulder."

"I wish that, too," Leslie said.

"What will you do? Can you check into a posh hotel for just tonight so you can take a hot bath and have some privacy so you can cry in peace?"

"Maybe, Mom. I don't know. I'll have to see. All I know is right now people are standing here waiting to use the phone. But I'll be okay, I promise. I'll think of something and I'll call you and tell you tomorrow night. I love you! Bye!"

Leslie hung up, leaving Val feeling helpless. How would Leslie handle her hurt? Would she check into a hotel and cry into her pillow in peace? Would she find some English-speaking students to share with? Finally, Val realized—thanks to her own AA training—that she was truly powerless over the situation, and that she'd have to let go of it. She had no choice.

Leslie phoned the next day and sounded like her old self. Once again, her voice was energized. She sounded almost chipper. "Mom! Guess what!"

"You sound better," said Val.

"So much better! Guess what I did last night?"

"Did you go to a hotel?"

"No. I went to an AA meeting! When I got off the phone with you I went for a walk. I walked around Brussels in the rain. It was so cold, and I was crying and feeling sorry for myself. Then all of a sudden I remembered those AA meetings you used to take me to when I was a little girl. I remembered how _good_ it always felt just to be there, the warmth. I wanted to be there again. Even though I don't even drink, I just knew that's where I _need-ed_ to be. So I found a phone and made a bunch of calls, emergency tourist numbers, stuff like that, and I ended up taking three buses to the outskirts of town to this little two-room English-speaking AA club in an apartment building. There was a meeting going on with about 10 people—and a fireplace. And Mom, they welcomed me! I sat by the fire and got all toasty. They let me talk. They let me cry. They gave me hugs. And after the meeting, they took me out to a coffeehouse, and then one of the members drove me back to the youth hostel. And you know what else? When I went downstairs to the front desk this morning, one of the AA people from the meeting had left me a red rose with a little note saying he hoped I was feeling better. Wasn't that the sweetest thing?"

By the time Leslie finished telling the story, Val was in tears. "It made me so grateful to AA. First they took *me* in and comforted and healed me, and then they did the same thing for my child. And to think I used to wonder if Leslie understood what AA was all about! She understood perfectly well what AA is all about—it's about *heart.*"

This is "the chain." This is how AA managed to grow from two people to two million people. This is what is responsible for the proliferation of 12-step groups themselves, so that now there are many such groups helping many more millions of people. And this is what enabled 21 very courageous women, who might otherwise never have met one another, to get together and share their 406 accumulated years of sober wisdom with you, turning this book into a kind of portable support group.

If you were to ask any of the interviewees in the book—in fact, if you were to ask just about anybody who's been sober in AA for a while—"If science invented a pill that cured alcoholism so you could drink normally and never have to go AA again, would you take it?" the chances are that most of them would say no.

Why? Because they wouldn't have wanted to miss out on the incredible journey they've been on! Ellen, our youngest interviewee, who has 14 years of sobriety, has this to say:

*I wouldn't trade having this much
time in AA for anything. When I
speak at meetings, I tell people, "If
you think you know what sobriety is
all about when you have two years,
keep coming back. If you think you
know what sobriety is all about
when you have seven years, keep
coming back. If you think you know
what sobriety is all about when you
have 12 years, keep coming back."
Now that I have 14 years of sobriety,
it's exciting to realize that I won't
know how wonderful it's going to be
to have 16 or 18 or 25 years of
sobriety until I get there.*

In sobriety, getting there isn't just *half* the fun, it's *all* of it.

How the AA 12-Step Program Works

The following excerpt is taken from the book Alcoholics Anonymous *and explains the basic principles of the organization's program.*

Rarely have we seen a person fail who has thoroughly followed our path. Those who do not recover are people who cannot or will not completely give themselves to this simple program, usually men and women who are constitutionally incapable of being honest with themselves. There are such unfortunates. They are not at fault; they seem to have been born that way. They are naturally incapable of grasping and developing a manner of living which demands rigorous honesty. Their chances are less than average. There are those, too, who suffer from grave emotional and mental disorders, but many of them do recover if they have the capacity to be honest.

Our stories disclose in a general way what we used to be like, what happened, and what we are like now. If you have decided you want what we have and are willing to go to any length to get it—then you are ready to take certain steps.

At some of these we balked. We thought we could find an easier, softer way. But we could not. With all the earnestness at our command, we beg of you to be fearless and thorough from the very start. Some of us have tried to hold on to our old ideas and the result was nil until we let go absolutely.

Remember that we deal with alcohol—cunning, baffling, powerful! Without help it is too much for us. But there is One who has all power—that One is God. May you find Him now!

Half measures availed us nothing. We stood at the turning point. We asked His protection and care with complete abandon.

Here are the steps we took, which are suggested as a program of recovery:

1. We admitted we were powerless over alcohol—that our lives had become unmanageable.

2. Came to believe that a Power greater than ourselves could restore us to sanity.

3. Made a decision to turn our will and our lives over to the care of God *as we understood Him.*

4. Made a searching and fearless moral inventory of ourselves.

5. Admitted to God, to ourselves, and to another human being the exact nature of our wrongs.

6. Were entirely ready to have God remove all these defects of character.

7. Humbly asked Him to remove our shortcomings.

8. Made a list of all persons we had harmed, and became willing to make amends to them all.

9. Made direct amends to such people wherever possible, except when to do so would injure them or others.

10. Continued to take personal inventory and when we were wrong promptly admitted it.

11. Sought through prayer and meditation to improve our conscious contact with God *as we understood Him,* praying only for knowledge of His will for us and the power to carry that out.

12. Having had a spiritual awakening as the result of these steps, we tried to carry this message to alcoholics, and to practice these principles in all our affairs.

Many of us exclaimed, "What an order! I can't go through with it." Do not be discouraged. No one among us has been able to maintain anything like perfect adherence to these principles. We are not saints. The point is that we are willing to grow along spiritual lines. The principles we have set down are guides to progress. We claim spiritual progress rather than spiritual perfection.

Our description of the alcoholic, the chapter to the agnostic, and our personal adventures before and after make clear three pertinent ideas:

(a) That we were alcoholic and could not manage our own lives.

(b) That probably no human power could have relieved our alcoholism.

(c) That God could and would if He were sought.

Reprinted from the book *Alcoholics Anonymous*®

INDEX